Mind
Magic

Mind Magic

How to Develop the 3 Components
of Intelligence that Matter Most
in Today's World

JOHN LAURENCE MILLER, PH.D.

McGraw·Hill

New York   Chicago   San Francisco   Lisbon   London   Madrid   Mexico City
Milan   New Delhi   San Juan   Seoul   Singapore   Sydney   Toronto

Library of Congress Cataloging-in-Publication Data

Miller, John Laurence.
    Mind magic / John Laurence Miller. — 1st ed.
       p.   cm.
    Includes bibliographical references and index.
    ISBN 0-07-143320-1
    1. Intellect.   I. Title.

  BF431.M495   2005
  153.9—dc22   2004003171

1 2 3 4 5 6 7 8 9 0   DOC/DOC   3 2 1 0 9 8 7 6 5 4

ISBN 0-07-143320-1

McGraw-Hill books are available at special quantity discounts to use as premiums and sales promotions, or for use in corporate training programs. For more information, please write to the Director of Special Sales, Professional Publishing, McGraw-Hill, Two Penn Plaza, New York, NY 10121-2298. Or contact your local bookstore.

This book is printed on acid-free paper.

For Joelle, with love and appreciation.

CONTENTS

PART III   MIND MAGIC AND CHILDREN

FOREWORD

I like this book because I can disagree with half its statements and yet feel at one with an author who virtually tells me not to accept what he says. By disagreeing I am agreeing with what I take to be the book's key passage: "There are many people only too willing to teach you what they consider to be 'the right way to use your mind.' The right way for them, however, may not be the right way for you. You may be far better off if you develop your own 'right way.'" Here I have only a slight disagreement: he should not have said *may be*.

The real point of *Mind Magic* is its provocation to do what, when I was younger and thought the world was simpler, I would have called "thinking about thinking." But that is too narrow. True, the provocation of the book is to stop being timid about applying your mind to your mind. But mind is more than thinking. It involves feelings as well as thinking, unconscious happening as well as conscious application, and intuition as well as logic. It is an amazing but true fact that we do not have a name for any such inclusive mind process. Our language is built firmly on the neat divisions. We think thoughts, we feel emotions; thoughts are right or wrong, feelings are good or bad. There is a serious shortage of words to talk about the more complex views of mind that, as Laurie Miller forcefully tells his readers, that have come in the wake of more complex lives.

So what can we do about it? One way is to get pompous and invent new fancy words and "unified" theories that will somehow combine all the disparate elements. I prefer Miller's way: stick with the ordinary unpompous ideas that are the fabric of real minds, throw them all together with homely stories and multiple interpretations of multiple theories into the witch's brew and let magic—your personal mind magic—do its tricks. If he wants support from on high I offer him two. A great scientist, Marvin Minsky, is fond of saying that understanding means understanding in many separate ways—not bringing them together. Poet Robert Graves writes, "Refuse to choose / When life seems to give / Love in alternative." In any case don't let anyone, even Miller (not that he is trying) tell you which is the right way to be you. Or even that there is just one.

Seymour Papert

ACKNOWLEDGMENTS

It is strange how small decisions can change your life. After my second year of college, a friend and I decided to take a year off school and travel to Europe. The year turned out to be wonderful but left me bored when I had to come home for my third year of college. One day, after walking out of a psychology lecture, I decided, on impulse, to write to Jean Piaget to ask if I could work with him. At the time, I was at least as interested in going back to Europe as in studying psychology. And I could not imagine that Piaget would even reply. But to my surprise, he did write back and said that I could go to Geneva on the condition that I could pass the university's French competency examination. The next September, I was in Switzerland.

The two years I spent in Geneva shaped the work that I have done ever since. It was a great opportunity to work and study with a number of first-rate thinkers. Foremost among them were Guy Cellérier (a brilliant man whose ideas have never been fully appreciated outside of Switzerland), Bärbel Inhelder, and Piaget himself. While in Geneva, I met the South African mathematician and educational theorist Seymour Papert. After I went to Harvard to do my Ph.D., Papert served as my mentor and thesis adviser. As it turned out, the time that I spent at Harvard corresponded with one of the most productive and exciting periods in twentieth-century psychology. The new field of cognitive science was taking root, and Papert and Marvin Minsky together were developing its most innovative ideas. I see Minsky and Papert as the original mind magicians. Without their seminal ideas, this book could never have been written.

The key concepts in this book grew out of theoretical and applied research as well as discussions with friends and colleagues and my attempts to solve practical problems in clinical, educational, and business settings. I especially thank Mary Louise Bat Hayim, who worked with me for ten years while we developed the Learning Therapy Program at York University in Toronto. Her ideas were particularly influential in the discussion of learning disabilities in Chapter 7. Other colleagues whose ideas and encouragement have been especially important to me include Richard Chase, Shalom Fisch, Annette Karmiloff-Smith, Thalia Klein, David Leiser, Anne Lopes, Ruth Lugo, Harold Minden, Corey Schwartz, and Marc Wilchesky.

To produce a book for a nonprofessional audience required that I become something of a writer in addition to being a psychologist. Early drafts of this book were written in a style that would interest few people other than professional academics. I am deeply indebted to my wife, Joelle Silverman-Miller, above all others, for the weeks and months she spent painstakingly reading and critiquing my book, chapter by chapter and line by line. During this time she guided me in re-creating my ideas in a form accessible to an educated but nonprofessional readership.

I would like to thank the following people as well for reading and offering helpful criticism of sections of this book: Ling Lukas, Sigle Magner-Skeries, Myriam Orozco, Elizabeth Saenger, and Nicholas Smith.

Finally, I owe a large debt to my agent, Jay Johnson. His editorial advice and business judgment, not to mention his skill in quickly finding the right publisher, have been consistently on target. I also deeply appreciate the help that I received from Judith McCarthy, my editor at McGraw-Hill. Throughout the process her editing and judgment were consistently sound. Her comments forced me to rethink many issues related to mind magic, in each case strengthening the analysis and presentation. I would also like to thank her assistant Mandy Huber, who has been a pleasure to work with.

INTRODUCTION
HOW TO GET AHEAD IN THE INFORMATION AGE

Alice laughed. "There's no use trying," she said. "One can't believe impossible things."

"I daresay you haven't had much practice," said the Queen. "When I was your age, I always did it for half-an-hour a day. Why, sometimes I've believed as many as six impossible things before breakfast."

—LEWIS CARROLL

Mind Magic offers a new way of thinking about your mind. It will provide a fresh perspective on the whole question of what intelligence is, along with practical suggestions of ways to increase and improve your mind's power. It will help you to cope with the complex and ever-increasing demands of life and to thrive and prosper in the changing world we live in.

The notion of mind magic may seem impossible. But it is entirely realistic. In fact, constant change in society and in the economy is making it more and more imperative to learn the tricks of mind magic. Like everyone else, you will soon need to learn in better and more powerful ways. If you do not, the growth of knowledge and advances in technology will make much of what you presently know obsolete. If you do, you not only will comfortably adapt to the future, but you will also participate in inventing it.

The Challenge of a New Era

Since the late 1970s, we have been living through a watershed in human history—the computer revolution. There is no going back to the way things were. Both our society and the economy are notably different from the way they used to be. The computer revolution has been changing the way we work and the way we form and conduct personal relationships. Indeed, it has been changing the way we live.

But what aspect of our lives is it changing the most? It has arguably had the deepest and most sustained effects on the way in which we use and understand our own minds. If you look at the profession of psychology, you'll see that the influence of computers and computer science is unmistakable. Consider, as an example, MIT psychologist Steven Pinker's 1997 book titled *How the Mind Works*, which draws largely on research based on computer models. Can understanding how your mind works help you to use it more effectively? As you will see, the answer unambiguously is "yes."

The computer age is different from the era that came before, but not just in the kinds of machinery or even the kinds of ideas that we use. As futurologist Alvin Toffler has repeatedly pointed out, we live in a world where change is faster, deeper, and more ubiquitous than ever before. The development of computer technology has contributed substantially to an increasingly rapid pace of change. Coincidentally, it is also the source of ideas that will help us adapt to and thrive in the world of perpetual change that it has helped produce.

Where do we see change happening? Look at the world of education. Think back a few decades. As recently as the 1960s and '70s, most middle-class parents believed that children who did well in school would grow up assured of a decent-paying and personally rewarding job. Today that kind of confidence seems more like complacency. What went wrong? Most people just do not trust the system that much anymore. In the 1960s most parents felt they could count on education as being a safe and certain road to their children's economic success. In 2005, parents no longer view their children's formal schooling to be any guarantee of future success.

Today preparing for the future means preparing for constant change. After all, what good is a head crammed full of facts if those facts will become obsolete in a few short years? At a time of change, less is more. Won't the people who can keep up with the speed of progress be the ones who will get ahead? Teaching children to adapt will prove far more useful than teaching them any concrete set of facts. Put simply, we should teach them mind magic.

Indispensable Qualities in a Changing World

The importance of learning adaptability is not limited to children in school. It pertains to you, too. Adapting to change is a crucial skill regardless of whether you are a CEO or you are just starting out.

The rapid pace of change is both good news and bad. It is good news for people who are ambitious and flexible. It means that the next technological revolution is probably just around the corner. And when it comes, it will inevitably create new and previously unforeseeable work and business opportunities. The bad news is for people who find change difficult. A rapid pace of change will make certain skills and related occupations obsolete.

If you can anticipate the next revolution from the beginning, you will have an enormous advantage in learning to use and profit from new inventions and discoveries. Furthermore, becoming a participant will give you a head start over people who watch from the bleachers. Conversely, if you cannot adapt to change, you will become its victim.

Is adaptability in itself enough? Here is another question: how well do you manage information? New information, if anything, is an even more potent force than new technology. And the speed at which new information appears and proliferates is at least the same as the speed of technological progress.

New information technology, such as the Internet, serves to speed up the dissemination of facts and data. Keeping up with the growth and spread of information has become just as important for you as becoming familiar with new technology.

Many managers have already begun to feel pressured to assimilate and evaluate larger quantities of information than they feel they can handle. This feeling has led a growing number of office workers to complain about what psychologist David Lewis calls *data smog*. How will you cope when confronted with a confusing mass of data? You will need to be able to dive in, pick out a few critical facts or concepts, and use them as hooks to hang a coherent picture of what the information as a whole is telling you. Having this ability will protect you from feeling overwhelmed by new data as they become available.

You will have to consider a third skill, namely the talent for creativity, or innovation. Like the other two attributes, creativity will also become essential for finding and keeping a good job. Why is creativity more important today than it was in the past? The answer again is the computer. In the past you could earn your living by diligently applying what someone had taught you in school. But the days will soon be over when a company will pay you to apply tried-and-true methods. Today companies can buy a robot to do that.

In the future companies will hire human beings to succeed in those areas where computers fail. Applying set procedures, mechanically and repetitively, has become the work of computers, not people. Companies have learned this. More than ever before, you will have to value and nurture your talent for innovation.

Developing creativity will be essential for you to define and shape your own economic niche, where technological progress is not likely to become a threat. It is a truism: computers cannot innovate, but you can. Even if you do not consider yourself to be especially creative, the fact remains that you are surely more creative than present-day computer programs. You need to recognize creativity as one of your true strengths, even if you have not viewed it as a strength in the past. Nurture your creativity, and it will reward you.

To recap, there are three indispensable skills that together will help you cope with unprecedented demands on your abilities. First, you must be able to easily and quickly adapt to change; second, you must become an adept manager of information; and third, you must develop creativity and innovation. This book will offer you practical information that will help you to master mind magic and prepare for success.

Adapting to Change by Expanding the Mind

How will you adapt to this new social reality? Many routes are open to you, from buying a more powerful computer to studying economics. For most people, one clear starting place is to concentrate on your own mind and to develop the capacities that new circumstances will reward. In other words, develop and expand your own intelligence.

Is it actually possible to increase your own intelligence? Many people still see intelligence as a fixed resource measured by IQ tests. Interestingly, psychologists have increasingly come to reject this view. In 1995 psychologist David Perkins, a professor at the Harvard Graduate School of Education, published *Outsmarting IQ: The Emerging Science of Learnable Intelligence*. In this book, Perkins spoke for a growing number of psychologists who reject the notion that intelligence cannot change.

What has caused this revolution in thinking among psychologists? Perkins and other psychologists came to realize that intellectual abilities are in essence no different from other kinds of know-how. Acquiring the knowledge that IQ tests measure is essentially no different from developing any other ability, such as drawing or swimming.

Virtually everybody can draw, at least to some extent, except for people who suffer from a severe handicap. Give children crayons or pencils and they will draw. Even crippled or disturbed children usually enjoy drawing. Nevertheless, except for a gifted minority, most people do not draw especially well. They can learn to draw well, of course, but only by study and practice. They can improve their skill even further by reading books or taking courses that present advanced drawing techniques and art theory. Drawing is a learnable skill. The proof lies in the number of people who have learned to draw.

Swimming is another learnable skill. If you want to swim well, you need considerable practice and almost certainly at least some instruction.

Now here is the crucial question: aren't intelligence and thinking just as learnable as drawing and swimming? Like drawing and swimming, exercising your mind is something that you do naturally. Nevertheless, without practice, your skill as a thinker can remain rudimentary. How can you strengthen your mind? The purpose of this book is to offer methods, tools, and information that can help you to use your mind more successfully. What your mind can achieve is indeed amazing. That is why I call this ability *mind magic.*

Adaptability or Power: Which Matters More?

Most people in the past have conceived of intelligence as being equivalent to what you may call *mental power.* To replace the centrality of the concept of power with that of adaptation represents a fundamental shift in how you see the mind.

Until recently almost everyone in our society, professional psychologists and the general public alike, considered you to be very intelligent if you had a powerful mind, regardless of whether or not you were particularly adaptable. A smart person was someone who could use his or her mind to do something that seemed difficult and complicated. You could appear intelligent if you were skillful at games that seem to require mental power, such as chess, or if you could intimidate people with your talent at winning arguments. On the other hand, if you were adaptable, most people would probably never have noticed.

One of the main problems with a power-oriented view of intelligence was that power intelligence often proved rigid and inflexible. It is the dinosaur of the intelligence world. And like the dinosaur in prehistoric times, people with power intelligence did indeed reign supreme, as long as conditions in the outside world were essentially stable. But when change replaced stability as the norm, these people quickly became lost. They were no longer in their element. And their old way of looking at the world, which they had built up over many, many years, was suddenly obsolete.

A second problem was that power intelligence often did not turn out to be useful, regardless of how much it could impress. Being good at winning arguments or chess matches can certainly impress people. But it does not necessarily help in earning a living. The world is full of people who can impress us with how much they know, but all their knowledge does not necessarily do them a lot of good in the real world. Think of all the people with Ph.D.s who end up earning a living as taxi drivers!

In times of rapid change, you will often do better to have a simpler, more schematic view of reality, one that captures the essence of things even if it misses some of the details. For starters, changing your mind becomes easier. It costs less in time and energy because you do not have to reexamine as many beliefs or reevaluate as many commitments. In a word, it makes you more adaptable.

In the future, adaptability is likely to prove more important than power. You will do better to have a simpler, sleeker, and more elegant mind that can reinterpret and revise what you already know in response to new information. People who immerse themselves in complexity might find themselves so weighed down by details that they feel unable to respond.

Free Your Imagination

Especially to people who see themselves as hard-headed realists, telling you to free your imagination seems like the worst possible advice. Perhaps you know people who feel that way. Self-styled realists often equate imagination with wishful thinking, and they see imagination as a way of avoiding reality, its unpleasant side in particular. For them, exercising their imagination is fundamentally opposed to facing reality.

But too much pessimism can be just as dangerous as too much wishful thinking, and perhaps even more so. The Danish storyteller Hans Christian Andersen describes its effects in his fairy tale "The Snow Queen."

As the story begins, the most wicked of all the gnomes, the Evil One himself, has devised a terrible invention. He has invented a looking glass with the peculiarity that anything good or fair disappears into nothing when reflected in the mirror, while anything bad or foul becomes much worse. In this mirror, the loveliest landscapes look like cooked spinach, and the most attractive people become ugly and stand on their heads. Anyone who has a freckle can be sure that it now covers his or her nose and mouth. Faces become so distorted that no one can recognize them.

You might expect that the people would keep away from such a wicked invention, but just the opposite happens. People go to the Gnome School, run by the Evil One, and proclaim far and wide that a miracle has happened. They hold up the distorting mirror so that everyone can see it. "Now at last," they say, "you can see how the world and mankind really look."

What they saw had no more to do with reality than would the contents of a mirror that reflected only what was beautiful and pleasant. But they had become so cynical and pessimistic that they could no longer recognize this. Pessimists who see nothing but bad are just as deluded as optimists who see nothing but good.

The people in "The Snow Queen" in effect suffered from a mild—or perhaps not so mild—form of depression. They had become so demoralized that they could no longer distinguish between being realistic and being pessimistic. There are a number of possible explanations for why this may have happened. Perhaps they genuinely had experienced such unhappy lives that they had no choice except to believe the worst. Perhaps they were poor at problem solving and became discouraged when they could not cope. Perhaps they were unduly influenced by pessimism in the surrounding culture. But whatever the reason, the effect was to undermine and cloud their judgment.

To believe that things can never become better is self-destructive. Too much pessimism saps morale and paralyzes the mind. It can make you feel so convinced things have to be bad that you unconsciously make them turn out that way. The optimistic belief that things can be better is the spark that ignites imagination. Imagination in turn enables creative innovation and adaptive change.

The Right Kind of Intelligence for the Times

The example of power intelligence illustrates the fact that the meaning of intelligence will be different depending on social and environmental context. What is intelligent at one time or in one social context may become unintelligent later. Power intelligence may have worked well in the world of black-and-white television and vinyl records, even if it has now become out of date in the world of artificial intelligence and the Internet.

The Australian actor and director Paul Hogan vividly made this point in the 1986 movie *Crocodile Dundee*. Dundee is a bona fide genius in the art of surviving the Australian outback. He combines the inventiveness of a master at improvisation with a profound sense of empathy for the land, the wildlife, and native Aborigine society. But when he moves to New York City, he is a fish out of water. The inventiveness and practicality that served him well in Australia prove useless in dealing with high society, modern technology, and the avant-garde. The genius of the outback has become the imbecile of Manhattan.

A person as naturally intelligent and adaptable as Crocodile Dundee could and did, of course, eventually learn the ropes of surviving even in Manhattan. But that is not the point. Even in adapting to Manhattan, he was no longer living in his native element. It is unlikely that he would ever handle himself with the brilliance and mastery that made up his daily existence in the outback.

To understand mind magic, you have to do more than measure what people know and examine how they reason. You also have to look at the world around them. And as that world changes, the meaning of mind magic must change as well.

How will it change? This book presents an introduction to and overview of mind magic as it exists today. You are invited to learn more about mind magic and to participate in its evolution by visiting the mind magic website, **power-your-mind.com**.

[All names throughout this book have been changed for privacy except for those of published authors and other public figures.]

PART I

ABOUT MIND MAGIC

CHAPTER 1

DISCOVERING THE MAGIC OF YOUR MIND

What makes a person intelligent? Can you increase your intelligence? Can you learn mind magic?

Fifty years ago most psychologists believed that intelligence was the same thing as IQ, a magical number that told you how much intelligence you had. That thinking has changed. Critics have discredited the old "official" view of mind in favor of something more credible.

Where does intelligence come from? In the old days, it was thought to be unchanging. Today most psychologists believe that intelligence develops at least in part as a result of life experience, and a growing number agree that you can learn what I call *mind magic*. The term *mind magic* refers to the collection of skills, concepts, and principles that allow people to think and act in ways that would normally be considered to reflect better-than-average intelligence but nevertheless did not result from an innate ability or gift. Mind magic is learned intelligence. It can allow people to think and act in ways that they would never have thought possible.

How do you develop mind magic? There are many people only too willing to teach you what they consider to be the right way to use your mind. The right way for them, however, may not be the right way for you. You may be far better off if you develop your own "right way." This book will help you to discover your own kind of mind magic, something that is right for you.

How Mike Lawrence Became a World Champion

Apart from chess, perhaps no widely played game relies on brainpower more than bridge. Do you think that bridge champions are born with an unusual amount of ability? Or is their ability something they acquire along the way?

Mike Lawrence has been one of the best bridge players in the world for more than twenty years. He has won three world championships and more than a dozen North American championships—truly exceptional achievements. Look at how he explains his own success:

> *In 1959, I began to play bridge. After two years, I had qualified to be a life master, but not a good one, by everyone's admission including my own. A kindly gentleman, named Lloyd Graham, the "father" of bridge in my small area, told me to quit the game and return to college. Naturally, I ignored that and played on. But without a clear idea of how to do it.*
>
> *In about 1962, I was playing bridge in a sectional and in the middle of a hand I was declaring, I experienced something not unlike a hot flash. It lasted for about thirty seconds. When it went away, I discovered that the hand was no longer a problem. Nor were the rest of the hands that day. In the space of thirty seconds, I went from a random card pusher to someone who was aware of what the game was about.*
>
> *What happened was, I think—and heaven knows how much time I put into wondering about this event—that my subconscious had been cogitating over all the information about bridge that had entered my mind via the conscious corridor. After sitting in my subconscious for a few years, it all came together into a useable format.*
>
> *Not having insights into such things, I cannot claim to know what happened, but it was such a powerful moment for me that I believe something did occur.*

This story suggests three important ideas. First, brainpower is not just something you are born with. If Lawrence had not devoted himself to bridge, he could have remained what he himself calls "a random card pusher." Second, acquiring mind magic is emotional as much as intellectual. It involves powerful experiences, such as Lawrence's "hot flash." These experiences change you as a person while also changing the way you think. And third, mind magic is holistic. It can reorganize your mind.

As you will learn, your mind is capable of the same kind of transformation that Lawrence experienced. The better you understand your own mind, the more you can use this capability to serve your own purposes.

A Revolution in Psychology

How unusual is what happened to Mike Lawrence? Thirty years ago most psychologists would have interpreted his experience of the "hot flash" as uniquely characteristic of the exceptional individual. Today we know better. Cognitive reorganization, of the kind that Lawrence describes, is a normal part of development. It can happen to anybody. We know this from the work of a revolutionary thinker, the Swiss psychologist Jean Piaget.

No thinker since Sigmund Freud has challenged our conception of the human mind as much as Piaget has. And his ideas may one day prove to be more important than Freud's theories. They are certainly notably different.

Freud's ideas are somber and disturbing. By contrast, Piaget's are bright and exhilarating. Freud told us that we are under the control of dark unconscious forces and of childhood experiences buried deep in our past. Piaget told us that our mind is an instrument of power far greater than we ever suspected. According to Piaget, the source of this power is our ability to adapt and grow. Freud argued that average people are not much different from the neurotic patients on the psychiatrist's couch. Piaget's assumption is virtually the mirror image of Freud's. He presumed that the mind of the average person and that of the most brilliant scientist each works according to the same principles.

Piaget would not have been surprised by Lawrence's story. Piaget found over and over again that even quite ordinary children undergo essentially the same kind of experience all the time. Is it any surprise to learn that your mind is capable of the same kind of transformation?

Know Your Own Mind

Piaget studied scientists as well as children. How did he think you could explain the way in which the finest scientists discovered their most brilliant ideas? Piaget used the same basic principles to explain how all people think. It did not matter whether he was talking about the greatest scientist or the most ordinary person.

It follows in the spirit of Piaget to look at how famous scientists understand the working of their minds. Can you use your mind in the same way that they use theirs? Few eminent scientists are willing to speak openly about their own thought processes. A notable exception to this rule was the distinguished geneticist Barbara McClintock.

During the 1970s McClintock began to receive recognition as a scientist of the first order. She is famous today for having discovered how genes interact with each other decades before biologists had discovered the molecular tools to dissect genetic material. Working with the corn plant all her life, she is best known for her discovery that fragments of genetic material move among chromosomes, regulating the way genes control cells' growth and development. For this work, she received the Nobel Prize in Physiology or Medicine in 1983 at the age of 81.

What made McClintock such a successful scientist? Some people think that you have to be born with a superior brain in order to win a Nobel Prize. Interestingly, McClintock had a very different explanation. As Evelyn Fox Keller wrote in her distinguished 1983 biography of McClintock, *A Feeling for the Organism: The Life and Work of Barbara McClintock*, McClintock felt that her most valuable asset was what she knew about her mind. As she saw it, her skill as a scientist was intricately connected with her understanding of her own mind.

At first this idea seems surprising to most people. It seems strange that a kind of knowledge, self-knowledge, can help you use your mind more effectively. Does it mean that you can increase your intelligence by understanding more about your mind?

Keller writes that McClintock saw her mind as being like a computer. It was "a computer that was working very rapidly and very perfectly." In describing her research of the late 1930s, McClintock says that she was conscious of nothing other than the specimens she was observing;

the computer of her mind did the rest. Keller's biography quotes her as saying, "When you suddenly see the problem, something happens that you have the answer—before you are able to put it into words. It is all done subconsciously. This has happened too many times to me, and I know when to take it seriously. I'm so absolutely sure I don't talk about it. I don't have to tell anyone about it. I'm just *sure* this is it."

Why should knowing your own mind make such a difference to a Nobel Prize–winning scientist? In the case of McClintock, understanding her thinking meant that she could manage her mind. She knew when to make it stop and when to let it go. She knew when to take it seriously and when to be suspicious. She knew when she had to discuss her thoughts with other people and when to keep them to herself.

Everyone's mind is unique in its own way. That was true of McClintock's mind, and it is also true of yours. What she discovered about her mind may or may not apply to you. You may or may not find that your mind works like a computer. You may or may not find that your subconscious does most of the work. You may feel the same way as McClintock about the value of putting your thoughts into words, or you may feel otherwise.

In spite of the many differences, there is one way in which McClintock is like everyone else. Understanding your mind improves your ability to use it. I call this kind of understanding *mind consciousness*. Mind consciousness enables you to manage your most valuable resource, your mind, more effectively. This idea is essential for learning mind magic.

How I Think Is Who I Am

Mind consciousness changes more than your thinking. It affects your emotions and your sense of who you are.

Allan Smith is a happily married and successful computer professional. But if his first grade teacher saw him today, she would not recognize him.

To say that Allan was a difficult student is an understatement. As early as first grade, his teacher identified him as a loser. Because of his poor school performance and his lack of discipline, the school insisted on a psychiatric assessment as a condition for allowing him to remain in class. The psychiatrist diagnosed Allan as having an attention deficit disorder and a learning disability.

Allan recalls many of his difficulties as a child. First, he confused certain letters and numbers. He could not reliably distinguish between *b* and *d*, *p* and *q*, or *6* and *9*. His handwriting was labored, and to most people illegible. (Today he writes in block letters because people still cannot read his cursive writing.) He stuttered. He remembers from third grade that he was never able to memorize the multiplication table. A couple years later, word problems were introduced in math, and he found these impossible. His difficulties with math persisted years later in college. He enrolled in a precalculus course for students who wanted to go into computer science but did not have the mathematics prerequisites. A few weeks into the course, he dropped out. Eventually, he was able to struggle through a college-level calculus course, but his grade was a barely passing D.

Paradoxically, Allan sees himself today as a very mathematical person. His skill as a programmer seems to prove that he is right. He realizes, though, that he thinks differently from other mathematical people.

How did he "become mathematical" to the point that he had the confidence to enter and succeed at a highly mathematical career? Two experiences years apart were crucial. The first is that his parents bought him a computer when he was in fourth grade. They wanted him to learn to use a keyboard because of his poor handwriting and problems with letter recognition. But the computer quickly came to mean much more to Allan. While at school he was failing math, at home he was programming in BASIC and playing the educational computer game *Oregon Trail*.

The second experience leading to his later success in math was a therapy group that he attended in college. The purpose of the group was to help students diagnosed as having a mathematics learning disability to overcome both intellectual and emotional barriers to success. For Allan, the therapy group became an opportunity to resolve his conflicting self-images as both a "smart" computer whiz and a "dumb" learning disabled kid.

The computer and the therapy group both had long-term consequences for Allan. He recalls, for example, that the computer motivated him to read. He had never been terribly interested in books. But now, while other children were reading novels and comic books, Allan read *Creative Computing*. It helped him in math as well. He remembers how intuitive algebra seemed to him: equations with letters were no different from assigning values to variables in BASIC.

Why was the therapy group important? First, it gave him inner strength. He saw all these other students who had struggled so hard to get into the university, and he felt for the first time that he was one of them even though he had neglected schoolwork so often and instead had pursued private interests. Second, he learned to observe his own mind. He realized that he did not learn the way people are expected to learn. For example, teachers were of little help to him. Instead, he learned best on his own, with the help of a good textbook. He noticed that he rarely used the same methods as other students used to solve problems; nevertheless, he got the right answers. Through the experience of therapy, he came to appreciate that it is OK to solve problems your own way.

Like McClintock, Allan came to achieve a rich and highly personal understanding of his own mental processes. He explains, "My memory is based on relationships." He remembers processes in terms of objects moving along a conveyor belt, from point A to point B, through endless repetition.

The Roots of Self-Confidence

It is hard to stick to your own private sense of reality when it flies in the face of what everyone else seemingly believes. Most people think that if it is me versus the whole world, who is probably right? McClintock was an exception. She persisted even when most of the rest of the world regarded her as a crackpot. On the one hand, her academic training taught her to respect the authority of the scientific community. You can appreciate what a terrible experience this kind of conflict represents to a young scientist. The conclusions of science are supposed to be entirely impersonal. In theory, anyone will come to the same conclusions if he or she follows sound procedures and applies them competently.

On the other hand, McClintock's own personal observation taught her that the rest of the world was wrong. What was the source of her tenacity and self-confidence? Her life experience taught her to question established principles that almost every other scientist took for granted. Consequently, she had room to trust herself. She had observed phenomena that no one else could see. The old ideas did not fit what she observed. What was she to do?

Many people know the experience of feeling that the "official" answers are not quite right. Have you ever had that feeling? You may be sitting in a classroom and suddenly notice that the teacher has made a mistake. Or you may be reading a book and feel that the world of the author is not the world that you know from your experience. Do you trust your inner sense or do you trust what the so-called expert says?

The experience of Allan Smith shows how finding people like yourself can be a source of strength. Throughout his childhood, Allan felt there was something wrong with him that kept him from learning the way other students appeared to learn. By participating in a math therapy group, he felt for the first time that it was OK to solve problems his own way.

Part of mind magic is coming to know when to trust your own inner sense. You will sometimes be right even when everyone else says that you are wrong. Through developing the magic of your mind, you will become better at knowing when to stick to your own beliefs and when to go along with the crowd. Very few people face the intense pressure that McClintock had to face. But if you have new ideas, you will almost certainly face some pressure to give them up. The examples of Barbara McClintock and Allan Smith show, in different ways, how people can find the strength to stand up to pressure when it comes.

McClintock came to believe that there are valid ways of knowing other than the ones conventionally espoused by scientists. In her view, what we call the *scientific method* cannot by itself give us real understanding. It may give us relationships that are useful, valid, and technically marvelous. However, they are not the truth. Similarly, Allan came to believe that there are valid ways of knowing other than the way espoused by teachers and professors. It is important to get the right answer, but it does not matter how you find it.

The Meaning of Intelligence in the Information Age

Among both professional psychologists and the general public, the last several years have witnessed a growing dissatisfaction with traditional conceptions of intelligence. Clearly, we need something new. I believe *Mind Magic* brings us closer to the new idea.

Two central notions defined the old view of mind. The first was the image of the brilliant scientist, a type embodied by Albert Einstein. People thought that the greatest scientists were the most intelligent people. The second was the IQ test. People thought that high IQ and high intelligence were the same thing.

Most people today, experts and nonexperts alike, have become skeptical about both of these old ideas. And their skepticism has created a vacuum. If the old ideas are no longer acceptable, then we need a newer, better idea that can take their place. One influential theorist, Howard Gardner, sees an answer in the concept of *multiple kinds of intelligence*. But the kinds of intelligence that he postulates seem to be top-heavy with skills that are generally taught in school. More and more psychologists feel that such a school-oriented theory cannot be right. They believe instead that we should attribute greater importance to ways of thinking that lead to career success and life success even if school does not reward them. In my experience working with university students and the general public, most nonprofessionals share this feeling.

Observing reality tells you that the meaning and nature of intelligence are always changing. Instead of looking for universal definitions, we need to look at the here and now. Let's look at what intelligence means in the world of the twenty-first century. This is the world of information, high technology, and global commerce. What is intelligence in the information age? *Mind Magic* will answer that question.

The experiences of Mike Lawrence, Barbara McClintock, and Allan Smith demonstrate three important points. First, you cannot expect to be born a master of mind magic any more than Lawrence could have been born a world champion. Mind magic is something that develops over time. Second, mind consciousness is a crucial part of mind magic. As McClintock discovered, the better you understand your mind, the more effectively you can use it. Third, increasing the magic of your mind changes more than the way you think. As Allan found, it also changes you as a person.

If an image of intelligence is any good, it should tell you something useful. *Mind Magic* does that. It will give you practical information and advice as well as insight into the meaning of intelligence today and in the future. This information should help you adapt to the demands of the information age. In terms of what today is truly relevant, it will also help you to extend your mind's magic further than ever before.

CHAPTER 2

MIND CONSCIOUSNESS: HOW TO EXTEND YOUR MOST VALUABLE RESOURCE

You have more power than you realize. Some people think power comes from position, others think it comes from money, and there are those who think it comes from education. These externals must surely count for something, but they are not the whole story. You have only to look at yourself to see where to find a vast source of power: it is the power of your mind.

Think of the mind of one man, Galileo. Galileo did not accept that our little earth was the center of the universe, and in the wake of this idea the civilization of the Middle Ages came tumbling down. Think of the power of a mind such as Sigmund Freud's. Freud believed that the child is father to the man and changed forever the way we see children and ourselves. Minds have created and destroyed empires and changed civilizations. *Mind power* is the power to change the world and the power to change your life.

Mind consciousness is the awareness of oneself as a being that thinks and learns. Consider the difference between mind consciousness and its first cousin, emotional awareness. Since the time of Freud (who lived from 1856 to 1939), we as a society have become skilled interpreters of how dreams, fears, conflicts, and emotional attachment affect our experiences and actions. In spite of our high level of emotional awareness, few of us achieve a high level of mind consciousness. Otherwise educated and sophisticated people have virtually no awareness of how they solve problems, discover ideas, assimilate and manage information, or adapt to change.

Is it important to develop mind consciousness? A human mind is an instrument of enormous power. The similarities between the workings of your mind and the mind of a major scientist (such as Galileo) or a revolutionary thinker (such as Freud) are great, while the differences are subtle. To make the most effective use of your mind, you need to be aware of what it does as you think and learn. Strange as it may seem, you only have to learn to use the magic of the mind that you already possess. That is why mind consciousness is such a powerful asset.

The Yin and Yang of Learning

You can never totally be the master of your mind any more than you could ever totally be the master of your body. Your heart keeps beating, your lungs keep breathing, your ears keep hearing, and the rest of your body keeps working, for the most part, whether you tell it to or not. In the same way, your mind keeps assimilating information and reinterpreting your experience. But neither are you obliged to let your mind master you. Think in terms of the analogy with your body. You can tell your eyes where to look and your feet where to step. With exercise you can influence how far you can run, and with training you can even affect how rapidly your heart beats. If you observe your mind and understand it, it will exceed your expectations. If you continually try to bend it to your will, it will try to defy you at the first opportunity.

Instead of trying to bend your mind, guide your own learning in the same kind of way that a government regulates a country's economy. Economists offer methods for the government to avoid both an overheated inflationary economy and economic depression. They track business cycles and prescribe remedies to contain the excesses that could derail economic growth at any particular point.

Your mind goes through learning cycles in the same way that the economy goes through business cycles. If you understand the cyclical patterns of your own mind, you will be able to keep the growth of your own mind magic on track as well.

The basic fact is that there is a yin and yang of learning. Mind consciousness involves becoming conscious of more than just the yin-yang process, but this process is nevertheless quite powerful. It offers a vivid example of how mind consciousness can extend the power of your mind.

According to the Chinese concept of yin and yang, nature is made up of two opposite principles that combine to produce all that comes to be. There is a yin and yang in learning as well. The yin is the intuitive expressive side of learning. You are finding new ways to use and express what you already know. One may call this period the *expansive phase*. The yang is the conscious and critical side of learning. Here you are changing and improving ideas that you developed during the yin phase, perhaps in reaction to making an error. One may call this the *corrective phase*. To learn well, you need to keep the two in balance.

Following are some examples of how learning fails when the yin and the yang are not in the right balance:

- Lesley, a high school student, is doing math homework. Every problem seems well within her ability. Then she hits one that just does not seem to have a solution. She tries everything she can imagine, but still she cannot find the answer. In the end she gives up in despair.
- Simon, a chef, has spent more than an hour on his specialty, *soupe de poisson à la marseillaise*. Today for some reason it does not taste right. He has no idea what he is doing wrong. He adds first one spice and then another, but the taste just gets worse. He decides to throw out the batch and start again, only to find that the second try tastes just as bad as the first.
- Julie originally went into genetics because she saw it as a promising route to finding a more effective treatment for breast cancer. As part of her training, she discovered that the scientific problems are far greater than she realized. So, like most researchers, she specialized in a particular theoretical problem that her professors considered important at the time. She worked on the problem for several years and made substantial progress. But the rest of the field never became

interested in her work. So she ended with few tangible rewards. She cannot understand what went wrong.

- Stella founded her own company, Cybertalk, five years ago, to produce and distribute translation software. The quality of the product was outstanding and sales grew rapidly. Then a year ago, a competitor began to produce a new product that did not work quite as well but cost only half as much. Stella's sales began to fall. She kept making improvements to her product but continued to lose market share.

- Doug has received much accolade for the exceptional craftsmanship that is obvious in his writing. Critics invariably praise his books, and other writers often call him for help with their work. But in spite of critical acclaim, his books do not sell well. Doug has responded to his poor sales by working harder than ever to perfect his skill as a writer. At the same time, he supplemented his income with college teaching and part-time work as an editor. But at the end of the day, his income seems meager to him for a writer of his ability.

- Harry thought he had a job for life. He worked for General Manufacturing, one of the largest and most profitable corporations in the world. But in the early 1990s his life took an unexpected turn. His employer was facing stiff competition from firms that were shifting their production abroad. They could offer much lower prices because the cost of labor in Mexico and Brazil was so much lower than American wages. The crisis came when, to reduce costs, General Manufacturing closed down the plant where Harry worked. Harry felt that his life was ruined when he lost his job.

These people stopped learning because the yin and the yang became unbalanced. Take Lesley, the high school student, for example. She was doing fine on her math homework as long as she could continue to apply what she already knew. But she hit a roadblock when she ran into a problem that demanded something different. To solve this problem, she needed to leave the expansive yin mode and switch to the corrective yang mode. Instead, like many people, she tried to squeeze more performance from what she already knew. Not surprisingly, she ended up confused and angry.

What happens in school also happens at work. Consider Simon, the chef. He was also stuck in the yin mode and arrived in a situation where proven methods failed to work. Like Lesley, he kept trying to apply techniques that he already knew. He, too, ended up feeling helpless and frustrated.

Unlike these first two examples, Julie, the geneticist, got stuck in the corrective yang phase instead of the expansive yin phase. She kept trying to improve what she knew. And in the process, she forgot why she had become a geneticist to begin with. Julie needed to backtrack. She had to recall why people considered her research problem important in the first place. Then she could begin to explain the significance of her results.

Stella, the entrepreneur, was also stuck in the yang phase. In the past she had succeeded because she produced an outstanding product. But over the long run, business success demands more. Instead of concentrating on the quality of her product, Stella needed to consider the needs of her customers.

Doug, the writer, found himself in a similar predicament. He kept trying to improve his writing but neglected to consider what the public wanted to read. His fine craftsmanship won him the respect of writers and critics, but he failed in the marketplace because the reading public could not appreciate it.

The case of Harry, the production worker, is perhaps the saddest of all. He was like the proverbial dog who could learn no new tricks. He learned his trade when he was young and stayed in the application-oriented yin mode after that. In middle age he found that he had lost the habits of change and self-correction. Therefore, he felt totally lost when his factory closed.

Yin and Yang in Harmony

Seeing the yin and yang in yourself is generally very difficult. Why is that? When you are in the act of learning, it is the subject being learned that usually commands all your attention. You have nothing left over to observe what your mind is doing. But seeing it in other people is sometimes easier. Often you will learn most when you observe children.

Watch how children change over time in the way they think about a particular person, thing, word, or idea. You will frequently see children become positively obsessed. You will also see that there are distinct phases in their thinking. There is the yin phase, when they apply their thinking to an ever-expanding range of contexts. There is also the yang phase, when they rethink their ideas and engage in self-correction.

One good example is a thirteen-year-old boy named Ethan. At one time Ethan became obsessed with the question of whether the TV program "Star Trek" was realistic. He started to wonder whether the technology (warp engines, transporters, holodecks) could ever exist, whether starship captains would really behave like Kirk or Picard, and whether real aliens would be like the aliens on the program. From there the question of fictional realism spread to other aspects of his life, including other TV programs, movies, and books. Ethan even began to wonder whether the idea of intelligent aliens was itself realistic. For a week he went around asking his parents, his teachers, and other adults in his life whether they thought there could be such a thing as an intelligent alien. He was fascinated to discover that serious scientists are actively searching for intelligent life in outer space.

Over a period of weeks, Ethan started to show the yang of self-correction as well as the yin of self-expression. For example, one day he suddenly said, "You know, I think I was wrong about 'Star Trek'—it really isn't all that realistic." For the next two weeks, he went through a period of self-doubt. His mood was more somber. After expressing an opinion about "Star Trek," he frequently added the qualifier "but maybe I am wrong."

He eventually decided that "Star Trek" was partly realistic and partly unrealistic. After that point he went through a second expansive yin phase. Once again he began to apply his ideas more and more broadly. He analyzed several fictional works, in a variety of media, in regard to the ways they were partly realistic and partly unrealistic. Although a television program first kindled Ethan's interest, in the end this interest spilled over into other domains of experience. He ended up even learning some astronomy.

Ethan's experience illustrates the process of *natural learning*. W.. is this? Natural learning is learning that take places in the absence of instruction or some other form of explicit direction or control. Learning how to speak and learning how to use one's body as a young child are both examples of natural learning. In adulthood getting to know a person, learning how to function in a new job, and finding out about a place that you visit on vacation are all examples of natural learning. Natural learning includes no curriculum, but nevertheless, it typically is efficient and productive.

As Ethan's experience shows, natural learning involves a movement back and forth between yin and yang. For a time your thinking expands as you apply what you know to more and more contexts. Then things start to go wrong, and you are forced to retreat. After a period of self-correction, you are ready for another period of expansion when you try your ideas out again in the real world. Unless you deliberately stop it, the cycle of expansion and correction, yin and yang, continues indefinitely.

Your Mind's Natural Power

The really surprising fact is this: strange as it may seem, the intrinsic power of your mind, its magic, once you become conscious of it, is greater than the most brilliant techniques and methods that other people can teach you. What in essence makes the human mind so powerful? The uniquely human ability to adapt and learn. That is what separates us most obviously from every other species.

It is amazing when you realize that human beings have successfully adapted to life under an incredible range of conditions, from the parched heat of the desert to the freezing cold of the Arctic. Perhaps one day humans might even adapt to life in outer space!

Adapting to life in the information age will in essence be no different from adapting to any other dramatic change in living conditions. Futurists (such as Alvin Toffler) and business experts (such as Peter Drucker) tell us that power in the information age will come increasingly from the mind. That can mean only one thing: in the future, even

fore, you will have to rely on your own natural ability.
ot be cause for alarm. Your natural ability is entirely ade-
as you are skillful in putting it to good use.

Natural Learning in the Real World

Can mind consciousness help you in the real world? Definitely! Tennis coach Timothy Gallwey has argued for years that you will do better at learning even a sport such as tennis if you become conscious of how your mind naturally learns. The same principle applies to most domains of experience.

How can mind consciousness help you in learning a sport? In teaching tennis, Gallwey continually encounters the frustration of novices who are unable to place their shots accurately in the opposing player's court. He does not try to teach these students better methods of aiming their shots. Instead, Gallwey tells his students to ignore where the ball lands and concentrate instead on the rhythm of the ball as it hits the ground and then bounces off the racket. Amazingly, their shots become more and more accurate.

Gallwey may not understand tennis better than other coaches do. But he does understand the yin and yang of learning. Gallwey knows that people's minds naturally go through a phase of self-correction in response to errors. He insists just that his students keep hitting the tennis ball. Their unconscious mind will take care of the rest.

Within the American education research community, Professor Donald Graves, who retired from the University of New Hampshire in 1992, is widely considered the leading expert on teaching children to write. Graves works with five- and six-year-olds who know almost nothing about spelling, grammar, or narrative structure. They do not even know that they should write from left to right and top to bottom or that they need to use letters of the alphabet rather than other drawings or marks. In Graves's classroom there is only one rule: the children must spend half an hour writing every day. That is the only rule Graves needs. As long as the children keep practicing, he knows that their writing will keep getting better and better.

Within two years Graves finds that his students can spell, use grammar, and create structured narratives. They learn to write in almost the same natural way that they learned to talk.

What Graves knows about writing is the same thing that Gallwey knows about tennis. The mind naturally self-corrects. The same knowledge is useful to you.

Re-Creating a Balance Between Yin and Yang

As you become conscious of principles such as yin and yang, you can use this understanding to solve your problems and to improve your learning.

Return to the example of Lesley, the frustrated math student. Most students in Lesley's position expect that they can use roughly the same methods to solve every problem. This will not work. A problem that resists solution is qualitatively different from other problems. To solve it, you need to switch gears from yin to yang. Stop trying to apply methods and techniques that you know. And start trying to improve your own thinking. You need to either find or invent a new method. Put differently, you need to stop worrying about the answer or product and start focusing on the thinking process itself.

Students in Lesley's position often go wrong because they expect the difficult problems to take only a little more time than the others require. But yang thinking is intrinsically slower than yin thinking. Solving one yang problem can take as much time as doing a whole homework assignment of yin problems.

What should Lesley do? First, she needs to switch gears. After quickly answering a series of questions, most students are already looking ahead to having the work finished within a short time. Lesley and students like her will suddenly reach a point when it becomes clear that the work is going to take longer, perhaps a lot longer, than they had expected. This recognition requires an emotional adjustment. Lesley is unlikely to make progress unless she experiences and accepts her feelings at this moment. These feelings may include annoyance, frustration, sadness, anger, and even mild despair. She may need to take a break from her math, lasting from an hour to a day, so that her negative feelings stop clouding her mind.

Next, Lesley should get to work finding a solution. The right choice of strategy depends on the specific mathematical topic and Lesley's own problem-solving style. A possible strategy is to compare the one difficult problem with the previous set of easy problems. Describing carefully what makes the difficult problem different may suggest possible solutions. For example, it may help her identify a specific concept or method in her previous course work that she had partially misunderstood. She may find the solution by reading about that concept in her textbook or course notes or by looking it up on the Internet.

The ability to switch gears may always be valuable. Nevertheless, even when it helps you find the best solution to your problem, that best solution may still be the best only of several imperfect alternatives. Simon tried to make his soup taste the way it used to taste. And he failed repeatedly. It is time for Simon to realize that he cannot make the same pot of soup twice. He needs to switch to yang thinking. Then he may try to invent his soup anew. It can be totally different from the way it tasted yesterday as long as the new taste also is delicious.

What happens to Simon, though, if his customers complain that the new soup is different from the old one? What was originally a technical difficulty in reproducing a specific taste has escalated into a potential threat to the customer base of his business. If his old customers desert him, he may have to look for new ones, and he may even have to change his self-definition of what kind of chef he is. What initially appears to be a concrete problem can end up requiring a change in self-concept. I will discuss how minds undergo this more complex kind of change in Chapter 3, which deals with adaptation.

Mind consciousness helps Julie, the geneticist, in a different way. In becoming so obsessed with refining her own thinking, she lost touch with the real world. She needs to tell herself to stop being so yang-oriented. When she actively tries to stop criticizing herself, she will feel lost at first. People like Julie become used to self-criticism. But if she maintains her determination not to be self-critical, her yin thinking will slowly begin to reemerge.

Julie's training and experience as a professional researcher have given her a wealth of knowledge that she could put to use in a wide variety of ways. But she has become blinded to her many options. Julie has so totally internalized the values of the research community that she sees her work as important only to the extent that it contributes to the growth of knowledge. Furthermore, she feels compelled to ensure that her work maintains the strict standards of the international research community. If she relaxes her pattern of yang thinking, she will start to notice what aspects of her work give her genuine pleasure and satisfaction.

Like Julie, Stella, the entrepreneur, has to escape from the cycle of yang thinking. But in Stella's case the solution is harder to find. Julie has to rediscover an original purpose that time has caused her to forget. Stella has to acquire a concern for customer service that she may never have felt before. Regardless of the degree of difficulty, the process is the same. Stella has to force herself to stop continually trying to improve her already outstanding product and instead focus on what her customers are looking for. Slowly, she will see yin thinking reemerge. It will suggest new directions for her business to take.

Doug, the literary craftsman, also needs to switch from yang to yin if he hopes to achieve commercial success. When he does so, might envious colleagues and critics think that he has sold out? As part of switching gears, Doug certainly must face this kind of fear. A writer like Doug often does best to make contact with his more ordinary emotions. He does not have to worry about necessarily being a brilliant writer. Instead, he can allow feelings to emerge that he shares with most people and try to write prose that relates to them. Or he can decide that his critical success is fulfilling enough and come to terms with making his living in other ways.

Harry, the industrial worker, may have the hardest time of all. People often repeat slogans such as "You can't teach an old dog new tricks." This kind of mind-set brainwashes the Harrys of the world into thinking they are too old to learn. Harry actively has to resist the prejudices of his culture in order to switch from yin mode to yang. He must first become used to criticizing his own thinking. Then he will discover in himself the necessary ability to adapt, perhaps by returning to school to acquire new credentials.

These six examples of how to overcome learning failure are all different from each other. Nevertheless, they share in common one fundamental attribute. The key to success in every case is the awareness that learning involves both a yin phase and a yang phase. Awareness of this fact empowers you to switch from one phase to the other when necessary. This awareness represents a powerful asset for breaking out of a cycle of frustration.

What Makes Mind Consciousness a Revolutionary Idea?

As you have seen, the learning cycle of yin and yang is similar to the cycle of growth in the economy. You can use this knowledge in the same way that government uses knowledge of the business cycle. Is there something revolutionary about this idea?

Before the Great Depression of the 1930s, governments knew about business cycles. But they never used this knowledge to improve the performance of the economy. They saw the business cycle as an inevitable process beyond human influence.

Many people today think of the growth of the mind in roughly the same way. They feel that genetic factors control intelligence and that, short of genetic engineering, there is no way to influence them. Some people are born smarter and others are born less intelligent. The former learn easily and the latter do not. *Que sera, sera.*

On the other hand, the theory of mind consciousness says that there is a way for you to increase what your mind has the capacity to understand and learn. How do you do it? It comes in part from understanding your own mind and in part from observing and understanding the thinking of people whom you might want to emulate. Specifically, you need to find people who are able to learn in the way that you would like to learn. You should be able to observe what they do and learn how to do the same thing yourself. (There is of course, another solution. To save time, you could read a book by a learning specialist who has studied the people whose learning methods you would like to emulate. Then, you can adopt the method presented. In fact, you can use many sections of this book that way.)

Which kind of people do you (or your learning specialist) need to observe? Suppose you wanted to learn in the same way as a brilliant problem solver. In that case, you might want to observe how an eminent scientist learns. Alternatively, suppose you wanted to learn in the same way as a successful persuader. Then perhaps observe how a brilliantly effective sales representative learns.

Here is what makes the idea of mind consciousness so radical. Most people believe that you can acquire specific skills (such as reading) and bodies of information (such as social anthropology). But can you acquire the higher-level skill of becoming more adept at the process of knowledge acquisition? And in general, can you acquire your ability to use your mind more effectively? The principle of mind consciousness asserts that you can. In other words, it means that you can learn mind magic.

Is the innate ability theory correct or is the mind-consciousness theory correct? The best way to judge the concept of mind consciousness is to give it a try. See if it helps you develop a new talent. Personal success is the best proof you could want.

How Will Mind Consciousness Help You?

As you come to understand the concept of mind consciousness, it can start to change your whole conception of what learning involves. You see the essence of learning more as a process of acquiring new ways of thinking. At the same time, you see it much less as a process of acquiring information.

Have you ever wanted badly to learn something but felt that it was virtually impossible? Society pursues better educational methods with the same perseverance that many people use when searching for the ideal weight-loss program. But do you need better teaching? Not necessarily. As Gallwey and Graves argue, the best learning begins from the inside, not the outside. You need to make better use of what you naturally do.

In practice, people usually have trouble learning because they demand too much of their minds too quickly and then become discouraged when it does not perform. Minds, like children, are idiosyncratic and temperamental. They will learn, but perhaps only when they feel like it. The answer is to become conscious of your mind's learning style and let it learn in its own way.

How does consciousness of the yin-yang process help you to learn more successfully? First, awareness allows you to see that mistakes are a natural part of learning. The only people who never make mistakes are people who never challenge themselves. Knowing this allows you to build in time for self-correction. Furthermore, you will be able to see your mistake as something to be anticipated rather than as a reason to think poorly about yourself.

Second, the yin-yang principle tells you to respect the expansive phase of learning as well as the corrective phase, the yin as well as the yang. Educational researchers continually see people who learn wonderfully in the classroom but then fail to transfer to other settings what they know from school. Such researchers consider the problem of transfer to be one of the most serious issues in education. They understand the problem but not the solution. What is it? To be able to use a new idea, you have to let it run. You need the expansion phase for it to become second nature.

Third, and most important of all, the yin-yang principle teaches you moderation. Do not become discouraged when you repeatedly have to correct yourself. This phase will not last forever. On the other hand, do not become overconfident when things seem to be going well. That phase will come to an end, too.

You Don't Have to Fix What Ain't Broke

The real beauty of mind consciousness is the way it combines simplicity and power.

Since the 1960s experts have been promising to teach people better ways of thinking. Today books on the subject are available at any major bookstore. Are such lessons necessary or useful for most people? Some of these "thinking lessons" presented genuinely powerful ideas. But it was extremely difficult for most people to learn and apply them. Other lessons were quite simple. But the simple lessons did not give people much mind power.

On the other hand, think about the idea of yin and yang. The idea is easy to understand, and you do not need to engage in extensive brain building in order to apply it. Why is this new?

As books on thinking were first appearing, a revolution was taking place in psychology. It left us with an infinitely richer and more sophisticated picture of how people think and learn than we ever had before. The concept of mind consciousness grows directly out of this revolution.

One principle was especially important. Earlier authors had assumed that you have to teach people to think effectively. A large body of research directly contradicts this notion. In a normal environment, mind magic develops adequately on its own. You do not need to help it along.

The Swiss psychologist Piaget is most famous for having made this point. This idea was so surprising that it transformed the way in which schools teach. Its influence on early childhood education has been so pervasive that in many places, it made Piaget a household name.

Piaget recognized how effectively the human mind does its job. Do you see your mind as needing improvement? You probably do not even begin to recognize how well it serves you already. The intelligence of even the most powerful computer is tiny in comparison with that of the most ordinary human being. Before you try to improve your mind, first make sure that it genuinely needs fixing.

Piaget was the first person to document systematically the intrinsic effectiveness of ordinary human mind magic. Paradoxically, this discovery grew directly out of his analysis of the role of errors. People commonly see one's being correct as a sign of being more intelligent and one's making mistakes as a sign of being less so. On the contrary, Piaget argued—mistakes can be a positive sign. The only people who never make mistakes are the ones who always play it safe. Mistakes are a sign of a living mind in action.

Piaget's perspective serves to counteract much unhelpful advice that so often undermines people's confidence and morale. Advisers will often tell you to have a realistic sense of your own limitations. It is certainly true that you should avoid self-deception. Unfortunately, this explicit piece of good advice often goes along with an unstated piece of bad advice. The implicit message is that you should see yourself as limited regardless of whether you really are or not.

It is indeed possible to increase the magic of your mind. But you should never let experts seduce you into giving up the considerable mind magic that you already possess. Piaget's data remain sound and his conclusions remain valid. Improve on your mind's way of thinking and learning, but do not change or replace what is already working well.

Hasn't the way you naturally think demonstrated its reliability to you over many years? If you are like most people, you have had to face numerous obstacles over the course of growing up and functioning as an adult in our society. You have probably been wrong some of the time. Nevertheless, most of the time your mind almost certainly has served you well. Your mind's strong track record shows that it cannot help but function remarkably well in many ways. Treasure the skill at thinking that you already have—only learn to make it even better.

Dealing with the Real World

There is ample evidence in support of the theory of mind consciousness. Indeed, it is reassuring to see that science and common sense both point to similar conclusions. What does science have to say about the power of natural mind magic? Take into account the importance of learning from a biological viewpoint. In particular, think about the role played by learning in the ability of human beings to adapt.

The natural abilities of most living creatures are well suited to dealing with the kinds of problems typically presented by their environment. Camels can survive in the desert because they can store water in their humps; giraffes can eat the leaves of tall trees because of their long necks. Human beings have comparable abilities.

Books on intelligence often show your true abilities in a bad light because they measure your skills using textbook problems. Those problems do not offer a fair description of your true potential. Real-world problems are quite different from the neat and tidy questions you see in textbooks. As part of everyday existence, you have to make decisions about how to organize your life. You have to deal with problems in your work. If you are a parent, you have to make decisions that will affect your children's future. These issues may not be easy to resolve; nevertheless, they are better suited than textbook problems to the way your mind naturally works. Even though it may not be the entire solution, making better use of your mind can significantly help.

In what specific ways are real-life problems different from the ones usually found in textbooks?

- Real-life problems will not disappear when you close the book or when you finish the course. Therefore, the amount of time you will choose to devote to solving them is many times greater than you would devote to a textbook exercise.
- Real-life problems are deeply embedded in what you really know. You may indeed have far more real-world knowledge that directly relates to your problems than anyone else has. (Book problems usually remain at the periphery of your knowledge.)
- Real-life problems engage your emotions. Solving them often involves emotional adjustments at least as much as inference and deduction.
- Real-life problems often require you to participate in a highly personal, even idiosyncratic, process to uncover a solution that you find acceptable. What works for you may be different in important ways from what works for another person.

The "right" methods for solving real-life problems are ones that you trust in your heart as well as your head. It is not enough that you believe in them intellectually. You also must feel comfortable with them emotionally. Your engagement with a technique that you know only from a

ot help but be superficial. A deeper sense of engagement can
y from personal experience.

Putting the Power of Your Mind to Work for You

The inscription on the oracle at Delphi in ancient Greece prescribed
"Know thyself." Today we can add a second prescription, telling you to
know your own mind.

Mind consciousness serves the needs of your head as well as your
heart. To understand the way that you think and learn is to gain at least
partial control over your mind. If you understand how minds work, then
you can deliberately put mind power to work for you.

Learning mind magic is by nature multifaceted. There is no reason
to believe that one specific aspect of your mind is the key to mind magic
as a whole. On the contrary, it is far more realistic, and more interesting, to explore the different faces of mind magic one at a time. What
are the most powerful components of mind magic? Among them are
the following: adaptability, creativity, information management, and
problem solving. The next four chapters address these aspects.

The more you know about the mind, the better you will be able to
tap into your own mind magic. In the information age, mind consciousness truly is your most valuable resource. You can learn what you
need to make it work for you.

CHAPTER 3

ADAPTING YOUR MIND TO FIT THE TIMES

You lose your job. A relationship breaks up. Someone falls ill. Major crises are a fact of life. They happen to all of us.

The fun side of learning is the yin phase, the period of expansion and self-expression. But we also have to negotiate the yang phase, the period of self-correction. The yang experience sometimes occupies only a small region of your mental space. You do not do as well as you expected on a calculus examination. You probably will need to reexamine your understanding of some parts of your mathematics course. Other times the yang phase can occupy your whole mind. After a painful breakup, you may feel, "We seemed so perfect for each other—how could I misjudge a person so badly?"

Many people try to avoid the yang phase. They feel that it is too depressing. But they pay the consequences. Other people are good at facing their problems but not at making the adjustments that will let them put the problems to rest.

Possibly the greatest value of mind magic is the help it offers you in adapting to changes in your life and your world. Where does this knowledge come from? Clinicians who treat trauma need mind magic to adapt their learning to the very real emergency situations they face. As we saw in Chapter 2, watching children develop is a great way to learn about mind magic.

Another valuable source is the history of science. Textbook science tells us stories of the great thinkers, such as Galileo and Newton, who changed the way we understand the world in which we live. But what happened to the less famous scientists, the professionals who needed to adapt when a Newton or an Einstein challenged the very foundations of their work? Adaptation to change is no harder or easier for scientists than for the rest of us. Scientists need to adapt successfully as a matter of course because change and progress are the very lifeblood of science. The ways in which scientists cope have valuable implications for how we can adapt to change as well.

Charles Darwin wrote, "It is not the strongest of the species that survives, nor the most intelligent that survives. It is the one that is the most adaptable to change." Regardless of your IQ or your history, you can learn how to be more intelligent and how to succeed in the constantly changing world of the information age. The key ideas to remember are adaptability, creativity, and information management.

Mind consciousness will not make the yang phase go away, nor will it necessarily make you happy. But it will help you negotiate hard times more smoothly and successfully as well as learn from these experiences. Mind consciousness helps you know when and how to intervene in managing your mind to make the process of adaptation happen more smoothly and perhaps more quickly. It also helps you monitor both the conscious and unconscious spheres of your mind and gives you feedback about whether you are adapting successfully.

Piaget

In this chapter we will pay special attention to the work of Jean Piaget, the most influential theorist of intelligence and adaptation in all of psychology.

According to a recent survey, members of the American Psychological Association consider Piaget the second most important psychologist of the twentieth century. The APA assessment is entirely justified. In terms of the depth and originality of his ideas, it is reasonable to compare Piaget with Sigmund Freud. Like Freud, Piaget came to believe that understanding childhood is crucial for understanding human psychology. But in other respects, Piaget was very different f. Freud. Freud was a theorist of motivation, personality, and p chopathology; in contrast, Piaget was a theorist of learning, thinkin₀, and intelligence. Freud's work has important links with literature and the arts, whereas Piaget's work has links with less easily accessible fields, such as epistemology, the branch of philosophy that deals with the origins of knowledge.

Why is Piaget important? For one thing, he is important as a source of mind magic. If the theory of mind consciousness is correct, then we should be able to turn to his discoveries as a source of information to help us use our capacity to adapt consciously and deliberately.

Intelligence Means Adaptation

The central concept in this chapter is the notion, proposed by Piaget, that we should see intelligence as the psychological mechanism of adaptation. We will look at what this idea means and why it is important to you.

Throughout his career Piaget was critical of both IQ tests and the theory that intelligence is an unchanging innate ability. He saw change as essential to life and to the structure of intelligence itself. Piaget earned his doctorate originally in evolutionary biology, not psychology. His background in biology made him sensitive to the ways in which living species change and evolve over thousands and millions of years. As a psychologist, he had a similar interest in the remarkable ways in which individual human beings change from month to month and year to year. According to Piaget, intelligence accounts for this process of change and development.

Piaget found in his research that the ability to change and adapt intelligently is a feature of all normal human beings. We all do it, even though we are not aware of when we do it, how we do it, or that we do it. One of his great accomplishments was to shed light on this amazing capacity.

Future Shock

When could it help you to understand the processes of intelligent adaptation? First of all, it can help you with learning, in all of its many forms. Second, it can help you in dealing with major life events and crises. Third, it can help you adapt to fundamental changes in society and in the world around us. In the rapidly evolving society we live in, adapting to social and technological change is a necessity.

For the last three decades, thinkers have been pointing out the psychological price that constant and rapid change can extract. In his 1971 book *Future Shock*, Alvin Toffler, the father of futurology, coined the phrase *future shock* to refer to "the disorientation and stress brought about by trying to cope with too many changes in too short a time." At the time, future shock was a potential threat; today it is a fact of life. Toffler held that it is possible to overload individuals, organizations, and even nations with too much change too quickly. If this happened, he argued, it would lead to disorientation and a breakdown in their capacity to make intelligent adaptive decisions.

In other words, the effect of future shock is to undermine people's familiar ways of thinking and feeling. As Toffler predicted, future shock did indeed become a common and widespread problem. Is there a solution? Toffler himself did not offer any answers apart from slowing down the pace of change—an unlikely scenario, to say the least. Perhaps we need to look elsewhere. The antidote to future shock in large part may be to appreciate what Piaget discovered about the human mind's remarkable ability to adapt.

With respect to the problem, the statistics speak for themselves. As Toffler predicted, the nuclear family has become fractured. We can no longer see as the norm the standard family structure so familiar at the time when Toffler published his first major work. The effects of future shock affect people's mental life as well as their social world. Consider the growing frequency of psychiatric illness. Since the start of the information age, mental health professionals have seen a steep and dramatic increase in the occurrence of all stress-related problems. One clear example of this trend is the incidence of post-traumatic stress disorder (PTSD). At one time the diagnosis of PTSD was extremely rare, limited almost exclusively to soldiers suffering from shell shock. Today the diagnosis of PTSD has become a standard diagnosis in an "average" psychiatric practice. During the weeks and months following the terrorist attack on the World Trade Center on September 11, 2001, the New York City region witnessed an epidemic of PTSD.

Just as alarming are the statistics on depression. Clinical depression is among the most serious and debilitating of all psychiatric illnesses. Epidemiological studies show that over the last half century, the rate of depression has increased approximately tenfold, or 1,000 percent. That is not a misprint—you did read it correctly. The figure is shocking. According to the National Comorbidity Study, sponsored by the National Institutes of Health, in 2003 more than 16 percent of Americans suffered from depression severe enough to warrant treatment. Depression is a cyclical disorder in which patients may be asymptomatic for several years between phases of the illness. Therefore, at any one time, the number of people suffering from depression will be much greater than the number who show symptoms. Nevertheless, in any given one-year period, thirteen to fourteen million people, about 6.6 percent of the nation's population, experience the illness.

Because some of this data is based on the rate of diagnosed depression, people sometimes suspect that this figure may reflect not the actual rate of depression but instead people's willingness to seek professional help. It is true that people are much more willing to seek psychiatric help today than they were, say, in the 1930s. Nevertheless, even taking this factor into account, the underlying reality remains unaltered. Research shows the same increase in the frequency of symptoms indicative to a clinician of depression, regardless of whether the person had sought professional help. Depression has become a pervasive feature of American society. The fact is undeniable.

In the case of women, the data are even more alarming. While the rate of depression in the general population was increasing tenfold, the rate of depression among women was increasing twice as fast. Taking into account all available evidence, it is clear that the rate of depression is a public health problem of the greatest urgency.

Victims of a depressive illness represent the extreme case. Most people do not suffer from a depressive illness even though they might not feel as happy or as satisfied with their lives as they would have a generation ago. But they still suffer from the effects of future shock. They need better methods to put their minds to greatest use.

Opinion polls reflect the fact that the mood of society has become increasingly somber. One reflection of this is the rise in public concern about the future. In the past America was known as a nation of optimists. For generations Americans have believed that the future would always be better. But as future shock has spread, Americans have lost their faith. Poll after poll shows this: during the decade of the 1990s, a majority of Americans became pessimistic about the quality of their lives improving, even following year after year of economic growth. Even more telling, most Americans came to foresee hard times for their children. According to the American dream, it was always believed that your children would do better than you did. Not many people believed that anymore. Every year the polls report faithfully the same message: most people expect their children to have a harder time and lower standard of living than they themselves enjoy.

The information revolution, however, does not have to cause hard times. New technology offers the tools to create new products and services, and it creates the possibility of new wealth. A global economy may mean foreign competition, but it also means foreign markets. Quite literally it opens up a world of consumers for excellent products.

Adaptation is a process of changing your thinking and your perceptions. What really helps you to cope with social change or technological change? When the world changes, your understanding of it must also change. It is not enough just to act differently. You have to think differently.

Clinicians who treat PTSD say that their clients need to construct a new personal narrative. What does that mean? We all have a perception of how the world around us works, which affords us a sense of safety and security. We feel that we can count on things generally to work in a predictable way.

Why was the World Trade Center attack (or longer ago, on December 7, 1941, the attack on Pearl Harbor) so traumatic for so many Americans? It was not just a matter of personal connection. People hundreds of miles away from the attack, and who knew none of the victims personally, still suffered symptoms of trauma. Nor did the trauma result purely from the number of lives lost. Natural disasters that take even more lives do not have the same effect. Was the experience so traumatic because human agents caused it? Even that is not a complete explanation. Acts of human terror at least as savage, such as genocide in Rwanda or suicide bombings in Israel, do not affect so many Americans so deeply.

A traumatic event is one that threatens and undermines our sense of reality. Americans were not prepared for the World Trade Center attack (or the attack on Pearl Harbor). For that reason, its effects were so disturbing. To cope with so shocking an event typically involves changing our sense of reality, constructing a new narrative, which acknowledges the reality of the disturbing events but still allows us a reasonable sense of safety. Years later, many people are still in the process of adjusting their sense of reality.

The information revolution may pose new challenges—the symptoms of future shock are all around us. But it also discloses new opportunities. If people learn to use the power of their mind effectively to adjust their sense of reality, they will join those who adapt successfully in today's world. This ability to adapt can open the door to a better future for them and their families.

How the Mind Adapts to Change

If you do not expect to be able to adapt, then you probably will not adapt. On the other hand, people who see themselves as capable typically live up to their expectations. There is no reason to doubt your ability to adapt.

When they talk about change, people often use phrases such as "adopting the new paradigm" or "jumping on the bandwagon" or "getting up to speed." All of these phrases make it sound as if adapting means coming around to what other people think. Perhaps for people highly predisposed to conform, it really is like that. But for everyone else, the process is more complicated. This is one of the reasons why the experience of paradigm shift in science teaches us a great deal. Professional scientists stand out as being predisposed to be more careful and critical of unfamiliar ideas than the rest of us. You would surely expect scientists to defy the "bandwagon" view if anyone does.

Seeing change as nothing more than conforming fails in many ways above and beyond the question of whether it fits paradigm shift in science. For one thing, it says nothing about the subjective experience of people in the midst of change. Change causes future shock with the associated experiences of anxiety and stress. Some embrace change regardless of the discomfort it may cause them. Others actively resist. But unpleasantness is quite often a basic fact of the process. An accurate description of adaptation must take this fact into account.

The view of change as conforming also ignores the role that you may want for yourself. Who is better able to serve your organization and community—a mindless conformist or a rational thinker? No one gets ahead of the crowd as long as he or she passively accepts whatever everyone else thinks.

Conscientious rational thinkers will accept a paradigm only after they have answered their own personal doubts. This means that from time to time they have to suffer through painful transitions. For these people, adapting to change is essentially a process of reinventing the old self but in a changed working environment.

Changing Your Perceptions

Many people think about adaptation in terms of changing their behavior. This is the "New Year's resolution" theory of adaptation. After losing a job or losing a relationship, people often say, "I have to make sure not to make that mistake again." Do they succeed? A few people, though not many, actually keep their New Year's resolutions. As we have seen, adaptation in the real world is more complicated.

Adaptation virtually always involves some significant change in our sense of reality. It is not as simple or as straightforward as making a New Year's resolution, but it is substantially more stable and more effective. However, you cannot just command yourself to see the world differently and expect anything to happen. What makes your sense of reality change? Let us return to Piaget to see his answer.

The Mind Magic of Adaptation

How do you get it when you just do not get it? What do you do when you have no idea what to do? How do you understand what simply does not make sense? Of all the achievements of the human mind, the "aha" experience of suddenly "getting it" seems to most people to be among the most magical, perhaps second only to the ability to produce an original creative work. In spite of its magical aura, this skill is one that all human beings share.

Piaget demonstrated over and over again that adapting to change and overcoming profound misinterpretations are regular everyday events. Although he first observed this process at work in children, it is not limited to any particular age group or developmental stage. Babies, children, teenagers, and adults all undergo the same experience.

Consider one example of mind magic at work. In this famous experiment, Piaget and his distinguished coworker Bärbel Inhelder showed children a plastic model of a countryside with a rich complex landscape. It featured hills, a river, roads, a bridge, buildings, and other landmarks. Psychologists usually call it the *three-mountain problem* because Piaget's original study used a landscape with three mountains. At first the child stood at one side of the landscape facing toward it, and Piaget placed a small doll right in front of the child looking forward. He asked the child to tell him what the doll saw. Even preschool-age children had no trouble accurately describing the landscape from the perspective of the doll, because it was also the child's own perspective.

The crucial step in the experiment is what happened next. Piaget moved the doll to a distant point far away from the child, facing a direction different from that of the child. Once again he asked the child to tell him what the doll saw. Not all children gave the same answer this time.

Around the age of four or five, most children attributed to the doll the same perceptions that they had themselves. If they saw a river in front of a road, they said that this is what the doll saw. They did not take into account if the doll was on the opposite side of the landscape and was therefore closer to the road than to the river. But by age nine or ten, children seemed to take into account differences in viewpoint. They knew the doll would see things differently because it was at a different vantage point.

As Piaget and Inhelder pointed out, these results directly contradict what most people then and now have believed about learning and adaptation. People generally presume that mistakes reveal a failure of understanding. For this reason adults feel embarrassed when they make mistakes themselves and feel compelled immediately to correct errors that children make.

Piaget and Inhelder insist that this is a poor and potentially harmful way to react to children's errors. On the contrary, making mistakes is a normal, healthy part of learning and adaptation. People who never make mistakes also never learn.

Before Piaget, if parents saw their five-year-olds having difficulty with perspective, they would worry that their children would never acquire this important skill. But as Piaget and Inhelder showed, there is no reason to worry. It is normal for five-year-olds to make this kind of mistake. And it is just as normal for nine-year-olds to give a more mature, adultlike answer. Something changes in most children between the ages of five and nine that alters both what they think and how they think about the three-mountain problem.

If Piaget and his colleagues encountered this kind of qualitative change in one or two experiments, the findings would be interesting and would raise many questions. But they would not change psychology. Piaget succeeded in changing psychology because he conducted not one or two experiments but hundreds. And these experiments were extremely varied in content and method. Taken together, they demonstrate that qualitative changes happen all the time in our thinking.

Think about it. This finding is odd. Most of us feel that it is very difficult to correct our own mistakes. On the other hand, research shows overwhelmingly that Piaget was right: correcting our mistakes is as normal for human beings as breathing. Like breathing, it is something that we do whether we are aware of it or not.

A Mistake Is Not a Crisis—but It Can Still Help You Learn How to Cope

What does correcting mistakes have to do with coping with crises? Do the two really have a lot in common? Correcting a mistake seems to be a purely intellectual process. It seems to make use of only the logical cognitive part of our mind. On the other hand, coping with a crisis demands that we make use of all our psychological resources, emotional as well as intellectual. It often seems as if the emotional resources are by far the more important.

Nevertheless, there are many similarities between correcting conceptual mistakes and responding to a crisis. In Chapter 2 we discussed the idea of a yin and yang of learning. The idea is that learning has two phases. It has an expansive yin phase in which we broaden our horizons and a corrective yang phase in which we reexamine and change our suppositions. Correcting the way in which we think about conceptual problems, such as the three-mountain problem, and coping with crises both represent the yang phase.

Piaget's analysis of self-correction reveals that correcting mistakes is a far more emotional process than people often recognize. In many of his experiments, Piaget was able to find subjects at the point of transition between two fundamentally different ways of thinking. He reports the sense of conflict and confusion that they experienced. Many would vacillate between two answers, one reflecting a more mature understanding and the other a less mature one. They kept going back and forth, never feeling able to settle on either one. He observes that others felt a subjective sense of confusion and uncertainty. All of these observations reveal a powerful emotional component at the heart of a supposedly intellectual process.

Go back to the three-mountain problem. The five-year-old child lives in a self-contained world in which she feels safe and sure of herself. She is utterly certain that she is correct when she says what the doll sees. Piaget and Inhelder tried all kinds of ways to shake the child's confidence, but none of them worked. Piaget or Inhelder would tell a five-year-old, "This morning I showed this problem to another girl. She said the doll would see the road in front of the river. Was this girl right or wrong?" This kind of countersuggestion almost never caused children to waiver. They insisted instead that the other girl was wrong and that their original (mistaken) answer was right.

Piaget explains that qualitative change involves a disruption and reorganization of some part of our worldview. Something happens that disrupts the equilibrium in the person's thinking. It punctures a hole in his or her safe, secure worldview. The disruption causes distress and anxiety that disappear only after the person returns to a steady, stable, secure state of mind. Sometimes stability reestablishes itself when the person returns to his or her earlier viewpoint, essentially disregarding or repressing the disruptive piece of information. Other times he or she progresses to a broader, more inclusive, and better-adapted narrative. This is real adaptation. It happens surprisingly often.

The many parallels between correcting mistakes and adapting to a crisis lend substantial credibility to the thesis that both reflect the same underlying process. Applying the lessons of one to solving the problems of the other makes the case that much more compelling.

If It Is Really OK to Make Mistakes, Why Do So Many People Think It Is So Bad?

Although Piaget may have spoken with more authority and evidence than anyone else, he surely was not the only person to have recognized the crucial and positive role of mistakes in learning. Many good teachers have pointed out that you learn nothing without making mistakes. They tell us that if you are not making any mistakes, you are not trying to do anything challenging.

So why has the idea been so slow to catch on? Why do so many people feel embarrassed when they make even a minor harmless mistake? Even in schools and universities, we tend to see mistakes treated as evidence of failure, not as signs of learning and ambition.

Our culture's fear of making mistakes is perhaps the most serious impediment to our being successful in learning and adaptation. Successful learners typically take mistakes in stride, learning something from them and then quickly forgetting them. Unsuccessful learners either refuse to admit their mistakes or, once having admitted them, go

to the other extreme, obsessing and fretting over them. People
adaptable treat mistakes as no big deal. People who have troubl
ing see their own mistakes and those of others as evidence of
inadequacy.

Why do so many people handle being wrong so poorly? I think there
are six common reasons.

1. Lack of knowledge
2. Experience with content experts who are not learning experts
3. Fear of losing face
4. Leftover effects of childhood
5. Personal ideology
6. Cynicism about Piaget and like-minded thinkers

Lack of Knowledge

Although most psychologists are familiar with Piaget's theories, his
work is still poorly known in the general community. Many people simply do not understand the place of mistakes in learning and adaptation.

Experience with Content Experts Who Are Not Learning Experts

Experts in many fields tell us to make a special effort to get things right
the first time around. They mean that we should not make mistakes.
They often warn us that mistakes at the beginning could lead to bad
habits later on and that bad habits are hard to break.

Are they right? Only if you lack the mind consciousness to know how
mistakes become corrected. These experts are really saying that they
know so little about learning that they do not know how to help people overcome bad habits. As a result, they become perfectionists when
instructing new learners. The effects are likely to be disastrous. Because
they lack confidence and familiarity, new learners need the freedom to
make mistakes more than anybody else does.

Insisting that students get things right the first time around is bad
teaching practice. The real solution is to teach these experts about how
people learn, not to make unrealistic and perfectionist demands.

Fear of Losing Face

There really are times when we need to be letter-perfect. You would be disappointed at the theater if the leading actor forgot his lines. The problem comes when we feel we must avoid mistakes all the time, not only when it counts.

You need to distinguish learning from performance. When you are on camera, you want to be letter-perfect. But in the privacy of your living room, you want to feel able to make a lot of mistakes. Too many people treat their private rooms as if they were public rooms. They hate themselves for making a mistake, even at a time when it would be unrealistic of them to expect to have gotten it right.

Leftover Effects of Childhood

Many of us grew up before Piaget's ideas were widely recognized. Therefore, we probably experienced discouragement or even punishment for our mistakes. Although it happened long ago, the effects can persist today. People feel ashamed or embarrassed about making mistakes not because they consciously see anything wrong with it but because they experience feelings that persist from childhood.

Personal Ideology

A certain number of people have an ideological commitment to educational methods that punish mistakes. They typically claim that they believe in setting high standards and criticize educational methods that avoid punishing mistakes as coddling. Paradoxically, you find many of these people working in the field of education, the very place where they do not belong.

If setting high standards is the same thing as a commitment to excellence, there is no need to punish mistakes. Surely a sincere commitment to excellence implies a commitment as well to educational methods, such as a tolerance of mistakes, that increases the chances of achieving it.

Cynicism About Piaget and Like-Minded Thinkers

Strange as it may seem, there are people who think that Piaget (and others) is really making excuses for personal failure when he points out the inevitability of mistakes. In the case of Piaget, he received many, many accolades for his work during his lifetime. How much recognition do you need to receive before you count as a success? (Well, Piaget never did receive the Nobel Prize, but neither did any of these critics.)

This kind of personal attack reflects close-mindedness, not thoughtful criticism. Its goal is to intimidate and embarrass rather than to refute.

Human Beings Are Brilliantly Adaptable (Even When We Feel Helpless)

People may expect their minds to do great things for them at times when their thinking is going well. What happens when you are in trouble? Can your mind show its magic even when you feel frustrated and helpless?

At times of crisis, or in the face of mistakes, people are especially prone to throw up their hands in despair. They become discouraged and depressed. They feel that things are hopeless. Surprising as it may seem, your mind can reveal its greatest power at times of greatest weakness. When things are going wrong is when you truly need the ability to adapt. Magically, if you do not undermine that ability, it is there.

Consider this: when are people most helpless? It is hard to imagine any greater helplessness than that of the newborn baby. Newborns can barely do anything. They cannot even perform an act as simple as telling their hand to grasp a toy that they have seen with their eyes. Yet a few months later, they are playing, smiling, babbling, crawling, pushing buttons, recognizing familiar things and people, and solving problems. How does the helpless newborn turn into the competent baby and mobile toddler? Does the adaptability of the newborn tell us anything about how we are able to adapt?

Before Piaget, most psychologists and pediatricians used to believe that the emerging competence of the newborn resulted from maturation of the brain. There was never any hard scientific evidence to show that known changes in the brain cause the amazing growth of competence that we observe. Professionals believed the brain-maturation theory because they could not think of anything better.

What changed? Most psychologists consider Piaget's most original and important research to be a series of studies of infant intelligence. This research reveals an amazing capacity to learn and adapt even during the first days and weeks of life.

Piaget's infancy research is extremely detailed and in places highly technical. The level of detail necessary in studying early infancy is sometimes off-putting to nonprofessionals. Nevertheless, it has revolutionary implications for understanding learning and adaptation in adults as well as babies. I will not go into great detail, but I will give you at least a taste.

In one set of studies, Piaget investigated the origins of eye-hand coordination. Most of us totally take for granted our ability to tell our hands to grasp an object that our eyes see. It is hard to imagine what it must be like to lack that ability. It is harder still to imagine how anyone could acquire this ability if he or she did not have it in the first place. But watch a newborn grasping for an object. See her arms flailing in space and her eyes moving about. She cannot do it. It seems almost as if different people control the eyes and the hands. There is no coordination between them.

Before I tell you what Piaget found, try to imagine a solution yourself. How can someone as helpless as a baby learn to coordinate vision and grasping? Spend a few minutes on this exercise. Why? Adults often find it impossible to imagine how their adult minds can adapt in significant ways. But they fail to recognize that imagining even how the mind of a baby can change and adapt was equally difficult before Piaget. In fact, the two are both versions of the same problem. The more you think about this problem on your own, the more you will admire Piaget's solution once you hear it.

Now here is what Piaget found. The ability to grasp objects intentionally is a complex skill that typically takes babies more than six months to master.

Babies are born with a grasping reflex—you put a finger in the hand of a newborn, and the hand will automatically close around it. During the first two months of life, the baby tries to grasp objects over and over again in what Piaget calls a *circular reaction* (circular because of its repetitiveness). With repetition, reflexive grasping gradually changes into a large array of differentiated grasping responses, each one suited to the shape and size of a different object. (Your hand needs to move differently to grasp a thin object, such as a piece of paper, and a round object, such as a small ball. If you are truly able to hold things, you also need to be able to grasp large objects that require two hands, and that is an entirely different response.)

Once grasping responses have become reasonably well developed, they begin to connect to other kinds of behavior. The first is sucking. Babies try to hold in their mouths what they are holding in their hands and vice versa. In fact, they coordinate sucking and grasping before seeing and grasping.

Next, grasping responses become connected with vision. This connection begins when the baby notices with her eyes that her hand and fingers are in motion. Babies go through a period when they spend a great deal of time just watching their own hand move. Full coordination of seeing and grasping begins days or weeks later with the baby watching her hand and using it as a guide for picking up an object, never letting the hand go out of view. The eyes focus on the hand, not on the object being picked up. It appears as though the eye and the hand are becoming calibrated to one another.

A while later the baby shows some signs of being able to grasp objects while focusing on the object instead of the hand. The ability remains limited. As long as the hand and the object both remain in her visual field at the same time, she can instruct the hand to grasp the object. But if the hand moves outside of her visual field, the coordination is broken. She cannot tell the hand to pick up the object. Indeed, when this happens she cannot use vision at all to tell the hand where to move.

Finally, when the baby is about six months old, vision and grasping become completely coordinated. The baby can grasp objects that she sees and look at objects that she is holding. This does not mean that eye-hand coordination is fully developed. For example, it will be many years before she can coordinate the two systems well enough to field ll or sew on a button. Nevertheless, she has acquired the basic

As has been emphasized, these studies are not just about eye-hand coordination or even just about babies. They help us to understand intelligent adaptation in general. Here are five facts about real-life adaptation that this example illustrates:

1. What the mind achieves is so amazing that most people at first glance have trouble believing it is even possible until someone spells out the details of how the process works.
2. The process involves a hodgepodge of many component parts. It has no simple elegant description.
3. The process takes a long time—weeks and months, not minutes and hours.
4. The process keeps moving forward, motivated by the small gains along the way, unconnected to any conception of the large goal that eventually will be achieved.
5. The process happens unconsciously. Even when vision and grasping are almost completely coordinated, most people, including the parents and the baby herself, are typically unaware that anything so important is happening.

Sometimes people expect that a brilliant sentence or two can tell them the solution to a challenging problem. Adaptation does not usually work that way. It takes time and it is messy. You need to do a lot of different things, none of them necessarily terribly complicated. But the cumulative effect can be wonderful. It offers one of the finest testimonies on behalf of mind power.

What Can You Do to Help Your Mind as It Adapts?

Does the fact that newborns adapt quite well without ever trying to do so imply that adults should do the same? Absolutely not. Mind-conscious adults can work with their minds to increase their effectiveness. This is the essence of mind magic. The example of the newborn shows that your mind can do remarkable things even when you are totally helpless. If you are not helpless, your mind can do a great deal more.

The lesson of the newborn is to avoid undermining the power of your natural instincts. Work with them, not against them. What you achieve will amaze you.

Ten Principles of Adaptive Thinking

Following are ten principles that allow you to cooperate with your mind's natural ability to adapt.

Principle 1: First of All, Do No Harm

This point is crucial: do not subvert your mind's ability to fix itself. Your mind often knows where it is going long before you do.

The Hungarian-born writer Arthur Koestler made this point in a revealing set of scientific biographies. Koestler's view was that many of the greatest scientists, such as Galileo and Newton, were like sleep-walkers. They moved science forward without realizing that they were doing anything so important.

As Piaget showed, we can say the same thing about babies and children. We can also say it about adults. Our instincts are often wiser than our sense of conscious purpose. Even if we eventually decide not to obey our instincts, we should at least listen to them.

As adults, most of us have an overly well-developed ability to muffle if not totally silence what our instincts tell us. We are able to become demoralized and say that something will not work. We can feel that a new course of action is too difficult or will take too long or will cost too much money. We worry that we will make mistakes and embarrass ourselves. Sometimes our instincts do fail us, but often they are surprisingly effective. If you want your mind to adapt, you need to give it a chance.

iple 2: Monitor Progress

As Piaget's example of eye-hand coordination shows, success quite often comes cumulatively through many small steps, not through one giant moment of insight. It is therefore useful to make note of the small steps as they occur.

The main reason for monitoring progress is to maintain your morale. It is human nature that you should want instant solutions—who doesn't? But when they do not come, you can begin to feel that you will never escape from your rut. Seeing small steps in the right direction helps you keep working, even when total success remains elusive.

Principle 3: Get to Know Your Personal Style

Although skill at adaptation is a universal human trait, methods of adaptation are not. While you are monitoring your own progress, make note of what seems to work for you and what does not. This kind of self-observation helps you identify what methods to keep trying and what to give up. It can also help direct your reading by suggesting what authors and books are likely to help you the most and whom to avoid.

Principle 4: Brainstorm

You remember that babies try grasping and holding objects in all kinds of different ways before they even begin coordinating eye and hand. Generating a large number of alternatives can be an important part of adaptation.

The equivalent for an adult is brainstorming. Generate lists of lots and lots of ideas. When you return to your list, most of them, and maybe even almost all of them, will be useless dead ends. But the one or two winners could be exactly what you need to make the next step.

Note that brainstorming is a learnable skill. You become better with practice. It also pays to return to the same problem for another brainstorming session. You often generate better ideas on the same subject when you come back to it for a second or third round.

Principle 5: Understand What Went Wrong and Why

A classic principle of effective thinking and problem solving is to understand the problem. Experts make it a top priority. It is just as important for you. Consider what happened after the tragic accident that resulted in the 2003 disintegration of the space shuttle *Columbia*. NASA engineers spent millions of dollars trying to understand what led to this catastrophe. Most public disasters are followed by a search for answers about what went wrong and why.

This strategy also applies to personal disasters. Dwell on the problem. Obsess about it. Consider numerous possible explanations—the far-fetched as well as the obvious. Investigate them to see if they could be right. Imagine what you might have done differently. A lot of the time, solving a problem becomes clear-cut once the problem itself is well understood.

Just describing the problem, putting it into emotionally neutral language, is often productive. It helps you to go beyond trying to justify your actions of the past, finding fault and blaming. Then it becomes possible to adopt a pragmatic perspective, looking for solutions instead of villains.

Principle 6: Read Around the Problem

Piaget believed in and followed this rule. It might help you, too. Reading books or other materials on related subjects will often suggest concepts that might not occur to you if you were concentrating only on the problem itself. These other sources can provide additional fodder for brainstorming.

Principle 7: Find New Ways of Thinking as Well as New Courses of Action

You often have to adapt your thinking as much as your behavior. Learning how various people think about the same problem can therefore be helpful. Of course, you have to listen in a critical spirit. Some people will have ways of thinking that are better than yours; some will have ways of thinking that are not as good; some will have ways that are equally good, just different.

One advantage of thinking about ways of thinking is that it is cheap. You may need nothing more than a pen and paper. Furthermore, finding a new way of thinking is often a solution in itself. Think about a problem, such as Piaget's three-mountain problem. The difference between the five-year-old and the nine-year-old is that the latter is using a whole new concept, the idea of point of view.

Principle 8: "Mourn" Old Ideas When They No Longer Work

In most respects, adaptation is easier for adults than for children. Adults have vastly more knowledge and experience to draw on, know many more people, and have more access to resources in the community, such as books, public services, and the Internet. Adults suffer from one disadvantage that comes from having lived for a while. Over time you develop attachments to certain ideas and assumptions. You want to hold on to them, even after they have become obsolete, because they have served you well in the past.

Adults sometimes need to "mourn" what no longer works. You need to recognize that an idea is no longer working, experience the regret, and then let go.

Principle 9: Be Open to Dialectical Solutions

Piaget often pictured adaptation in terms of a dialectic between opposites. For example, in the three-mountain problem, a subject might feel at first that the doll would see the road in front of the river. A moment later another part of his mind might feel that the doll would see the river in front of the road. When this happens people often begin to experience a sense of conflict as the two parts of the mind fight it out. The dialectic gets resolved, and a state of equilibrium is reestablished only after the two rival interpretations have become integrated into some larger synthesis.

Adults as well as children can adapt their thinking by finding dialectical solutions. This has certainly happened many times in science. Is light really a particle or a wave? For a long time, scientists were divided between the particle school and the wave school. Each one tried to prove that the other was wrong. The conflict persisted until someone proposed a new, more complex theory of light that combined particle-like and wavelike properties.

Principle 10: Look for New Connections

Trying out new connections can sometimes lead to surprising discoveries. Children do this all the time. The infant learning to grasp objects tries to connect grasping with other action patterns that he knows. Sometimes looking for connections fails to produce any interesting new insights. But other times it works quite well.

It certainly works for babies. Their first big attempt at integration is to combine sucking and grasping. Putting objects you hold into your mouth can be helpful if you are holding food, but otherwise it does not do a lot of good. It may even cause harm if you are holding something dirty. But the next attempt at integration is to combine seeing and grasping. The resulting skill is the development of eye-hand coordination, a major achievement.

Techniques That Usually Do Not Work

Just as effective strategies work together with your instincts, harmful ones serve to undermine them.

Perhaps the best common example of a bad strategy is the experience of being proven wrong. Has this ever happened to you? With the best intentions, someone gives clear and compelling arguments to show you why you are wrong. He or she thinks that the proof will change your mind. But proof does not work like that.

The trouble with proofs is that they are persuasive tools rather than problem-solving tools. When you are right, proofs are great at demonstrating this fact to other people. They are great at increasing your own confidence in a solution that you found. They also provide a useful check in case you made a mistake.

The mathematics class is one of the places where proving people wrong is especially common. More than other subjects, mathematics emphasizes proof and certainty, at least to the extent that certainty is possible. Proving is so much a part of math education that it makes sense to speak of a "math teacher's fallacy"—namely, the mistaken belief that proving to a student that her answer is wrong will help her find the right answer.

The trouble with proving the student wrong is that it typically serves to discourage without providing a path for change. The effect on morale of being proven wrong, especially if it happens often, can be devastating. I suspect that it is a significant contributing factor to the amount of math phobia that we see in schools. Furthermore, being proven wrong does not usually tell you how to be right. Thus it leaves students demoralized and frustrated.

With strong students, often just pointing out a mistake is very helpful. By knowing where a problem exists, the student can try to figure out the precise error on her own. The act of finding it in itself can frequently provide much of the solution.

With weaker students or when the mistake is serious, a more promising response is to begin with what the student does right. Was one line of the solution correct, even if the rest was wrong? Did the student have one or two promising ideas about where to look for a solution? Did the student successfully solve a similar or related problem? Work from strength. In the case of difficult problems, building on good ideas almost always is more successful than tearing down bad ones.

Another experience that undermines good instincts is despair, losing hope and giving up. Remember that failure, even repeated failure, is a normal part of learning. If you are trying to do something challenging, you can expect quite a bit of failure before you achieve success.

Interestingly, Piaget himself experienced his share of failure. One especially difficult period was during the 1940s and '50s. In his laboratory he was making astonishing discoveries, many of which later became recognized as his most influential and important. But at the time, virtually the entire world ignored him.

Many years after, I asked his close associate Bärbel Inhelder l
Piaget coped during this difficult period. She told me that he was nev
demoralized. How did he keep up his spirits? The answer, not surpris
ingly, is that he understood then what we now call *mind magic*. He
appreciated that ideas and viewpoints go in and out of fashion. Before
psychologists could appreciate his more recent work, they would have
to undergo a yang period of self-examination and self-correction.
According to Inhelder, Piaget felt sure that intellectual fashions would
eventually change—and events proved him more than right.

You do not have to be Piaget to deal successfully with repeated dis-
appointment. During the 1930s and early '40s, a whole generation in
succession experienced the stress of the Great Depression and then
World War II. You may have parents, grandparents, or perhaps great-
grandparents who have personal recollections of that difficult time. In
spite of the hardship people of that generation endured, hopelessness
and despair were much less common then than they are today.

Perhaps it was easier to cope during the 1930s, at least emotionally,
because so many people were facing the same, or similar, problems.
Nevertheless, there are many people today who continue to function in
the face of serious difficulties.

As an example, think about Keisha, a single mother in her early thir-
ties who worked as a toy designer for a Connecticut-based toy manu-
facturer. Her life at the time was hard enough as a result of a painful
divorce, loneliness, and a worldview that made worrying a constant
companion even when things were going well. But matters became
much worse when, during the recession of 2000, she lost her job, in the
first of what proved to be many layoffs at her company.

How did Keisha cope? She channeled her fear and energy into the
day-to-day problems of looking after her daughter. More than a year
later, she responded to an ad from a children's television company. Getting the new job was the catalyst to turning her life around. She is now
remarried and very happy.

External conditions beyond your control can change rapidly and
unexpectedly. Despair is a terrible poison, because it can blind you to
unanticipated possibilities when they suddenly appear. Losing hope

shuts down the parts of your mind that are trying to adapt. It keeps you from changing and tragically can become a self-fulfilling prophecy.

Do Children's Methods Solve Adult Problems?

The claim is sometimes made that adults learn in markedly different ways from children. This idea seems to argue against applying findings from research with children to adult problems. In reality, do adults and children learn in the same way or not?

Before trying to answer this question, it is helpful to carefully look at the thinking that lies behind what they say. This point of view is more closely associated with a school of thought known as *adult learning theory*. It comes from a time before Piaget's work was well known and certainly before its implications were well understood. Its advocates' real quarrel is not with Piaget but rather with older ideas of children's learning that Piaget and his colleagues also criticize.

As we have seen, Piaget's impressive body of research makes clear that children have an amazing ability to adapt their behavior and their thinking to the increasingly complex world that they are always facing. Adult learning theorists have no reason to question this fact. They insist, however, that adults need a sense of purpose in their learning and a feeling of control over the process. Significantly, the practice of mind consciousness is intended precisely to allow this sense of purpose and control.

As adults, we have not lost our childhood ability to adapt. On the contrary, we have added years of formal education and real-world experience to what we could do as children. Unless some kind of external pressure has caused us to repress the skills that we already have, adults become better at adaptation than children.

Impediments to Adaptation in Adult Life

If we have not lost our ability to change, what makes adaptation in adult life sometimes so very difficult?

Whether they realize it or not, adults sometimes prefer : change. Change can be difficult because people face it with so reluctance. Adults often have good reason to resist change. They may genuinely believe that their old familiar way of thinking is better than any newer alternative. If it is not broken, why fix it? Alternatively, as people get older, they may feel that adaptation is just not worth it. The unpleasantness of giving up an old trusted way of thinking or the uncertainty of trying something new may be too great. Fair enough.

But other times adults genuinely do want to adapt. A veteran librarian with no technology background may sincerely want to learn how to set up a computerized card catalog and search online databases. An experienced unilingual English-speaking manager may genuinely want to learn Spanish at a time when his company is transferring much of its manufacturing to Latin America. An established first grade teacher may truly want to understand and apply new student-centered educational methods, such as process writing and constructivist mathematics. These people may want to adapt in quite fundamental ways. Is that possible?

As with so many other aspects of intelligent adaptation, the experience of professional scientists can show us a great deal. There may be no walk of life in which change of worldview can be so crucial as scientific research. What happens when a paradigm shift forces scientists to think about their field in an altogether different and often unfamiliar way? What happened to astronomers when Nicolaus Copernicus and Galileo argued for a heliocentric, rather than a geocentric, view of the universe? What happened to biologists when Charles Darwin presented his evolutionary explanation of the origins of the species? What happened to physicists when Werner Heisenberg argued that they needed to take observer effects into account as part of his quantum theory? When fundamentally new ideas come forward, are scientists able to adapt or do they remain trapped in the old paradigm?

As happens in any occupation, individual scientists may react to the same new paradigm in totally different ways. Some may eagerly embrace it. Others may staunchly resist it, even to the point of trying to engineer a "counterrevolution" that rejuvenates older ideas. But for most scientists, the process of coming to terms with a new paradigm is difficult and often slow. Indeed a large number remain committed to the older paradigm long after a new generation has understood and accepted the newer alternative.

What does it feel like to live through a paradigm shift? According to historians, it can be incredibly difficult. The experience is typically one of stress and anxiety. Many scientists admit to feeling confused and disoriented. Thomas Kuhn, a distinguished historian of science, reported that a surprisingly large number of physicists consulted a psychiatrist during the period when quantum mechanics was first being accepted (1926–1928). So much for the stereotype of the scientist as cold, rational, and unemotional!

You can understand the difficulty of an experience if you consider what can be at stake. Thinkers who propose a new paradigm can ask their colleagues to consider some disturbing ideas. Sometimes a new paradigm puts fundamental religious beliefs in doubt, such as Galileo raising doubts about the literal truth of the Bible when he claimed to have observed the moon around the planet Jupiter. Other times it calls our everyday sense of reality into question, such as Einstein suggesting that space contains four dimensions, regardless of the fact that it seems so plainly three-dimensional. No wonder that new paradigms cause stress.

In fact, many scientists never make the transition to the new paradigm. Historians point out that scientists have trouble giving up the points of view that they learned in graduate school. Science typically progresses because a younger generation with new ideas takes over.

Nevertheless, there are many scientists who do succeed in negotiating a paradigm shift. How does such a major change in their thinking occur? The process of paradigm shift in science seems much like change in a clinical setting and the kind of developmental change that Piaget described. It includes the following features:

- A period of adjustment sometimes lasting months and years
- Gradual recognition of the limitations of old ways of thinking
- Gradual acceptance of new ideas that previously may have seemed too wild or far-out
- A reappraisal on the part of an individual of how the new paradigm fits with the rest of his or her thinking

- Construction of a new narrative that places one's understanding (
  some part of the past in relation to the new present
- Investment often of strong emotion as well as intellectual change

Five Rules for Emerging from Crisis

Progress from coping to emerging out of transition involves the whole
personality. In that respect, it serves as a prototype for problem solving, creative thinking, organizing information, and any other example
of serious learning. None is just processing information.

It can sometimes seem as if the crisis will drag on forever. Is achieving closure out of your control? Not completely. There are actions you
can take to smooth out the process of finding the end.

Allow Time for Adjustment

Most people have no sense of how long a period of adjustment takes.
They often expect it to pass far more quickly than it will. How long
does it really take? You can usually make a small adjustment after five
or six hours of concentration. Significant changes in your thinking can
happen after six to eight weeks. A fundamental shift in thinking, such
as a paradigm shift, can take a year or two.

During much of the time, it may seem as if very little is happening.
Why? First, building concepts takes a great deal of time. According to
Piaget, we spend the first decade and a half of life primarily engaged in
just this. It should not surprise us if it takes time as well in adulthood.
Because we have little awareness of this process, most people fail to real-
ize that it is happening at all. Second, a lot of adaptation involves gen-
erating many new directions and trying out what prove to be dead ends.
People often mistakenly fail to see this process as productive.

A final moment of insight may take just a few seconds. People
sometimes think that they should be able to have the insight without
all the preliminary work. Forget it. There would be no quick moments
of insight without hours, months, and even years of preliminary
spadework.

Know Which Way Is Up

Try to understand where you are really going. Is your worldview becoming more complex or is it becoming simpler and more coherent? Is it becoming more accurate? Is it becoming more consistent? Are you feeling fewer conflicts and sources of anxiety? Are you feeling more competent and confident? Your worldview may not be moving in the direction that you thought.

Piaget made the observation that success comes before understanding. Our minds can often find the right direction for us long before we become aware of where we are going. Piaget found this to be true even for physical actions. As he discovered, people are able to throw a ball accurately at a target long before they can describe how they did it or explain it to someone else. Arthur Koestler made the same point in his description of Galileo and Newton as sleepwalkers. They succeeded in laying the foundation of modern science, but no one at the time, including Galileo and Newton themselves, understood that they were doing anything of such historic importance.

The same principle applies to such life skills as adaptation. Solving the problem comes first. Understanding comes later. If you misunderstand where you are going, you can obstruct your mind and slow it down. A better understanding makes the process of change more efficient.

Welcome Positive Steps

As Piaget emphasized, change happens through stages. It usually does not come all at once. We all make mistakes along the way when we are trying something difficult. Recognize that coming closer to your goal is positive even when it does not immediately give you the whole answer.

A recent consulting project brought this point home to me. My client Jim is the president of a world-famous company that publishes educational books for children. In recent years Jim's company had been losing market share to rivals, and Jim wisely decided that it was time to undertake a major evaluation of one of his products.

Jim wanted a panel of ten to twenty educators to evaluate the educational quality of the product. As an alternative strategy, I recommended that we ask two educators to offer an initial evaluation. I told Jim that their recommendations would help him to formulate clearer and more precise questions. We could use these questions to ask two more reviewers to make a second pass. I proposed that we continue this process of hiring pairs of evaluators and refining our questions until we had a definite picture of the product's strengths and weaknesses. This strategy of successive approximations in the end proved quite successful. Asking a panel to offer recommendations based on our first set of questions would never have worked as well. Furthermore, the successive approximations strategy was much less costly, because we ended up using fewer reviewers and the workload per reviewer was quite light, especially at the later stages in the process.

Prepare to Assert a Different Side of Yourself

After a period of change, you often become dependent on skills and knowledge that have stayed in the background. An interest that you abandoned years ago or a subject that you never especially liked as a student can suddenly become crucial for you. You may have to start thinking of yourself as a somewhat different kind of person.

The sooner you become comfortable with changes in who you are, the easier it will be to emerge from the transition.

Don't Expect Other People to See the Process of Change the Way You Do

If you discuss the experience of change with people who know you well, they may perceive the process entirely differently from how you do. Do not be surprised if this happens.

You may think that you were withdrawn and preoccupied by your own thoughts. But other people may say that you were your normal self. You may feel that you went through a period of keen insight. Other people may see this as a giant rationalization.

As in Piaget's three-mountain problem, things always look different depending on your perspective. If the events happened in the past, the capacity of our—and other people's—memories to change and distort undermines all claims of objectivity.

Changing Your World by Changing Your Mind

When as a student I first studied Piaget's work, I was dazzled by experiments such as the three-mountain problem. That five-year-olds everywhere are so much the same that they all produce the same mistaken solution seemed surprising enough. But the transformation between ages five and nine seemed utterly amazing. Imagine the mind-set of a person who does understand that the same reality appears very different depending on your perspective. How can anyone change the underlying filters through which he or she sees the world?

Piaget showed that the structure of how we think can indeed adapt. Furthermore, it is possible for adults as well as children to adapt their thinking. Remember that adaptation, for Piaget, does not simply mean changing your mind. And it certainly does not mean replacing your old way of thinking with somebody else's idea. Instead, it means achieving a larger, stronger, and more stable equilibrium. It means finding a synthesis that adapts your old way of thinking by responding to perturbations that come from the outside.

Piaget's discovery has such profound implications that the whole world should know about it. Consider all the problems, both public and private, that people could solve by deliberately taking advantage of this piece of mind magic.

All too often people feel trapped by their ways of thinking as if a mental straitjacket held them tight. When that happens they begin to lose hope and can easily become depressed. This may be the main reason why more people should be familiar with Piaget's work. It opens up possibilities that most people would otherwise have failed to notice.

PART II

HOW TO USE MIND MAGIC

CREATIVITY: A LEARNABLE SKILL

In Molière's classic farce *Le Bourgeois Gentilhomme*, the protagonist M. Jourdain is famous for remarking, "Good heavens! For more than forty years, I have been speaking prose without knowing it. All that is not prose is verse; and all that is not verse is prose."

Many people believe that creativity is a rare and exotic talent. The truth, however, is exactly the opposite. Being creative is as common as speaking in prose. You have been doing it all your life. Anything not copied is creative; anything not creative is copied.

Although almost everyone is creative, almost no one produces creative work. Why not? Sometimes people prefer to follow the tried-and-true. There is a good reason why they feel this way: you know almost by definition that proven methods work. Nevertheless, often people want to innovate but fail to do so. The reason is not that they lack creative potential. What they lack is the knowledge of how to manage that potential in the service of conscious purpose.

Learning creativity means learning to manage what you already have instead of learning something entirely new. This chapter offers a practical guide for putting creative ideas into action.

Listen to Your Unconscious

Although your unconscious is always an important part of intelligence, its influence is especially significant in the case of creativity. If you try to force yourself to have an original idea, you will not succeed. Indeed, you may often be more successful if you just let your mind wander and daydream, afterward making note of what materializes. The idea has to bubble up on its own from the cauldron of your unconscious mind.

Many people are less creative than they could be because they have grown up feeling unnecessarily afraid of their own unconscious. In our culture the dominant image of the unconscious comes out of the Freudian conception. Hence, people see it as tormented and tumultuous, a source of psychological conflict, and the seat of powerful sexual and aggressive impulses.

You may be interested to know that there is an alternative conception of the unconscious. It is more neutral and upbeat than Freud's picture and at least as old. During the early 1900s, at approximately the same time when Freud was writing about dream interpretation and slips of the tongue, the French mathematician Henri Poincaré proposed his own theory of the unconscious. Poincaré knew nothing of Freud's theories, and Freud knew nothing of Poincaré's. It is no wonder then that their theories are as different as night and day.

Poincaré pictures the unconscious as a system that does mixing and matching. It takes the contents of your mind and tries to put them together in every possible way. There is no need in Poincaré's theory for defense mechanisms that protect the ego because nothing especially threatening ever emerges. On the contrary, the unconscious described by Poincaré is a rather friendly place. It tries to gain your attention only when it finds a combination that satisfies its own sense of balance and beauty.

Poincaré developed his conception of the unconscious as part of a theory of creative problem solving. In his view solving a problem involves three distinct stages.

In the first stage, you devote your attention just to understanding the problem. You may have a few ideas about the solution at this point, but Poincaré advised people to treat them lightly. They are almost certainly wrong.

The second stage was the crucial one. Poincaré's advice at this point was strange and paradoxical. Here you forget about the problem, at least consciously. During this second stage, according to Poincaré, your unconscious becomes very busy trying out huge numbers of possible ideas—but not bothering to tell you about them.

The third stage begins when your unconscious has come up with what it considers a nice idea. It tells you the idea, and now you begin to work with it. One possibility is that the idea is brilliantly creative and successful; alternatively, it may be so close to success that you can make it work with a few small changes. The worst case is that the idea fails; then your unconscious begins working on it again.

Why should Poincaré's theory matter to you? Poincaré had a valuable insight that remains valid today: to think creatively, you need to allow room for your unconscious. You need to feel able to walk away from a problem in the middle, trusting your unconscious to do its part.

The main reason why adults in our society are so rarely creative is that they actively censor their unconscious. Is it your perception that children are usually more creative than adults? Adults are better off than children with respect to almost every resource that contributes to creative thinking: adults have greater knowledge, greater experience of the world, greater incentives, greater intellectual maturity, and greater familiarity with other creative work. The main advantage that children enjoy is a greater willingness to give their unconscious free rein.

The point here is not to deny the obvious. There are certainly many times when you as an adult are correct to censor yourself. If you are making a public presentation, you want to make sure that your remarks are controlled and well prepared. Nevertheless, in the privacy of your own home, you have to feel free to hear the thoughts that cross your mind, even if they sometimes embarrass you. Poincaré's main insight was correct. Freeing up your unconscious contributes in many ways to the magic of your mind, and it is essential for creativity.

Creativity Deromanticized

Apart from listening to your unconscious, you will have to deal with a second major obstacle in the way of becoming more creative. This second hurdle is the exaggerated images of the creative individual that permeate popular culture.

When you think of a creative person, what name comes to mind? The first picture to enter most people's minds is the image of someone such as Wolfgang Amadeus Mozart, a brilliant composer who produced notable original works at an early age. People think to themselves, "I could never do what Mozart did. Therefore, I guess I am not creative."

You have to ask yourself why Mozart was able to do what he did. You quickly see that Mozart enjoyed a number of advantages over many other people who might have just as much creative potential. One important fact is that Mozart's father was a musician. From earliest childhood, Mozart listened to the finest music in the world. For all we know, many other children have been born with the same innate talent; however, their parents lacked the knowledge to help them develop their skills.

Another important fact is that Mozart's family encouraged his interest in musical composition. Imagine what would happen to a musically gifted child with parents who have a low regard for music. Many fathers regard musicians as effete or impractical; they would far prefer to have a son who can earn lots of money or play shortstop.

A third noteworthy fact relates to the time and place in which Mozart lived. Austria in the eighteenth century was quite a musical society, the home of the greatest musicians in the world. Music was in the air; the broader society valued musical talent. Mozart's fate would have been entirely different if he had lived during the same period in New York or Calcutta.

These facts certainly don't refute the idea that some natural gift made him better at composing music. Nevertheless, they should force us to wonder how many gifted children there really are. And they should help us to see that we, too, may simply need to broaden our exposure to ideas in order to tap our own creativity.

You Don't Have to Be Born Creative

According to William Shakespeare, "Some are born great, some achieve greatness, and some have greatness thrust upon them." In this respect, creativity is no different from greatness. Even if you were not born creative, you can still learn how to achieve it.

The Hungarian writer Arthur Koestler argues that creative people are like sleepwalkers: they produce their best work in spite of their best intentions, not because of them. Do all or even most creative people fit this image? If you study the lives of creative people, you will see that many, perhaps most, deliberately set out to produce innovative work. Thomas Edison's remark that "genius is 1 percent inspiration and 99 percent perspiration" embodies the very opposite picture of creativity. For every Mozart, there was an Edison.

You also arrive at a different image of the creative process if you think about creative artists other than Mozart. Consider Michelangelo. Michelangelo worked for popes and princes who had their own definite ideas of what his works should express. He was essentially a craftsman. Like Edison, he refined and improved his talent through practice and experiment and used his abilities to serve the wishes of his customers.

Every psychologically healthy person from childhood on has the capacity to innovate. Learning creativity means learning how to subordinate this capacity to some consciously recognized and productive purpose.

If you want customers to pay for your creative work, as was the case for Michelangelo and Edison, you will have to manage your natural ability to serve their needs and goals. Thus learning creativity is as much an intrinsically social process as psychological. It is social because it requires you to understand both your customers and your specialty.

Five Myths About the Creative Process

Our society has developed such a mystique surrounding creativity that most people have lost the sense that creative thinking is as commonplace as speaking prose. Creativity is as much a skill as writing computer programs or preparing income tax returns. As with any other skill, the people who master creative thinking deserve our respect for their accomplishment. On the other hand, we should see them as being no more exceptional than any other skilled person is.

If you want to learn creativity, you first have to free yourself from the myths that surround it. Following are five of the most insidious.

Myth 1: Creative People Are Naïve and Innocent

The first myth is that creative people are by nature naïve. You may remember the movie (and play) *Amadeus*, which presented a stark contrast between genuine creativity (embodied in the spontaneous and unruly but naïve Mozart) and clever imitation (embodied in the sophisticated and corrupt Salieri). The theme of *Amadeus* resonates with the myth of the naïve innovator: according to the stereotype, sophistication by its very nature subverts creativity.

As with many stereotypes, this one is worse than inaccurate. It is virtually the opposite of the truth. After all, what people have the most sophisticated understanding of how the world really works? More often than not, people think of a serious writer or some other creative individual; such a person is subtle enough to offer genuine insight into human nature and life. Furthermore, creative people have often needed to deal effectively with the wealthy and powerful. You need to think only of the artists of the Italian Renaissance, such as Leonardo da Vinci and Michelangelo. Artists and sculptors of the period needed real sophistication to obtain support for their work from princes and churchmen. History shows that creative people are usually far more sophisticated than the average person is.

Myth 2: Creativity Is Beyond Your Control

The second myth is that creativity depends on forces beyond your control, such as inspiration from a muse. The American psychologist Howard Gruber, a leading authority on the subject of creativity, has devoted his career to debunking this myth. As he has repeatedly pointed out, creative thinking is purposeful work. Why do people forget this fact? The myth persists that creativity depends on inspiration and magic. In fact, inspiration will often come but only after you have become immersed in the work itself. As Edison pointed out, creativity and hard work go together.

Myth 3: Creativity Is the Prerogative of Exceptional Individuals

Related to the image of the inspired genius is the myth that creativity is the prerogative of the exceptional individual. The one implies the other. If you need inspiration to be creative, it follows that the uninspired majority of people will never be able to create.

This myth, like the other ones, is mistaken. From childhood on, most people demonstrate all the components of creative thinking. They have the potential to produce creative work if they ever choose to use it.

Myth 4: Creativity Is the Opposite of Rationality

The fourth myth is that creative processes are irrational. Are creativity and rationality complements or opposites? Many people see the two as incompatible. According to this image, creativity is the epitome of spontaneous and uncontrolled thought; on the other hand, rationality is the epitome of conscious control. Those who see creativity and rationality as incompatible interpret certain findings from brain research as providing anatomical evidence that creativity is right-brain thinking and rationality is left-brain thinking. If they take place on opposite sides of the brain, does that not prove they are psychologically as well as anatomically opposite?

The short answer is "no." Let us ignore for the moment the fact that brain organization is far more complex than any simple left-brain/right-brain dichotomy suggests. Even if creativity and rationality were anatomically separated (which they are not), that would in no way mean that they are psychologically separated.

In reality, rationality and creativity belong together, not apart. Creative thinking almost always involves a great deal of logic and rationality; furthermore, the best rational thinking requires creativity. You separate the two at your peril.

Myth 5: The Creative Individual Is by Nature in Conflict with Society

The fifth myth is that creative people by nature are alienated from the society around them. Some artists and writers use this myth to define the essence of their identity. The talented American playwright Edward Albee used to title his public talks "The Playwright Versus Society." He once explained his feeling that the title could never fail him. Being a creative playwright inevitably, in his view, put him in conflict with society.

Novelists, playwrights, and artists themselves sometimes use this myth to establish their own authority and credibility. It lets them present themselves, for example, as disinterested observers of the society around them; hence, they can claim to be more objective in their perceptions than the rest of us. This myth can also serve as an ego defense for creative people at times when their work is commercially unsuccessful. It is understandable why they might be attracted to this myth, especially if their work is genuinely good but temporarily out of fashion.

Like the other myths, this one reflects the viewpoint of a particular subculture instead of inevitable truth. Why must creative work always serve to criticize society? The history of the arts shows that creative people can be radical, moderate, or staunchly conservative. Creativity refers only to the process of invention. It can serve you and your values, regardless of what they may be.

You *Can* Learn to Produce a Creative Work

You can see creative innovation as a two-step process. The first step is to have an original idea that is good enough to pursue. The second step is to shape, refine, criticize, and develop that idea to the point that it becomes a viable piece of work. Many people succeed at one step but then falter on the other. Some people are able to forge many good original ideas; however, they may lack the perseverance to turn them into a finished product. Other people are able to work diligently and persistently; however, they may lack the boldness to devise an original concept.

Can you negotiate both steps successfully? Yes, as long as you devote enough attention to both parts of the process. If one comes naturally to you, you can learn the other.

How to Devise a Concept

Even winning ideas rarely start out being brilliant. What you want to begin with is an idea that has promise. You can tolerate a multitude of imperfections as long as that glimmer of promise is there.

How are promising ideas born? Surprisingly, for most people the hard part is emotional, not intellectual. You have to be able to believe in yourself and your work, even when nobody else does. Most of us have a voice in our head telling us to trust what the rest of the world thinks, even when our instincts are telling us something else. To believe in yourself when you feel alone is not arrogant—it is courageous. For most people, it is also very difficult.

Original Ideas Take Courage

Even though you almost certainly have the capacity *intellectually* to do creative work, it may not suit you *emotionally*. If you have good new ideas, they will inevitably make you feel out of step to some extent with people around you. Many people prefer to fit in instead of standing out. Are you sure that you want the loneliness and sense of alienation that creativity so often brings?

On the other hand, the social and emotional cost of being creative is much less if you already feel alienated or dissatisfied to some extent. In fact, your feelings of dissatisfaction are the seed of your original idea. Here is one of the most useful secrets in doing creative work. You can almost always reformulate dissatisfaction with something bad as the kernel of a vision of something better.

Devising an original idea is quintessentially an act of courage, similar to the courage of the first immigrants or explorers who travel to a new land. Like them, you know little about the places where your idea will take you. Will these places be rich and fertile or will they be barren and harsh? Perhaps they will present unexpected dangers. The journey at times will surely be lonely. You can expect the folks who stay at home to see you as a little crazy. (If you fail, or even face temporary but significant setbacks, you can expect some of your old neighbors to say, "I told you so.")

Having the kernel of a creative idea means having the will to act on your dissatisfaction. There is never any guarantee that you will be able to implement your idea successfully. So why do you leave the comfort and security of the old ways? Creative people usually find old ideas so oppressive and confining that they feel they have no choice.

What are some examples? Immigrants to America resented religious persecution in the old country, so they imagined finding another place, a new country, where they would have freedom to practice their religion. Inventors resented the backbreaking effort of physical labor, so they envisioned machinery that would do the hard work for them. Musicians felt bored with the repetitive rhythms of traditional music, so they created the syncopated rhythm of ragtime. In all of these examples, you see the seminal influence of dissatisfaction. If Willis Carrier had really enjoyed sultry summer afternoons, do you think he would have invented air-conditioning?

To feel dissatisfied is easy; to act on it is very hard. It takes unusual people in unusual circumstances finally to muster the courage to do something about what bothers them.

Being an Outsider for Once Is an Advantage

The Swiss psychologist Jean Piaget offered these three golden rules for doing creative work:

1. Read *everything* on your subject.
2. Read *nothing* on your subject.
3. Have a target to attack.

The first rule makes intuitive sense to most people, but the second one seems surprising. Why did Piaget say this? Published authors almost always have better ideas than novices do because they have spent years on the subject. You will feel overwhelmed if you read their published works too soon. The experience will probably kill your personal point of view even before you start working on it. You first need time to develop your own viewpoint; then you can assimilate the ideas of other authors into your own framework.

Piaget's third rule is similar to Albee's conception of the playwright versus society. According to Piaget, your target does not have to be society; in fact, it can be anyone or anything at all. Nevertheless, you need to have a target. Without one, your work will lack focus.

Features of creative innovation (such as the need to have targets) make it fundamentally different from more conventional kinds of work. You would generally expect people to have an easier time succeeding if they seem like the kind of people who have traditionally had the most power. Why do we usually assume that the odds of success are greater if a person is white, Anglo-Saxon, and male? In most kinds of work, these attributes are indeed an advantage.

Paradoxically, however, in creative work, especially in the arts, belonging to an otherwise disadvantaged group can be an advantage. Creativity of necessity comes from dissatisfaction with the status quo. If you belong to a disadvantaged group, you almost certainly have reasons to feel dissatisfied. A great paradox, for example, is that many of the most celebrated figures in English literature were not English at all but rather were Irish. The list includes Jonathan Swift, James Joyce, George Bernard Shaw, and many others. Although being an outsider is usually a disadvantage, in devising a creative work, outsiders are often more productive.

How to Transform Your Vision into Reality

It is obvious to most people that creative innovation requires new ideas. But what do you do with an idea once you have it? Thinking up ideas is only a small part of the work; the large part is shaping, refining, improving, and eventually marketing.

Very few good ideas spring from your brain fully formed the way the goddess Pallas Athena in Greek mythology emerged from the forehead of Zeus. Nurturing and developing your idea are usually what makes it sparkle. You can ruin a brilliant idea if you develop it poorly, and you can turn a mediocre idea into a good one by caring for it properly.

Is your vision the kind that is easy to turn into reality? Be aware that "easy" does not mean "better." Implementing a vision is like passing through an obstacle course. You learn and become stronger from every hurdle that you overcome. If implementation is easy, it gives you too few obstacles. Here is a big surprise: the more and the harder the obstacles you are successfully able to negotiate, the better the quality of your final product.

To strengthen your idea, you need to thoroughly and ruthlessly examine it from all angles. Find all its potential weaknesses, and then change the idea so that the weaknesses disappear. Then find some more weaknesses. Actively seek out criticism. If nobody can find things to criticize, the idea is probably too bland and boring. In that case, you have to make your idea spicier to provoke people into criticizing it.

You begin by dealing with criticism of your own. Later you will continue to improve your work as you receive criticism from other people. That will include constructive criticism (from friends, respected colleagues, and experts) and destructive criticism (from people actively unfriendly to your work and even critics who may be either irresponsible or unfair).

The peer review process for evaluating academic work illustrates how much the experience of seeking out criticism can offer. At its worst, peer review serves as a filtering system to protect privilege and keep out change. But at its best, peer review allows a creative thinker to improve and deepen theories and concepts in response to a broadening range of criticisms.

As a graduate student, I saw the value of this process in the working practices of the brilliant American linguist Noam Chomsky. While working on new theories, Chomsky taught courses that included not only graduate students in linguistics and related fields but also half a dozen of the preeminent professional linguists in the world. The course served as a testing ground for his theories. The members of the course were generally sympathetic to Chomsky's theoretical perspective and offered high-quality but friendly criticism of his work. Later, after publication, Chomsky further revised his theories in light of the harsher criticism he received from his intellectual opponents.

No matter how unpleasant the experience, learning from criticism is what makes your ideas flourish. No matter how surprising, this fact remains true: most creative work consists of responding to criticism.

As you implement your vision more fully, you will have to respond to many different kinds of challenges. What are they? You should ask yourself the following questions to identify and overcome potential obstacles.

Does It Satisfy You?

People typically try to produce a creative work in a domain where they have some significant personal experience. Their experience has given them standards of quality. Maybe you aspire to satisfy the generally accepted standards of your field. Maybe you reject traditional standards and hope to replace them with standards of your own. In either case, the first question to ask is whether your work satisfies you.

Should you expect to feel satisfied quickly? Creative people differ so much in temperament and working style that no single answer fits everyone. Some people produce great first drafts that need little revision. Other people have a perfectionist nature and keep finding more problems each time they come back to the same work.

If you are like most people, you will probably find that you see more and more to criticize in your own work as you gain experience. Why is that? First, you will have been exposed to more criticism from other people. With experience, people often learn to revise their work in anticipation of criticism. Second, you are probably an expert on your topic and understand the common problems of the domain where you work as well as or better than anyone else does. You will be the first person to know when something does not work correctly, to detect errors of logic and inconsistency, and to recognize flaws.

Does It Satisfy Your Friends?

Creative scientists have long used a process of peer review to solicit comments and criticism from people they respect. You may not belong to a formal community of peers, but you can still seek out experts and ask friends if they are willing to offer candid opinions of your work. It may be disconcerting when a friend notices your embarrassing mistakes; nevertheless, it is far more embarrassing when an unfriendly critic notices them.

It is noteworthy how often personal friends working in the same domain produce creative works, including major innovations. The early impressionists were personal friends and often exhibited together. The collective of early twentieth-century British writers who formed the Bloomsbury group were also personal friends. Even artists who work alone often benefit from having one or two close friends who can double as friendly critics. T. S. Eliot's masterpiece *The Waste Land* only assumed its final form after his friend and fellow poet Ezra Pound thoroughly edited it.

What kinds of people do you want to include in your community of peers? Ideally, your peers should be able to serve as your alter ego. You want criticism from people who have almost the same expert knowledge that you have and whose judgment you trust. If you are fortunate enough to have a respected mentor, he or she is often the best source of criticism.

Creative people sometimes worry that peers (or even their mentor) might abuse the role of critic. You may be afraid, for example, that peers will try to impose their own ideas for reasons that have nothing to do with your needs. That includes both traditional ways of thinking (that you may have already rejected) and the peers' own pet ideas. You may worry as well sometimes about the risk of plagiarism, that a peer might steal your work.

Both kinds of fears are legitimate. If you feel either way, you need to think seriously about whether you should find a different peer group.

How Do Your Partners Feel?

If you can produce your work entirely on your own, you belong to a privileged minority. During the Renaissance, some artists (such as Michelangelo) and scientists (such as Galileo) had rich and powerful backers. Still today most creative people depend on the help of their partners—backers, collaborators, assistants, and outside services—to produce their work. Think of the numbers of associates needed to produce a feature-length film, such as Orson Welles's *Citizen Kane*, or a major architectural work, such as Daniel Libeskind's proposed model for the former World Trade Center site. Even though they may understand only one narrow aspect of your entire project, partners' comments can often prove to be an invaluable source of constructive criticism.

If you maintain a trusting and comfortable working relationship with them, your partners are most likely to feel free in offering their opinions. How can the criticism of partners help you? First, skilled partners usually know enough to have good reason for giving the advice they offer. Second, your partners will usually do a better job for you when they believe that you respect their ideas.

What Do Your Critics Say?

Responding effectively to critics ultimately depends on your ability to understand the relationship among diverse perspectives. You have to be able to see the same facts from many different points of view without in the process compromising your commitment to what you genuinely believe.

Reacting to friendly critics rarely poses a problem. It is easy as well to know how to respond to blatantly unfair critics. (You ignore them.) The tough cases, however, are critics who are unfriendly but not necessarily unfair. How do you know whether or not to accept their criticism?

Here is a secret to help you effectively handle unfriendly criticism: always read critical comments on at least two separate occasions. The first time, read them from the viewpoint of the critics. Bend over backward to see the critics' viewpoint and give them the benefit of the doubt. Assume for the sake of argument that critics are always right and you are wrong. Then the second time, read criticism from the perspective of trying to understand the critics' biases and background. This time you are trying to see if their negative comments reflect their own shortcomings instead of being a fair appraisal of your work. By comparing these two entirely different readings of what critics say, you will end up with the fairest and most balanced appraisal of your work.

You can gain enormously from the comments of an intelligent critic, even if the comments are harsh. For one thing, a critic can open your eyes to the ideas of people whose entire outlook is completely unfamiliar to you. Few experiences are more broadening. The eighteenth-century German philosopher Immanuel Kant praised his adversary, the Scotsman David Hume, for waking him from his "dogmatic slumber." Kant's most important works followed directly from Hume's stern criticism. Piaget, too, made his most significant discoveries after critics pointed out that his earlier research had relied too much on verbal methods. If you have such a critic, you should consider yourself lucky, even if it hurts your ego.

Does It Satisfy Regulators?

At some point in your project, you should begin to understand any laws that affect the kind of work you do. You do not want to spend months or years on a project that turns out to violate federal or state regulations. Could your idea somehow represent a violation? That may be reason to either modify or abandon a project quickly.

Copyright and patent laws are the ones most likely to affect a creative work. You may need to verify that your work does not infringe on somebody else's copyright or patent. Similarly, you may need to protect your work from infringement by somebody else in the future.

Does It Satisfy the Marketplace?

Should you care whether your creative work sells? The history of civilization is full of figures who died in poverty, the quality of their work unrecognized. These include the scientist Gregor Mendel (the father of modern genetics), the artist Vincent van Gogh, and the writer Franz Kafka. If creative work is a hobby for you, commercial success may not be important. But if it is your livelihood, you will want to avoid the fate of Mendel, van Gogh, and Kafka. You will therefore have to face the problem of marketing your product.

Unfortunately, for many creative people, selling is the highest hurdle of all. Are you bothered by the thought of having to market your work? Our society is full of talented people who cringe at any hint of commercialism. No one should feel surprised at this. We educate our students to believe that the artists and scientists to admire the most were the ones who worried the least about selling. Within the world of high culture, the term *commercial* is almost always derisive. Furthermore, our popular images of the salesman carry overtones of sleaziness and deception. No wonder then that so many artists and scientists shy away from the marketplace.

You have to think of marketing as just one more obstacle to overcome. How can you cross it? Our society is aware that creative people often have problems selling, and solutions have evolved to help cope with them. If you are a writer or an artist, you should definitely consider finding an agent. For a share of your eventual earnings, this person will take much of the work of selling out of your hands. An agent is a good investment. If you are a scientist, the best course is probably to follow the accepted practices of your profession for publicizing new work, such as speaking at the major conventions and publishing in the most widely read journals.

Make It Personal

Marketing is different from earlier stages primarily because it forces you to adopt a fresh mind-set. Up to this point, you have been striving to make your innovative idea be, in some impersonal sense, as good as possible. When you start to sell, you have to stop being impersonal. You have to think about the particular individual people who might potentially buy your product and find a way to make it as good as possible at serving their needs.

Does serving the marketplace mean compromising quality or improving it? If your customers were foolish or had poor taste, you might have to "sell out" in order to serve them. If you care about quality, you would therefore be wise to look for intelligent sophisticated customers who can appreciate the excellence of your work.

Remember an important principle: being good means being good for someone. If your product does not serve somebody's real needs, then it is not a good product. For this reason, understanding the needs of your customers should place additional standards of quality before you. Your customers in a sense are like your critics and friends because they serve to broaden your understanding of what constitutes good work.

Who Is Your Market?

Look at your innovation and ask yourself: who needs it? You may be surprised when you discover the people who need it the most.

Believe it or not, marketing was a serious problem even for Piaget. You might think that the world would beat a path to the door of such a famous psychologist. Yet for many years, this did not happen. Who would want to know about children's mind magic? Then Seymour Papert, professor of mathematics and education at the Massachusetts Institute of Technology (MIT), came up with a brilliant marketing idea. He suggested selling to engineers!

Would you expect engineers to be interested in child psychology? Neither did Piaget. Surprisingly, the idea worked. Indeed, several members of the MIT Electrical Engineering Department became fascinated with Piagetian psychology. Piaget's theories provided the stimulus for breakthrough research that served to lay foundations of the science of artificial intelligence.

Successful marketing requires a willingness to look in unexpected directions. It demands creativity just as much as your original innovation did.

Sell Yourself to Marketing Experts

Do you see yourself as expert in producing innovations instead of selling them? In the end, the job of selling your product may belong to retailers and marketing professionals, not to you. Nevertheless, you are still wise to keep marketing questions in mind. For one thing, marketing people respond to your appreciation as much as your other partners do. They will do a better job for you if they feel that you understand their task and are trying to help them succeed.

You can help the marketing people by anticipating problems. Start with the name you give your innovation; the wrong name might keep customers from looking any further. Maybe Shakespeare thought "a rose by any other name would smell as sweet," but he was wrong. It is lucky for florists that nobody ever called it a "skunk-flower"!

Next, think about your product description. How detailed should it be? If you have the good fortune to have extremely well-informed customers, you can (and must) describe the design features of your product, even in technical terms. If you are selling a computer chip to IBM, you can trust the customer to have experts on staff who can figure out the benefits to their company on their own as long as you give them the specs. On the other hand, the general public usually does not have the time, interest, or know-how to draw that kind of inference. You will usually serve your customers best by telling them about your product's benefits instead of its features.

Finally, be prepared to improve and even totally reconceptualize your product if necessary. The value of an idea to customers is often entirely different from what the creator ever imagined. Do you know what the Internet was originally supposed to do? The U.S. Department of Defense first developed this network in the late 1960s as a proprietary medium for military communication highly resistant to disruption. They never dreamed that consumers would use the same technology thirty years later to buy books and airplane tickets, among many other things.

Evaluate your product from the customers' viewpoint. What good is it to them? What matters to you may be different from what matters to them. Add features that enhance its value to customers and remove the ones that mean little to them. Realize that your idea might have value for customers beyond anything you may have imagined.

Beyond the Impractical

The better you understand the creative process, the more you realize that it is a lot like a magician's tricks. A skilled performer is able to dazzle the uninitiated because they do not know the technique. It is also like magic in another respect. Once you know how it works, you gain a renewed admiration for the skilled practitioner, but of a different kind. Now you understand the technical ability and practice required for skillful performance, and you admire the master who succeeds in achieving it.

Does that mean creativity is nothing more than parlor tricks? Of course not. Nevertheless, the difference has more to do with the significance of the result than with the process. Creative works open your eyes to new possibilities; that is the source of the creativity mystique.

The information revolution has made it more urgent than ever for us to demystify the creative process. It did not matter twenty or thirty years ago if the majority of people saw creative work as beyond them; they could find work doing something relatively routine. However, that is no longer the case. Every year computers are doing an increasing number of the routine jobs; therefore, people have to commit their future to a kind of work that computers will not do.

You may wonder if computers will one day also be able to think creatively. The safe answer is "not yet." Scientists have been trying for more than two decades to design computer programs that think creatively, but their accomplishments so far have been modest. It is a reasonable conjecture that things will not change substantially during your lifetime.

People often lament the number of routine jobs lost to computers, but they don't think to rejoice in the associated gain as much as they should. Creative work is intrinsically far more interesting than the routine jobs that computers are replacing. The demands of creativity stimulate your mind, whereas the old routine work led to mind-numbing monotony. The rewards of having an active mind are enormous. We are truly fortunate to live during a period of history that offers so many opportunities for creative thinking.

INFORMATION YOU CAN OWN

Can you recall the last time you saw a speaker or seminar leader who seemed to have total control over the information that she was presenting? It can be impressive. Those kinds of speakers seem to have all the facts at their fingertips. They seem to have thought the subject through to the point that they welcome tough questions as an opportunity to demonstrate how well they understand it.

You can see that their level of knowledge even affects how they feel about themselves. Other people may be nervous in front of a demanding audience, but they remain poised and self-confident. Their confidence comes from the inside because they know that their knowledge is real. They do not have to fake it.

The dawn of the information age has been an era of paradox. As information becomes more and more available, you might expect to find an increasing number of people who attain, and display, a sense of information mastery. In reality, the opposite has happened. The growth of knowledge has made people feel burdened by information instead of being empowered by it. The result is information overload.

What are its symptoms? The *APA Monitor* (1998) reports that according to many psychologists and researchers, the information that "bombards us every day may be making us ill by interfering with our sleep, sabotaging our concentration and undermining our immune system." The British psychologist David Lewis is internationally recognized as an authority on information overload. He has identified a clinical disorder caused by information overload that he calls *information fatigue syndrome*. At worst, information overload causes indigestion, hypertension, and heart problems; in milder forms it provokes irritability and jeopardizes work productivity.

There is no need for you to suffer from information overload. You can achieve the kind of confidence that can only come from control over a body of knowledge. Information mastery is a skill like any other; you can learn it in the same way that you can master other aspects of mind magic.

Own Your Information—Don't Just Borrow It

The secret of successful speakers and seminar leaders is that they own the information they present instead of just memorizing it. You can be just as effective as these individuals are. However, you first have to understand (1) what *owning* information means and (2) how to achieve it.

What does it mean to own information? Simply put, it is a subjective feeling of mastery. People who own information feel able to offer their own interpretations of the facts. Like many other subjective feelings, it expresses itself in your actions and changes your entire manner. Remember the successful seminar leader. You could recognize her sense of mastery in her manner, and you also knew that it came from the inside. There was no need for her to put on an act.

Here is another example. Compare the way that Nobel Prize–winning scientists talk about their discoveries (which they own) with the way a journalist (who is borrowing) reports on a subject. Responsible journalists are usually careful to stick to the information given and not draw conclusions or inferences of their own. But listen to the scientists. They feel free to speculate and pass judgment because they know their information inside out.

To own information, you do not have to be a recognized expert. Most people own what they know about their friends and colleagues. Children own a lot of information, too—they own a myriad of facts about their families, their homes, and their daily routines. Once you own information, you gain enough confidence to organize it intuitively, without having to follow formal procedures.

If you do not own information, you will always treat it gingerly, like a borrowed cup and saucer. But once you own information, you start to feel in control. When you own information, you are the authority: if other people challenge you, you will keep your cool. The main benefits to you are increased flexibility in your thinking and a reduction in your stress level. Owning information makes it easier for you to think on your feet. You can examine and evaluate the various components to determine which ones are solid and which ones are shaky. Finally, it helps you to expand your knowledge base in the future, by serving as a point of reference.

The opposite of information ownership is surface understanding. The most extreme form is rote memorization. People can recognize that, too. It makes your presentation seem wooden, like that of a public speaker who keeps repeating the same stock phrases and seems to be following a well-rehearsed script.

Don't Make Information More Complicated than It Has to Be

Why do so many people suffer from information overload and so few people achieve information mastery? The answer has to do with the way you picture information to yourself. Consider the following. College and high school graduates usually know many ways of representing information. Unfortunately, though, the representations that they know are usually the wrong ones. Believe it or not, these representations can actually make it harder to learn a body of information and gain a subjective sense of ownership.

Think about the most popular formats for representing facts, such as tables, flowcharts, pie charts, equations, and graphs. As a way of communicating information to other people, they can be wonderful. They can even be useful to you for organizing a body of information you have already mastered. Sometimes you might use them to summarize a set of facts. Other times they reveal properties of the information that you would otherwise not notice. But do they help you at the point when you are first becoming comfortable with a new domain of knowledge? The answer almost always is "no."

You use graphs and tables to communicate information because they summarize a lot of data succinctly with a few lines on a page. When you are first learning new information, however, you usually want everything to be loose and expanded instead of tight and compact. If you are like most people, tables and graphs will help you only if they are ones that you already know well (and own). You normally want all the details and qualifications and special circumstances to be written in full. That way you can devote your mind power to identifying and understanding the main facts.

Here is an example of how I make sense of tables. Recently, a financial analyst from an educational software company met with me to discuss a return on an investment model for one of her company's products. Her model was in the form of a spreadsheet. She began going through the model, explaining what it meant line by line. My eyes glazed over. To understand this model, I knew that our conversation would have to change direction.

So I concentrated instead on her goal: to convince my client to purchase her company's product. Then I asked myself what her main argument was. It turned out that there was one key cell in the spreadsheet. If the figure in that cell was correct, then her product genuinely was more attractive than the competition. If that figure was wrong, my client ought to choose a different product.

So I circled the key cell and asked her to confirm that this value was the crucial one. She confirmed this. Then I wrote that figure on a new piece of paper, with a note saying what it meant. After that the problem became to verify whether or not this crucial figure was correct or not. By now I was doing most of the talking. I started asking her to explain how the key figure had been calculated. It turned out that I needed only a few select pieces of information to evaluate her entire argument.

Different people like to represent new information in different formats. A colleague of mine likes to make pictures. I prefer a long list of point form notes. Some people are most at home with tables and graphs.

Do not feel captive to the format in which you receive the information. The best form is whatever makes it easiest for you to understand and evaluate the facts.

The Principle of Self-Knowledge Revisited

How do you become the owner of your information? The principles that help in learning other kinds of mind magic will help as well in gaining ownership over information. The basic principle is to know yourself and your own mind.

When most people think about their own learning, they have in mind the way they acquire information at work or their experiences as a student. But think about the times in your personal life when you have had to do a substantial amount of learning. When you learn out of choice rather than necessity, things for some reason are a lot easier. A case in point is when you meet a new person or make a new friend. Within a short time, you learn a lot about a new friend—and you did not spend any time cramming for an examination. Furthermore, in the process you gain ownership over what you are learning.

Another example is moving to a new area. Almost everyone knows an enormous amount about his or her hometown. When you move to a new place, you acquire most of this information quickly. Just by going places and finding things, you get to know your way around. Significantly, even people who do poorly on psychological tests of spatial reasoning seem to have no trouble finding their way around the neighborhood.

Most people usually start out by recognizing specific landmarks, such as their own home, the office, the downtown, the corner store, the homes of friends, and so on. With time they start remembering routes that connect individual landmarks to one another. After a while they develop a whole map in their head so that they know implicitly how all the routes and landmarks fit together. You can see this knowledge at work when they discover shortcuts or when they seem to know, automatically, the correct route for a previously unfamiliar journey.

Landmarks to routes to maps; points to links to networks. That is how you naturally learn, and that is how you come to own knowledge.

If it works in your personal life, it can work in your professional life as well.

What Is the Natural Way to Learn Information?

Getting to know a new friend and learning your way around the neighborhood are only two examples of natural learning. There are many others. If you think about it, you will realize that you feel totally different about information acquired in this way. What are the differences? Here are three of the most important:

1. **You did not have to wait a long time before your learning paid off.** Formal study often requires years of work before you know enough for it to be useful. Natural learning is not like that. Each step along the way offers a payoff in terms of knowledge that has immediate value. (Knowing a landmark is valuable in its own right, as well as helping you later for constructing routes and maps.)
2. **Acquiring information was integrated with the rest of life.** People do not usually separate natural learning from everything else they do. Rather, natural learning is an integral part of normal everyday life. It happens automatically and unconsciously. People seem to pick up the knowledge they need without requiring deliberate study.
3. **You had a sense of owning your knowledge from the beginning.** If you were to measure it, you would find that the amount of information you acquire naturally is vastly larger than what you acquire in other ways. Nonetheless, it never causes any of the stresses and symptoms associated with information overload. On the contrary, most people have a sense of absolute ownership over it.

There are good reasons why natural learning is so stress-free and formal learning is so stress-prone. Each step in the process of natural learning grows smoothly out of what you knew before. The new step quickly establishes a rich network of connections with your earlier knowledge. These connections typically have emotional significance as well as intellectual meaning. On the other hand, formal learning rarely

engages a rich array of emotions. It also has few connections with w
you knew before, especially when you are beginning to learn a new sui
ject. People usually experience it as an abrupt shift instead of as a
smooth transition.

Would you feel more comfortable and more in control of information if you could learn everything in this naturalistic way? Almost certainly, you would. Remember the speaker who conveyed by her manner
a total mastery of what she was presenting. She most likely achieved that
sense of ownership because she learned it in almost the same naturalistic way that you learned your way around the neighborhood.

For some reason, most people give up the habit of natural learning
as soon as they consciously start trying to learn something. Wouldn't
you be happier and more successful if you could assimilate information
at work as automatically as you do in your private life? One reason why
mind consciousness matters so much is that it enables you to learn deliberately in a naturalistic way. Following are some facts that will help you
to do this.

Nine Important Facts About the Way You Naturally Acquire Information

Acquiring information by gaining ownership requires more activity
than rote memorization. Nevertheless, the activity is so much more
pleasant! You will probably not experience it as work. Listen to people
who are skillful at acquiring and using information. They use phrases
such as "getting used to new information," "appropriating it," "seeing
the big picture," "getting a feel for it," "seeing how it relates," and "getting a sense of control over the information." Every one of these phrases
touches on the same essential idea. People do not learn by passively
copying information into their memory the way that you enter data into
a computer. The human way to learn instead is to transform information in some way that gives it personal meaning.

The better you understand the way your mind naturally assimilates
and transforms information, the more you will be able to use this
knowledge to gain ownership of new information.

zing Facts Is Hard; Assimilating Facts

on recently with David, an eleven-year-old who had to
...mes of plant parts for school. He found the exercise
extremely difficult. His teacher thought the assignment should be easy
because it was "just memorization." Unfortunately, she did not understand David. David (like most people) finds it easier to assimilate information into a framework than to memorize meaningless nomenclature.
He would actually have found it much easier if she had given him certain
kinds of "more complicated" information about plant physiology, dis-
eases that affect plants, the way in which plants develop from seeds into
their adult form, or even the evolution of plants across the millennia.

If you assimilate information, you own it; on the other hand, if you
just memorize it, you never feel in control.

David is not alone in this. If you talk to medical students, you will
discover as a rule that they also find memorizing anatomy quite difficult. They will tell you that anatomy becomes much easier if you learn
it along with development. Seeing how their developmental precursors
led to the emergence of each structure gives you a context for understanding it. And this in turn makes it easier to learn the anatomy.

The implication of this fact for you is clear: avoid memorization.
Your recall will be much better if you spend your time understanding
and assimilating information instead of trying to memorize it. What do
you do if you receive a lot of meaningless information with no framework for interpreting or understanding it? Try either to find or to create a framework of your own. Sometimes the experience of other people
suggests a framework that would be right for you. That is what usually
happens in the case of medical students. Senior classmates will tell more
junior students that development gives you a framework for understanding anatomy and pathology gives you a framework for understanding physiology.

When you have to develop a framework on your own, it is often
helpful to concentrate on one or two simple examples. For instance,
imagine that you want to understand how the industrial revolution
changed the nature of work. You might choose to investigate thoroughly

the lives of a few individuals from diverse walks of life. The life gle individual can give you a framework that integrates the nu, social, economic, and technological forces at work during a pe rapid change.

Fact 2: Familiarity, Not Intrinsic Complexity, Is What Makes Information Easy or Hard to Understand

I spent two years in high school taking Russian. I found the language incredibly hard to learn, but the student sitting beside me always seemed to find it easy. Why did he find it so simple? The answer, as it turned out, is that he spoke Ukrainian at home. Ukrainian and Russian are quite similar to each other; therefore, he could learn the Russian by thinking of similar words and grammatical forms in Ukrainian.

Many people think that quantity or technical content is what makes information easy or hard. That is not the case. What makes information easy is familiarity. Even large quantities of information and highly technical facts can be easy to master once you have enough experience with similar material.

There is a well-known rule that states, "Understand the new by relating it to what you already know." This is a good rule. It has a corollary, however, that is just as useful but not as well known. The corollary states, "If you cannot easily relate it to what you already know, you will find it almost unlearnable." You need to expect that anything very unfamiliar is likely to be quite difficult.

Having recognized this fact, you should keep in mind that there are ways of making unfamiliar ideas seem less foreign. Some techniques are harder on you. These methods usually work faster, but they can also provoke more stress and are generally more demanding. Other techniques are gentler. They are more pleasant, but they also take longer to produce results.

The best understood of the "hard" techniques is called *immersion*. This is the sink-or-swim method of learning. A typical example of immersion is to learn Spanish by living in Mexico or Argentina. You learn because you have no other choice. Everyday exposure to the language makes words and phrases start to seem familiar. Research shows that immersion is extremely effective, even though immersion programs can also be quite stressful.

"Soft" techniques use a divide-and-conquer strategy. They work from the principle that you can approach an unfamiliar subject step-by-step. A good example is the use of what educational researchers call *transitional objects*. These are objects that exist both in the concrete physical world and in the world of knowledge that you are trying to master.

Consider the way computer companies try to help customers feel comfortable with their products. They deliberately use terms from everyday life such as *clipboards, files, notebooks, Web pages,* and *cutting and pasting* to describe processes in the computer. In effect, these terms serve as transitional objects. The purpose of using them is to make these processes seem less foreign. Using names that are both descriptive and familiar makes the processes themselves seem familiar as well.

Fact 3: Your Mind Works by Interpreting Reality Instead of Copying It

Your mind always feels more comfortable when you let it do the kind of thing that it does best. One of the things it prefers is to create its own interpretation of the world around you instead of having to make a photographic copy.

You may be surprised to hear that your mind dislikes making pictures of the world. There is an old saying that a picture is worth a thousand words. We all know that people find it extremely easy to watch pictures, especially moving pictures. Doesn't this prove that your mind enjoys making pictures? There are even books on the market that teach you how to improve your mental imagery.

Although your mind may enjoy pictures that someone else makes, forming pictures of its own is another matter. Art students quickly become experts on how poorly a person's mind makes pictures of the world. They are constantly discovering how much you miss, even if you are an artist in training. To a large extent, the purpose of studying art is to train the artist's mind to see all the details that they normally miss.

Professional artists are experts on this subject as well. It is utterly erroneous to say that art imitates life. A significant part of the painter's skill is to fool your mind into seeing something that is not there. The fact that artists can create illusions in so many ways shows just how poorly your mind's eye imitates reality.

Should you be bothered by your inability to see what is in front of you? You definitely should not. Your mind does a brilliant job of picking out what is truly important. It hardly matters if it misses the other details.

Indeed, you are not alone in preferring to interpret. Living things everywhere have the same preference. A case in point is the lowly frog. Do you think the frog can see everything that passes before its eyes? Scientists have found that the frog's eye notices little about the world around it; nevertheless, the things it notices are the important ones. For example, the frog's eye contains cells called *bug detectors* that recognize small black dots about the size of the bugs that the frog likes to eat. There are other cells that respond only to large looming shapes, the size of predators that might threaten the frog.

You see another good example if you look at children's drawings. Have you ever seen the way four-year-olds draw a human being? The drawings tend to look like Figure 5.1.

Psychologists call this figure *tadpole man*.

The first thing a lot of people notice about children's drawings is how inaccurate they are. But take a second look. You see that tadpole man has a face with the eyes above the nose and the nose above the mouth.

Figure 5.1

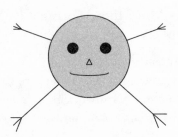

The arms and legs are also there. Do you see now what children do? Instead of making a copy of reality, their drawings are really interpretations. Furthermore, these are usually quite good interpretations because they capture so many important features.

We as adults may be far more sophisticated than children are; nevertheless, we still retain a preference for interpreting instead of copying. When you are trying to understand a new domain of knowledge, it will help you a lot to keep this fact in mind. You will find it much easier if you are able to create an interpretation of what the body of knowledge means, instead of having to remember everything that it actually says.

How do you go about creating an interpretation? The essence of interpretation is to let yourself respond subjectively to what you see around you and then to analyze your responses. Think about how you might devise an interpretation of a book you read. It would be a mistake to try to describe accurately and objectively everything that the book says. That would drown you quickly in boring details. Instead, start with your subjective response. Ask yourself whether you like the book or not. Then ask what component or components of the book were most responsible for making you feel this way. Answering these two questions gives you the nucleus of an interpretation. You can make your interpretation richer and more complex by trying to understand your subjective reactions more fully. Ask yourself why those components colored your reactions in the way they did. Also ask yourself how the book compares with others that you have liked (or disliked) in the past.

People respond subjectively to everything in their lives, even to things that seem cold or abstract. You can ask yourself what sections of a business report you liked best. Formulating and understanding your answer are the first steps toward creating an interpretation of the report.

Fact 4: Learning Is More like Making a Repair than like Filling an Empty Vessel

Have you ever heard people compare a mind to an empty vessel waiting to be filled with knowledge? Do not believe it. From the beginning every normal person's mind is filled with all kinds of ideas, including some accurate information, some outdated information, some half-truths, and even some outright errors. Furthermore, you are lucky that your mind is full. A full mind has all sorts of ways of relating to new information. Remember the principle that you should "understand the new by relating it to what you already know." A blank mind can just stare dumbfounded at its own emptiness.

It is extremely useful to have a mind full of information, even if the information is incomplete or partially mistaken. When someone presents you with new information, you do not have to make sense of it out of nothing. You only have to ask yourself, "How is this *different* from what I have thought all along?" The next step is evaluation: which one is more credible, the new information or your previous assumptions?

It substantially reduces your workload when you only have to adjust previous knowledge instead of starting all over again from the beginning. If you have to repair just a small number of misconceptions, that is a lot less work than having to master a whole new body of facts.

Fact 5: What Looks like a Whole New Body of Information Is Often Something Familiar but Seen from a Different Perspective

When you see the millions of volumes in a large university library, you probably feel overwhelmed by the enormous amount of knowledge that scientists and scholars have accumulated. Certainly, most people do. You would probably feel somewhat less overwhelmed, however, if you knew more about what those books contain. To a great extent, the growth of knowledge consists of reworking the same ideas over and over again in a slightly differently context or from a slightly different perspective. Although impressive, it is less overwhelming than most people usually assume.

Here is a case in point. The psychology of thinking seems to be worlds apart from the design of computers. The first has to do with understanding human nature, and the second has to do with engineering. Nevertheless, if you read the most widely used college texts on both subjects, you will find that most of the ideas in the psychology texts are only slightly different from many of the ones in the engineering texts. For example, the concepts that psychologists use to describe human memory are for the most part similar to if not identical with the concepts that engineers use to describe computer memory.

Or compare English literature and sociology. You would be surprised how much contemporary scholarship in English literature is a reapplication of ideas from sociology. The study of literature today devotes an enormous amount of attention to the way an author's culture determines the way he or she portrays such attributes as race, sex, and ethnicity. The questions and concepts that shape this research have their roots squarely in sociology.

When is it important to think about finding new perspectives? It is most useful when dealing with information about an unfamiliar subject. Ask yourself whether the ideas remind you of anything you have seen before. You will be surprised how often they do. When you recognize the similarity, you have an entry path into the new subject.

Fact 6: All Facts Are Really Interpretations in Disguise

Is there anything you can accept as "objective truth," including the findings of science? Most people think that Galileo (or Nicolaus Copernicus or Johannes Kepler) proved that the earth rotates around the sun. Someone may argue, therefore, that the orbit of the earth is surely objective truth. It is not. All scientists today believe that the earth orbits the sun; nevertheless, the real reason to accept this idea is that it is a simple and elegant interpretation of what astronomers observe. It is not something objective.

In other words, all knowledge is really an interpretation. Even the most well-established scientific knowledge is the result of an interpretation. Does a body of "facts" seem awkward or intimidating? If it is not objective truth, then you have the right to challenge it. You can ask what makes a supposed statement of fact useful. If information is difficult to understand, there should be a good explanation for why it has to be that way.

The psychologist Piaget called reality a *construction*. He was making the point that your mind is continually trying to invent better interpretations to make sense of the world around you. It is possible for your

interpretations to become better in many ways: they can become subtler, more complex, more powerful, or better informed. Still, no matter
how long you live and no matter how much you study, your knowledge
remains a construction. You can never go beyond interpretation to the
point of objective knowledge.

This fact is most useful to you on two occasions. The first occurs
when a new discovery puts one of your old and perhaps favorite beliefs
in question. You will have trouble changing your mind-set if you
thought that your old ideas were objectively accurate. On the other
hand, it is much easier to modify and change in light of new experience
if you recognized all along that it was just an interpretation, not objective truth.

The second occurs when you feel less than comfortable with another
person's account of "the facts." Your feeling of discomfort is a warning
to you that you should think of digging deeper. Instead of being the
only respectable account, it may just be one interpretation among many.
You may be able to find an alternative account that works better.

Fact 7: Understanding New Information Is Itself a Kind of Creative Thinking

You probably know people who see creative thinking and understanding information as absolute opposites. Do not believe them. Those people have too passive a view of how to assimilate information. They are
probably the same people who think that learning is a lot like filling an
empty vessel.

If you want to gain ownership over information instead of just memorizing random facts, you will almost certainly need an interpretive
framework. Perhaps you will be lucky and find some ready-made framework that you can comfortably accept. More often than not, you will
have to invent a new interpretation of your own. Nevertheless, even if
you have to do nothing more than customize someone else's interpretation, you will still have to think creatively.

Once you see acquiring information as a creative process, you will
realize that it takes on all the dynamics of creative discovery. You

remember the eureka experience, the flash of insight that accompanies the moment of discovery? People normally think of the eureka experience as part of creative thinking, but it is also part of acquiring information. You can have the same feeling when you land on a plausible interpretation of facts as when you make a creative discovery.

Fact 8: Active Interpretation Also Implies Active Self-Criticism

Once you recognize the role of invention in understanding, you can come to appreciate that soliciting criticism is also part of acquiring information. Why do you need criticism? As long as you are just copying someone else's account of the facts, your personal contribution remains minimal. On the other hand, if you are reorganizing and reinterpreting, then you will want to evaluate the validity of the framework you propose. Friends and colleagues can help you in trying to understand a body of information in much the same way they can help you with any other kind of creative thinking.

If you have the right to challenge other people's interpretations, then shouldn't you question interpretations of your own as well? The first interpretation that comes to mind may not be the best. You need to seek out its shortcomings. Here are some possibilities. First, you may have adopted a familiar framework even though it is not the best one for the job at hand. Second, you may have chosen one because it suits your personal interests or tastes. Third, you may have chosen your framework because it is currently fashionable. Fourth, it may be one that you know your supervisor favors. Fifth, you may have been attracted to a framework that seems quantitative or rigorous or for some other reason likely to impress people. None of these considerations justifies using a framework that really does not suit the information at hand.

Interpretations, unlike facts, are your own personal invention. This reality entails a new level of responsibility. Although you may not be responsible for facts you report, you are responsible for interpretations you propose. Criticizing yourself is the only way to ensure at all that you have fulfilled that responsibility.

Fact 9: How You Perceive Your Mind Affects How Well It Serves You

Professor Robert Rosenthal of Harvard University discovered many years ago how powerfully your perceptions of people can affect their behavior. The same principle applies to your perception of yourself.

In 1968, Rosenthal and his colleague Lenore Jacobson reported a study of what they called *Pygmalion in the Classroom*. The title refers to the George Bernard Shaw play about the way in which a linguist shaped the speech of a Cockney flower girl. Rosenthal and Jacobson discovered that perceptions can affect even children's measured level of intelligence. They divided the children in this study into two groups. He told teachers that the children in the first group had a high IQ and that the children in the second group had a lower IQ. In reality, however, there was no difference in average IQ between the two groups. At the end of the school year, he measured the children's IQs again. What do you think he discovered? The teachers' perceptions had actually changed the children's IQs! Now the children perceived as having the higher IQs by their teachers really did have higher IQs than the ones perceived as lower in IQ. Since then many other experiments have confirmed the same fact. Your perception of people itself often becomes a self-fulfilling prophecy.

What causes the Pygmalion Effect? Teachers often give more help and encouragement to certain of their students even though they consciously try to treat all children equally. Sometimes the differences are overt. Certain students may receive more attention in class or more stimulating assignments. Teachers often genuinely feel that it is appropriate to favor certain students in this way. They may think that the most able students require more attention than the others do if they are going to develop their special talents.

Sometimes the differences are subtler. If an "intelligent" student gives a wrong answer, teachers are likely to attribute it to laziness or carelessness. They will therefore encourage the student to work harder or to be more careful. On the other hand, if an "unintelligent" student gives the same wrong answer, teachers are likely to attribute it to lack of ability. They will expect neither extra effort from the student this time nor a better job next time.

Pygmalion Effect research tells us that other people's perceptions of you influence your performance. The corollary to that finding is this: how you perceive your own mind can have an even more powerful effect than how other people perceive you.

Compare two people, Anita and Josée. They both perceive themselves as intelligent; nevertheless, their sense of the source of their mind magic is quite different. Anita views herself as having been blessed with an unusually fine mind. She sees evidence of this in her ability to master large amounts of information. Her mind sometimes seems to her like a sponge, because it soaks up information so quickly. Josée views herself as having been born with rather average abilities. She considers herself as unusual only in her ability and determination to surpass her supposed limitations. In other words, Josée plans to be an overachiever. Even though she may not start out being particularly good at organizing information, she believes that she can learn to become much better.

What happens if you observe Anita and Josée over the course of several years? At the beginning Anita does well assimilating information, and Josée has a great deal of difficulty. Look again, however, a few years later. By this point Anita is still where she started. On the other hand, Josée has learned so much that she has become just as successful as Anita is. Come back after another year and Josée has clearly surpassed Anita.

Why did Josée improve so much while Anita did not improve at all? You will find the explanation in their respective images of themselves. In the case of both, having a positive self-image served to create a powerful Pygmalion Effect. Nevertheless, no matter how useful the Pygmalion Effect was in the case of Anita, its significance was greater in the case of Josée. Why was this? Seeing yourself as competent at learning is more powerful than seeing yourself as competent in other ways.

Josée believed that she could learn to improve; Anita believed that her skill depended on innate ability. In both cases, their image of their minds affected their performance. The difference between them is that Josée's sense of herself as intelligent relied on confidence in her own ability to learn. This is what gave her an advantage over the long run.

As you have more experience, you will come to understand your mind better and become more skillful at taking advantage of your unique abilities. Belief in your own ability to learn and change is one of the most powerful assets that you, as a user of information, can have.

A recent study by Joshua Aronson of New York University and his colleagues confirms this principle. Aronson compared two groups of African American college students: one group says intelligence is a fixed ability that does not change; the other group was encouraged to see intelligence as changeable. Otherwise, the members of the two groups were interchangeable. They found that the students who saw intelligence as changeable not only on average earned a higher grade-point average but also reported enjoying the academic process more.

Those occasions usually put the lie to a highly elevated sense of one's innate ability to organize information. On the other hand, being good at learning is much less rare. For that reason, many of us can be like Josée. We have the ability to learn as long as we are able to remove all the mind blocks that happen to get in the way.

Four Tricks for Simplifying Complex Knowledge Domains

Why do so many people find complex knowledge domains, such as math and science, so difficult to master? One reason is lack of familiarity. Their content is extremely foreign to most people's experience; they have no alternative except to spend a great deal of time and effort to master an unfamiliar collection of facts, procedures, and ways of thinking.

A second reason is the way our society perceives learning. If we taught them well, the majority of people would never have difficulty learning math and science. Nevertheless, society presumes that the current state of affairs is somehow normal. That expectation in turn becomes a self-fulfilling prophecy itself.

You can do nothing about the first reason because it has to do with the nature of the material itself. Nevertheless, you have the power at mitigate the force of the second factor. Following are four tricks ll help you simplify complex knowledge domains.

Begin with Something Concrete

It is hard to learn anything without actually seeing it. If you want to learn business management, get to know an entrepreneur. If you want to learn about electricity, visit a power plant. If you want to learn about farm animals, visit a farm. Seeing real things almost always makes them more understandable.

Doing something concrete is most important when you first start learning the subject. Later on, when you confront abstract theories, your early experience will give you actual specific examples that will make the theory meaningful to you.

Understand Theory in Relation to Practice (and Vice Versa)

Learning is almost always easier when theory and practice go together instead of being kept separate.

Take an example of two topics that should be studied together at one time. The first is a practical topic, genetic testing. The second is theoretical, the science of genetics. Students should learn as part of their education that genes cause certain illnesses and represent risk factors for other illnesses. They should know what genetic testing is and how reliable the results are. On the other hand, they should also know something about what genes are and how they determine traits.

Usually, schools teach these two topics separately. They teach genetics as part of biology and genetic testing as part of health studies. Imagine, though, that schools taught them at the same time. Students would become better able to evaluate the significance of test results if they ever underwent genetic testing themselves. The reason is that they would understand the theoretical rationale. Students would also see the practical relevance of biological theory. The theory would become less dry and abstract because students would see its practical significance in their lives.

When you are learning theories, it is natural to ask yourself what is the good of these abstract ideas and why anyone should care about them. Seeing practical applications will tell you, first, why other people consider them useful and, second, whether their particular uses relate to your interests. On the other hand, when you are seeing practical applications, it is natural to wonder why they work. Learning the theory behind the concrete applications at this point will give you an explanation.

Learn Complex Ideas by Understanding Their Historical Context

As you have seen, lack of familiarity is the main enduring reason why complex knowledge domains are so intimidating. You can make them seem a little less alien if you understand in human terms why people developed the knowledge in the first place.

It is no surprise that so many people see science as cold and bloodless. The way we usually present the history of science makes it seem as if scientists care only about the growth of knowledge. The same is true of complex knowledge domains outside of science. It is commonplace to present famous thinkers as if they were selfless idealists. In reality, the people who shaped our intellectual tradition had all kinds of motives. Some were practical (John Milton); some were mystical (Fyodor Dostoyevsky); some were committed to a particular community (Winston Churchill) or a particular cause (Martin Luther King Jr.); some quite simply were eccentrics who got lucky (Ezra Pound). If you see theories and ideas as disembodied works of genius, you lose the all-important human bond with the inventor. Ideas often come to life only when you begin to see how a human being could think of them as a response to a felt need.

Indeed, if you trace the process through which a particular idea emerged in history, understanding the idea itself will become much easier. Your own thinking can vicariously take the same steps. Think of students who want to understand Isaac Newton's theory of motion. It helps them enormously if they know how people explained motion before Newton developed his theory. In part, they will want to know something about the theories of earlier scientists, such as Kepler and Galileo. But they will want other information as well.

For example, Newton incorporated certain unscientific intuitions into his theory. Before Newton many people believed that angels were behind the planets, beating their wings and pushing them in their orbits. That idea does not sound at all scientific. Nevertheless, Richard Feynman (1965), Nobel laureate in physics, has pointed out that the image of angels pushing planets lay behind Newton's concept of inertia. Inertia was an unexplained force that kept planets in motion for Newton. It served the same function within his system as the medieval concept of pushing by angels had previously served. In effect, Newton reformulated the earlier notion of angel power to fit his own mechanistic framework.

It helps as well in learning Newton's theory if you understand how people in ancient times comprehended motion. Educational researchers have explained why this is so. Most students' intuitive understanding of motion is quite similar to what the ancient Greeks thought. It helps students to know something about how Newtonian science came to replace the science invented by the Greeks. Through understanding the history of the "Newtonian revolution," students can experience a similar revolution in their own knowledge.

Take Complex Ideas Down from Their Pedestal

Understanding the history and psychology of knowledge has the positive effect of bringing it down from its pedestal.

As a society, we have gotten into a habit of creating a superhuman image of complex knowledge domains, especially the sciences. All too often we make it seem as if you need a superior kind of mind even to understand them, let alone discover them. No wonder people find them so difficult. At the same time, we create the impression that someone once delivered the knowledge from on high and no one can ever challenge or change it. These images implicitly tell people to fear and respect knowledge instead of trying to own it. Ironically, this habit is diametrically opposed to the way scientists themselves say we should regard their work.

No symbol encapsulates this myth of the scientific genius more succinctly than that of Einstein. As the French social critic Roland Barthes observed in his book *Mythologies*, Einstein "is commonly represented by his brain, which is like an object for anthologies, a true museum exhibit." Popular legend pictures Einstein's brain as superior to the brains of other people. People imagine that Einstein was able to understand laws of nature too complex for other people to fathom. Barthes points out the absurd limits to which the cult of Einstein sometimes went. He describes a famous photograph of Einstein, lying down, his head bristling with electric wires. As Barthes explains, doctors were recording Einstein's brain waves to understand what made this organ special. Barthes reports as well that two hospitals fought for the gruesome privilege of obtaining Einstein's brain after he died. Their goal apparently was to discover the source of his mind magic by studying his brain anatomy.

No one ever found any significant differences between Einstein's brain and other human brains. Should that surprise anyone? Contrary to the myth, it does not require an unusual kind of brain to understand Einstein's ideas. Many thousands of very ordinary students use their very ordinary brains to learn Einstein's ideas every year. If you cared to devote enough time, you could probably master them with a normal amount of diligence and effort.

You will understand complex ideas more easily if you see them as ingenious solutions to specific problems in a particular human and historical circumstance. You will no longer have to feel in awe.

How to Beat Information Overload

Information management is increasingly becoming an essential skill for students and for people in the workforce. Many people—perhaps most people—feel that they have too much to read and too many facts to keep track of. Even deciding which facts and documents are the most important takes time. Is there any way to cut down the required reading?

Psychologists have documented what many people know all too well from their personal lives: the effects of information overload can be devastating. Information overload can cause psychological symptoms of stress, such as anxiety and irritability, as well as physical symptoms, such as an upset stomach, headaches, hypertension, and even heart disease. For many people, it has become critically important to learn better ways of organizing information.

How do you beat information overload? The main reason why many people so often have trouble mastering a body of information is that they tend to equate learning facts with rote memorization. Such a self-defeating theory of learning is the first link in a chain that leads to failure and frustration.

Out of the memorization model of learning grows disinterest, dislike, and eventually fear of information. It can make the experience of learning facts seem so unpleasant that you begin to avoid and fear it. This chapter has presented an alternative view of information management that focuses on ownership and interpretation instead of memorization. Following are some strategies for gaining a sense of ownership when you find the amount of information that you face overwhelming.

Think Before You Read

People almost never have to master information that is totally new (and it would be extremely unfair if anyone expected you to do so). New information almost always is related to familiar concepts and facts. Therefore, even before you start reading, you can make an educated guess about what you will eventually think.

So start by being bold. Guess what the main ideas will be and how you will interpret them. These guesses will help you to read more actively and purposefully. The one caveat is to realize that your opening guess almost certainly will be at least partly wrong and that you need to be open-minded enough to change it later.

Find a Friend

Unfamiliar information is intimidating. Finding a friend can make it less so.

A friend is an author, a theory, a concept, or even a word that connects the new information to something you already know (and with luck, also like). Ideally, your friend will offer you a perspective on the new subject that will make you feel that it is almost the same as . . . [fill in the blank] except for . . . [fill in the blank again]. It is OK even if that feeling of familiarity later proves to have been exaggerated. Your friend got you into the subject. That is an important step. Paradoxically, even an author you dislike can be a friend in the sense being discussed here, as long as you are quite familiar with how the author thinks. Find out what that author thinks, knowing in advance that you will disagree. Now look. The act of disagreement has helped you start organizing a new body of facts.

Sometimes there may be no familiar authors or theories to give you a perspective. Glance through your list of titles and notice key words. Specialized subjects usually assign new meanings to key terms. Find out what those words mean in the subject, and decide if you consider their meaning helpful, insightful, and appealing. When nothing else is available, a key word or two can open up a subject.

Read in Depth, but Do It Selectively

People often make the mistake of reading all documents with the same care. The process is exhausting. Instead, select a small amount of material, maybe one or two chapters or a couple of articles. Pore over them with meticulous care. Go over them two, three, or four times, until you feel that you really understand what they are saying. Then take a break.

Why read just some material with such care? Documents in most fields tend to be repetitive in vocabulary, in structure, and often even in content. Reading a few chapters or documents in detail will teach you the basic elements, and later documents will be much easier to comprehend.

How do you choose the right documents to read with care? Choose the most important, if you know what they are. If not, choose anything that looks typical. It will probably teach what you need to know.

Actively Challenge Yourself

As you start to become familiar with the subject, seek out documents that might force you to change your mind. Why? First, it will protect you from becoming overly influenced by your preconceptions. Remember that you began by creating interpretations based on guesses rather than knowledge. Actively challenging yourself will make sure that your later and more sophisticated interpretations reflect the facts, not just your worldview.

Second, it will make your own understanding of the subject richer, subtler, and more complex. If you can find paper after paper that will force you to rethink the subject in some way, you can achieve substantially more depth in understanding. Third, it can bring you to a point where it becomes difficult to find anything that will genuinely challenge you. When this happens you can feel with some confidence that you have mastered the main issues.

Changing Your Relationship with Information

Fear of information comes part and parcel with a broadly pessimistic view of oneself as a learner. Victims of information phobia become trapped in their own despair. They have difficulty in suspending their disbelief, even for a moment, to consider the possibility that they just might be able to learn more effectively than they thought. After you begin to despair, you stop caring. When you no longer care, you do not learn.

Information phobia has its most damaging effects on performance in the workplace. People find it increasingly difficult to acquire the information that they need for their jobs. Their job performance begins to decline. They have a harder and harder time obtaining promotions. Eventually, job loss can become a very real possibility.

What makes it especially sad is that the problem should never have arisen in the first place. You can learn to assimilate and organize information in the same way that you can learn other aspects of mind magic. If everybody learned how to organize information successfully, information overload and information phobia would cease to be serious problems.

The solution needs to be twofold. The first step must be to understand and change the way in which you have come to see yourself. The second must be to change the way in which you respond to information.

Many victims focus only on the times when they felt overwhelmed by large quantities of information. You have to learn to take into account the positive experiences as well, such as the way you acquire information in your private life and in your family.

You can begin to change the way in which you handle information once you have recognized that organizing information is not a magical skill. Understand the difference between owning information and borrowing it. Recognize that the former makes you feel in control, whereas the latter makes you feel stressed. You need to realize another important fact. To become a skillful user of information is an emotional change as much as it is intellectual. You have to start feeling differently about yourself.

Years of difficulty in organizing information can have a deep effect on how you see yourself. If "trouble handling information" has become part of your self-concept, your image of yourself can become a self-fulfilling prophecy. You can learn the most effective techniques for organizing information, but it will do you no good as long as you see yourself as lacking competence. So you must not let your self-concept interfere with how well you learn. Increasing your skills and rethinking your self-concept have to proceed hand in hand.

The next important step for you is to transform your method of assimilating information from passive accumulation to active interpretation. If there is no reason why a particular piece of information should matter to you, then you should not waste your time with it. If it truly matters enough and you accurately interpret its significance, then it will become memorable.

Because you are unused to applying a rich method of interpretation, you can expect things at the beginning to be harder. For a short time, the added work may even make you feel more overloaded with information than before. Nevertheless, you should stick with it. Your mind will adjust to a new style of responding to information, and you will notice a change. You will feel in control of the information, and your feelings of fear and stress will diminish.

When you become the owner of your information, even your manner will communicate your sense of control. People will notice it. In the process, you will have learned more than how to organize information. You will also have become more skillful at learning mind magic, and you will be able to apply that knowledge everywhere.

CHAPTER 6

HOW TO SOLVE PROBLEMS LIKE AN EXPERT

How do you become an expert? Many people think that you will become an expert if you study hard and gain a lot of experience. Study and experience may be necessary to become an expert, but in and of themselves, they are not sufficient. People who think otherwise can work for years and years before they finally realize that they were wrong. In all domains experts have more than just a lot of knowledge and experience. Because they think differently, they are able to solve problems that stump everyone else.

How is an expert different from a competent person who is not an expert? Take as an example the distinguished neurologist Norman Geschwind, until his death one of the leading experts in the world. Most competent doctors are products of their professional training. The more highly competent they are, the more meticulously they follow the accepted rules and principles they were taught. On the other hand, an expert like Dr. Geschwind is someone who understood when accepted knowledge applied and when you needed to find something different. Experts listen to their instincts even when most other competent people would go along with the crowd.

In the mid-twentieth century, when Geschwind entered medicine, an antilocalization bias dominated neurology. At the time, neurologists did not consider the specific part of the brain damaged to be especially important. This was particularly true in the case of aphasia, a neurological condition that affects people's ability to understand and produce language. While working in an aphasia unit, Geschwind noticed that there were marked differences from one aphasia patient to another. In spite of his lessons from medical school, it was obvious to Geschwind that differences among patients were associated with the location of the brain damage. As a result, he was able to offer precise diagnoses that eluded his more conventional colleagues.

If you observe real experts, you will notice they differ from one another as much as they differ from everyone else. Why is that? Experts tend to develop their own personal working style. Some are systematic and orderly; others wait for the moment of sudden discovery. Some think about design and aesthetic issues right from the start; others prefer to begin working on functional problems and only integrate design later on. Some like to wake up early and finish early; others do their best work late at night.

Can't you learn to solve problems like an expert? To become an expert problem solver, you first need to know the techniques that the best problem solvers use. But you cannot just rigidly follow other people's methods. You also need to think about your own natural problem-solving style. You can know the methods that even the most eminent scientists use. But you will not become an expert problem solver until you integrate these techniques into your own natural style.

Mind consciousness can help you learn to solve problems like an expert just as it helps to extend your mind in other directions. If you could learn problem solving simply by reading a book, mind consciousness might be superfluous. The process is different when you need to integrate something new into your existing style of thinking. It makes sense to begin by understanding your own natural problem-solving style.

The Tortoise and the Hare

Do you remember Aesop's fable about the race between the tortoise and the hare? The hare had a lot of speed, but he became careless when he got close to the finish line. On the other hand, the tortoise was not as quick as the hare, but he was more persistent and made fewer mistakes.

The tortoise and the hare personify two markedly different problem-solving styles. Some people rely on the brilliant flash of insight (but have to learn to be careful in case their brilliant insight turns out to be wrong). Other people are more methodical and gradually come to a solution.

Aesop believed that the tortoise's strategy was better. He said that "slow and steady wins the race." In the real world, things are not so clear-cut. Sometimes slow and steady wins. Other times quick and inspired works better. Most of the time they tie, even though they reach the "finish" by different routes.

There is not just one method of problem solving that is always right for all people. Instead, there are different kinds of people, with different kinds of personalities, who can and should approach problems differently. No approach is perfect; different methods work on different problems, and different methods work for different people. You will generally do best if you choose the kinds of methods that usually work for you. Other methods may be better in theory; they may even work well in practice for somebody else. But if they make you uncomfortable, they will probably serve you poorly.

In any given occupation, people with different kinds of personalities often come up with different kinds of solutions, all of which may be equally good. For years the chess championship of the world was in essence a contest between two different personal styles. One contestant, Bobby Fischer, was better at logical analysis; the other contestant, Boris Spassky, was better at devising elegantly beautiful strategies. The two players were virtually opposite in their style of play. Still they also were both brilliant.

Personality and style affect even how scientists approach problems. For certain, there are some scientists who follow the top-down logical textbook model; on the other hand, many successful scientists do not. You need only think of someone such as the American Nobel Prize–winning geneticist Barbara McClintock. She solved problems in biology by understanding the individual plant. She drew larger conclusions by moving from the individual organism to the broad generalization, or bottom-up instead of top-down.

Which One Are You?

Are you a tortoise or a hare? Find out by completing the following short questionnaire. Read each of the twenty statements. If you agree with the statement, circle the word *Agree* at the end of the line. Otherwise, circle the word *Disagree*. Do not skip any lines.

There are no right answers. The purpose is to help you determine your problem-solving style. Different problem-solving styles are equally good, but it can be helpful to know which one is yours.

1. I have trouble staying concentrated for a long time.
   Agree   *Disagree*
2. Slow and steady wins the race.
   Agree   *Disagree*
3. I am good at thinking on my feet.
   ✓ *Agree*   *Disagree*
4. A person who hurries a lot will inevitably do a worse job.
   ✓ *Agree*   *Disagree*
5. When I was in elementary school, I particularly disliked spelling.
   Agree   ✓*Disagree*
6. I like everything in its proper place.
   Agree   ✓*Disagree*
7. I often forget to dot the i's and cross the t's.
   Agree   ✓*Disagree*
8. I like to do things one step at a time.
   Agree   ✓*Disagree*
9. I do not know how ideas come to me; they just appear.
   ✓*Agree*   *Disagree*
10. The harder a person works, the better the results.
    ✓ *Agree*   *Disagree*
11. I trust feelings more than thought.
    ✓ *Agree*   *Disagree*
12. Practice makes perfect.
    ✓ *Agree*   *Disagree*
13. I dislike doing things by the book.
    ✓*Agree*   *Disagree*

14. Quick decisions are usually sloppy ones.
    Agree ✓*Disagree*
15. In some way I am unusually talented.
    ✓*Agree* *Disagree*
16. Success is 1 percent inspiration and 99 percent perspiration.
    ✓*Agree* *Disagree*
17. I easily become bored.
    Agree ✓*Disagree*
18. I believe in checking and then double-checking.
    ✓*Agree* *Disagree*
19. I prefer it when someone else takes care of the details.
    Agree ✓*Disagree*
20. I am my own harshest critic.
    Agree ✓ *Disagree*

Total: ___11___

Scoring

For statement 1, put an *X* over the word *Agree* if you circled it. Do nothing if you circled *Disagree*. Do the same thing for statements 3, 5, 7, and all the other odd-numbered statements. For statement 2, put an *X* over the word *Disagree* if you circled it. Do nothing if you circled *Agree*. Do the same thing for statements 4, 6, 8, and all the other even-numbered statements. Then count the number of *X*s. If there are fourteen or more *X*s, you are a hare. You prefer to solve problems through sudden insight. If there are six or fewer *X*s, you are a tortoise. You prefer to solve problems by working methodically. If there are between seven and thirteen *X*s, you have a mixed problem-solving style. You sometimes work like a tortoise and sometimes like a hare, depending on circumstances.

You can become exceptionally good at problem solving if you combine an understanding of your natural style with the tested methods of experts. Both used together, successfully integrated, are more effective than either one of them on its own.

Why Not Learn from the Best?

Where do you go if you want to extend your natural ability as a problem solver? It seems only common sense that you should learn a skill from the people who are at the top of their field. If you want to learn how to play tennis, you would do best to hire a tennis pro as your teacher. If you want to know how to fix your car, you should learn from a professional mechanic. If you want to understand anything, you should find an expert willing to teach you. This principle applies to problem solving, too. If you want to learn how to solve problems, see what the experts do.

In our society, who are the experts at solving problems? The real experts clearly are mathematicians and scientists. They are the people we hire to solve our most difficult problems. They discover the forms of treatment that cure our most serious illnesses; they discover the methods of production that are continually raising our standard of living; they are increasingly the people who solve our most pressing social problems.

When we as a society have a problem, we ask the scientists to find a solution. On the other hand, we almost never look at what scientists do when we want to learn how to find solutions ourselves.

Let's look at how scientists solve problems to see if we can apply the same methods in our private and professional lives.

Professional Puzzle Solvers with a Tradition

To understand what makes scientists expert problem solvers, we have to do more than ask them how they unravel complex problems. For one thing, scientists often do not know how they do it. Even the ones who think they know often turn out to be totally mistaken.

Fortunately, many people have wondered what makes scientists so good at solving difficult problems. Psychologists and historians have been interested in this question for quite a while. Even many scientists themselves have wondered about the reasons for their success. The results are interesting, surprising, and often extremely useful.

What is a scientist? On the surface, the answer seems almost obvious. Most people conjure up an image of a person with test tubes and a white laboratory coat. If you think about it, though, you will see that we call a huge and diverse group of people scientists. They range from laboratory scientists to naturalists who work in the field. They include experts in observation who peer through telescopes and microscopes, specialists in experimentation, and theorists who work with pen and computer.

What is it that scientists all have in common that sets them apart from the rest of us? School textbooks, even today, present something called the *scientific method*, which scientists everywhere are supposed to use. But what is this so-called scientific method? If you look at what scientists really do (as opposed to what school textbooks say they do), you will find that there is no such thing.

A more valid description of the scientist comes from historians of science. Observing scientists, past and present, historians have found that the vast majority of scientists are what they called *puzzle solvers*. In other words, the essence of being a scientist is to be an expert at solving problems. Historians point out that a very few "revolutionary" scientists do not quite fit the puzzle-solver image. Nevertheless, if you look at what the majority of scientists do, you see that they are professional problem solvers. Furthermore, you can learn a lot about how to solve problems yourself if you observe their methods.

People are sometimes reluctant even to think about learning problem-solving methods from scientists. For one thing, they are afraid that the methods of scientists inevitably are overwhelmingly complex. They are concerned also that scientists' methods will be too technical or too tedious. In this chapter you will see methods that scientists really use, freed of their technical complexity. There will be no equations and no obscure symbols. You will see instead the kinds of intuitions and inferences that guide them when they find the solutions to complex problems, before they even think of writing down a formula.

Rules You Can Break

When you call scientists problem solvers, you are not saying that they all deal with problems in the same or even similar ways. In some branches of science, scientists use methods as crisp and precise as a military operation. You can call these methods formal. In other branches, scientists rely to a surprising extent on improvisation and guesswork.

The systematic study of problem solving is a little more than fifty years old. Soon after the end of World War II, the Hungarian-born mathematician George Polya proposed a new field of inquiry, which he called *heuristics*. Polya wanted to improve the quality of mathematics education. His idea was to teach students not just the content of mathematics but also the methods of mathematicians. With this goal in mind, he described and catalogued the methods that mathematicians use in their work.

It may have been better if Polya had used a more familiar-sounding name than heuristics. Even though the word itself may sound obscure, its meaning is not. The word *heuristic* means nothing more than "rule of thumb." Because of Polya we are stuck with the word *heuristic*. It is a good idea to get used to the term. If for no other reason, familiarity with this word will help you to understand other books on the subject.

Polya had a relatively narrow goal. He wanted to help mathematics students. But understanding heuristics is far more useful than Polya recognized. Problems arise in all walks of life. Virtually everyone can benefit from knowing more about problem solving.

Clearly, scientists need to have both formal and heuristic methods. Much of the time you would surely hope that they would follow formal methods precisely. There can be no margin for error when scientists test for a serious illness or measure the safety of an aircraft. In everyday life, though, as opposed to science, the cost of making mistakes is usually small. If you make a mistake, will anything serious go wrong? If so, you have to be as careful and precise as possible. If not, educated guesswork will usually serve you better than strictly formal methods.

The main advantage of heuristic methods is that they are quick. Formal methods are notoriously slow, and in everyday life people rarely have the time to wait. Heuristic methods normally give you the right answer anyway. So you usually need a good reason to choose the slow road. Note that the time difference can be great. It can sometimes be a difference between seconds and hours or between minutes and days! Heuristic methods are also usually simpler. They rarely require the same effort or as much training as formal methods.

Formal methods in science are widely publicized and easy to find. They make up a large part of what instructors teach in high school and university science courses. Heuristics may well be the most useful aspect of scientific know-how, but they are much harder to find. They are like the intuitions and rules of thumb that master craftspeople pass along to a select group of apprentices. Successful scientists usually pass this knowledge along only in small seminars and tutorials, which generally take place only at elite universities. Furthermore, the professor usually limits attendance to only a handful of favored students.

Being most definitely a tortoise himself, Polya praised habits of thought, such as devotion, patience, and sound principles. To most tortoises, his advice seemed like good common sense. On the other hand, to hares, it usually sounded pretty stodgy. Fortunately for the hares, things have changed considerably since Polya's time. The Maltese writer Edward de Bono, for example, became famous by criticizing what he called *vertical thinking*, his name for the kind of methods that Polya recommended. De Bono argued instead for more *lateral thinking*. He was saying, in effect, that problem solvers should be less like the tortoise and more like the hare.

De Bono's harelike advice in no way represents the last word on the subject. By the beginning of the twenty-first century, the world of problem solving was discovering Polya's tortoiselike viewpoint. Stanford professor Alan Schoenfeld, a leading expert today on problem solving, explicitly acknowledges his debt to Polya's seminal work.

Most people rarely see heuristic methods described in print, and when they do, the place is usually a technical scientific publication. Nevertheless, of all methods used by scientists, they are the easiest for most people to understand. They are also the ones that you can integrate most easily into your natural problem-solving style.

Ten Genuinely Useful Problem-Solving Principles That You Can Learn from Scientists

Have you ever felt totally at a loss, without any idea what to do in the face of a new problem? When you have a good lead, staying at work on a problem can be easy. When you have nothing, it is terribly discouraging. If your problem-solving style is that of a hare, a lack of inspiration makes further progress all but impossible. If it is that of a tortoise, you may be able to keep slogging it out for a while. But feeling blocked for an extended period of time can utterly demoralize anyone, regardless of your problem-solving style.

Having a good set of problem-solving practices is useful at all times in keeping you on track. It matters the most, though, when you do not have any idea what to do, because it keeps you from giving up. The same principles are useful to tortoises and hares. But your problem-solving styles will almost certainly influence how you choose to apply them.

Principle 1: *Do* Make a Lot of Guesses

When in doubt, guess. The worst that can happen is that you will be wrong. Furthermore, even when you are wrong, correcting your mistakes in itself often suggests new answers. The worst thing you can do is to do nothing at all.

In the business world, people usually appreciate the relationship between risk and reward. It is difficult to take financial risks; therefore, the market rewards risk takers over the long run with higher returns. Think of a successful investor, such as George Soros. He was successful in acquiring wealth primarily by making excellent guesses about which currencies were going to rise and which would fall.

The same principle applies to the pursuit of knowledge and the pursuit of wealth: over the long run, risk taking (in the form of guessing when you are not sure, thus risking the shame of being wrong) pays off. As the Austrian-born English philosopher of science Karl Popper pointed out, bold guesswork is what drives scientific progress. In science the great risk takers are the theorists. Figures such as Isaac Newton and Albert Einstein changed the world by making good guesses that later experiments largely served to confirm.

Recognize that the ability to make good guesses benefits from practice. Make a lot of guesses, and you will usually become better at it. Successful investors (such as Soros) and successful theoretical scientists (such as Einstein) made one bold guess after another. Each guess put their intuitions to the test so that they could learn to improve their guesswork. Realize as well that skillful guesswork in one domain does not often transfer into others. Linus Pauling was brilliantly successful in molecular biology but brilliantly unsuccessful when he began to advance theories of health. In spite of his success as an investor, Soros has been quite unsuccessful in trying to promote himself as a philosopher.

Why don't people guess a lot? On the surface, this fact seems strange. You lose nothing materially by making a wrong guess, and you usually gain useful information when you see if your guess was right. The explanation is that there can be a psychological cost even if there is no material one. Many people hate to be wrong—and if you make more frequent guesses, you will be right a lot more of the time, but you will also be wrong a lot more often. Some people lose face even if no one except themselves knows that they were wrong. Are you like that?

How does problem-solving style affect your willingness to make guesses? Tortoises suffer from "fear of guessing" far more than hares do. Tortoises are often supercautious, therefore they avoid making guesses and for that reason often miss a great deal of useful information. Hares' thinking style usually forces them to live with the experience of being wrong, no matter how unpleasant. On the other hand, tortoises can often last well into adulthood still believing that with enough care, you can avoid being wrong.

The only way to avoid making mistakes is if you never take risks by guessing. If you stop guessing, you stop learning—and your world of experience freezes solid.

Principle 2: *Do* Be Prepared to Question the Legitimacy of the Problem

In the history of science, some of the most important advances occurred when researchers realized that they had been asking the wrong questions. A hundred years ago, physicists tried to discover whether light was really a wave or a particle. They achieved a real understanding of light only after Werner Heisenberg came to recognize that there were other options.

Problem-solving experts call this *unasking the question*. Much of the time when problems are difficult to solve it is because there is something wrong with the question you are asking. When you run into a lot of frustration, you should reconsider your question to see if it is somehow sabotaging you.

Many problems are like the riddle "What is the sound of one hand clapping?" You cannot answer this because clapping requires two hands. There are many reasons why a specific problem may be impossible to solve (or impossible for you to solve, given your particular circumstances). The meaning of the problem may be vague and ill defined. The solution may require more time or money than you could possibly afford. There may be something intrinsically paradoxical about the problem that makes it unsolvable. Discrediting a problem is often as legitimate as solving it.

Your boss may not appreciate it if you say directly that he or she is asking you the wrong question. But there is an alternative way of handling illegitimate questions. You can find the right question, the one that provides the information that your boss really needs—and then you can answer that one. For example, a maker of edutainment products asked me a number of years ago to develop a method for teaching arithmetic. It is a challenge to make arithmetic entertaining to children, yet it was imperative for the company's products to be entertaining. Also, the company's products did not lend themselves to genuine instruction, even though they definitely had educational value. I therefore proposed a collection of educational games that dealt with a broad range of topics in early mathematics, such as counting, measurement, classification, and sequential ordering. Although there was no real teaching involved and very little arithmetic, the company was happy. Why? I had told the company what it needed, even if I had not actually answered the question that was asked.

Unasking the question seems to many people like breaking the rules. As they see it, if you unask the question, you are evading the problem instead of solving it. Tortoises are usually more careful than hares about respecting established practices. Therefore, they are often the last people to doubt the legitimacy of the problem itself. Are tortoises wrong to feel this way? Certainly, you can be too cavalier. That happens when you give up trying to solve the problem before making a reasonable effort. On the other hand, after a certain amount of time, sticking with a problem becomes as unproductive as beating your head against a wall. You have to weigh the alternatives. That is a good time to consider unasking the question.

Keep in mind that finding the "right" answer does not always solve the problem. Especially in the real world, an answer can be technically right but still not good. It can be right in the sense that it satisfies all the conditions stated in the problem. But it still may not be good, because it fails to tell you what you really have to find out (regardless of what the problem literally asks). Other times, answers are not good because they are too complicated and too clumsy or because they fail to point to a useful direction for the future.

Indeed, you can miss valuable information if you think every answer has to be either right or wrong. Some answers are neither totally right nor totally wrong: they embody a partial solution, which you then need to modify and refine. Vague or ambiguous answers can be both right and wrong at the same time. Your answer may be right in one sense but wrong in another.

In the early 1950s, soon after the production of the first computers, the eminent English mathematician Alan Turing raised the question of whether or not computers could be genuinely intelligent. What was the answer? Half a century later, we still do not know. Even though it never yielded a clear answer, the question was still an excellent one. The attempt to create artificial intelligence, directly inspired by Turing's question, was one of the most productive chapters of late twentieth-century science. It led to significant advances in computer science as well as important practical innovations. Time-sharing, a standard feature of computer design, came out of artificial intelligence. Artificial intelligence researchers first invented the industrial robots now essential in heavy manufacturing. It even inspired a feature-length Steven Spielberg movie.

One reason why Turing's question was so hard to answer involves the notion itself of intelligence. How would we ever know if a computer were genuinely intelligent? One significant consequence of Turing's question was to force psychologists to think more clearly about the meaning of this important concept.

Principle 3: *Do* Consider the Problem's "Psychology"

What is it that makes a problem difficult? Most people usually believe that the difficulty is something objective. They may think that they need additional information (such as a book to consult or a person to ask) or better technical resources (better equipment, better lighting, a more powerful computer). Sometimes the solution really is out there, and better resources will help you find it. But much of the time, the real problem is in your head. You began with some mistaken assumption, and you will not find the solution until you correct it.

This kind of thing has often happened to scientists. You may know the story of how astronomers in the Middle Ages tried to map the orbits of the planets. The maps were all quite complicated, primarily because scientists thought the planets were all revolving around the earth. As soon as they accepted instead that the planets were revolving around the sun, the solution became much clearer.

People usually take their unstated assumptions so much for granted that it is virtually impossible to see them. Children probably do this more than anyone else. Here is an example taken from Piaget. Give a four- or five-year-old child a set of six eggs and six eggcups lined up side by side, as shown in Figure 6.1.

Now ask the child if there are more eggs or more eggcups or just as many of each. Almost all children answer that there are just as many of each. Next, spread out the eggs. Ask the child again whether there are more eggs or more eggcups or just as many of each. You still have six eggs, but the length of the row is much longer because there is more space between them. Most four- and five-year-olds say that there are more eggs.

You can argue the point with the child in various ways, but it will do almost no good. You can ask her how she knows that there are more eggs. She will answer something like this: "Because the eggs go from here to here [spreading her arms out wide], but the eggcups go from

Figure 6.1

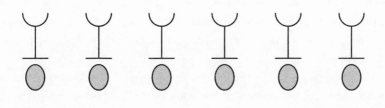

here to here [holding her hands close together]." As far as she is concerned, this argument proves her point. You can also remind her that she had said a moment earlier that there were just as many of each. Your argument will have no effect. As far as she is concerned, there are now more eggs, regardless of the way things were before.

Why do young children fall prey to this kind of error? The reason has to do with their unstated assumptions. Adults know that there is a difference between the numerical concept of *more* and the physical concept of *longer*. But four- and five-year-olds assume that they are the same. Children have to change their underlying assumptions before they can successfully solve the problem.

It is possible, however, to become aware of your unstated assumptions and then correct them. What is the proof? Ask an eight-year-old the same question. She will probably laugh and then give the right answer. Somehow between the ages of five and eight, she has corrected her erroneous conclusion. If children can correct themselves, then surely adults can do the same thing.

It is difficult for virtually anyone to recognize his or her own unstated assumptions, tortoises and hares alike. Many tortoises feel certain that they are using the right methods as long as they are doing what the instructions say. Hares often feel just as sure of themselves but for different reasons. They sometimes feel overly confident of their own natural ability, so they cannot imagine that it might have let them down.

But no one is right all the time. You need to examine ways that you may have led yourself astray.

The textbook image of problem solving draws a sharp distinction between what is given (the terms of the problem) and what you produce yourself (solutions). In the real world, this distinction often becomes muddy. What you do yourself will sometimes change the problem and at times even make it worse. Solving problems in the real world requires at least that you consider how your actions could have become part of the problem.

People change and influence the phenomena that they are trying to understand, even in physics, the hardest of the hard sciences. Scientists have recognized for a long time that the process of observation can even affect the phenomenon being observed. It can influence something as impersonal as the motion of light. (The act of observing rays of light in motion has measurable effects on their behavior. Heisenberg's discovery of this uncertainty principle led to a revolution in the thinking of physicists.) Think how much more influence you as an observer might have when the situation involves human beings!

Even if the problem is in your head, that does not mean it is an illusion. It is real, and it needs to be treated with respect. Regardless of the reason, mapping the orbit of the planets was a very real problem for hundreds of years. Being in your head means only that you have to begin questioning your own assumptions in order to solve a problem.

Principle 4: *Do* Bite Off More than You Can Chew

A hundred fifty years ago, few people—other than scientists and science fiction writers—imagined flying machines. Engineers might have been designing submarines as long ago as the late-sixteenth century; but in the nineteenth century when Jules Verne wrote about a voyage to the bottom of the sea, few people believed that such a journey would ever be more than fantasy. It seemed like an impossible dream in 1961 when President John F. Kennedy challenged Americans to commit themselves to landing a man on the moon within a decade. No one knows which present-day scientific fantasies will become reality in twenty or a hundred years.

Why are scientists prepared to try to do the seemingly impossible when other people generally are not? Knowing the stories of scientific successes of the past must surely give them a lot of encouragement. Another, perhaps deeper, source of encouragement is having detailed technical knowledge. Why should knowing a lot of technical details matter? Not only does it force us to doubt what most people naively consider impossible, but it also tells you what technical problems you have to solve in order to turn seemingly impossible fantasies into reality.

Tortoises usually have more trouble than hares do when it comes to thinking big, even though they are more likely to own the kind of detailed technical knowledge that makes big scientific conjectures work out so much more often than other ideas. What goes wrong? The problem for most tortoises is that they get lost in the details that they know so well. Every once in a while, they have to remind themselves of the big questions. If you are a tortoise, remember from time to time to ask yourself what questions got you interested in this field in the first place. Contemplating that will do wonders in refocusing you on larger concerns.

Trying to do the impossible can have enormous consequences, even when you fail to achieve your intended goal. When Christopher Columbus sailed west from Spain, he had no desire or intention to discover America. Instead, he was looking for a westward route to China. As it turned out, there was a vast continent that stood in his way. Was his mission a failure? He never got to China. Yet what he did discover was surely more significant than the sea route he was seeking.

Even though you may not achieve your stated objective, it still pays to think big. Why does it help? Seriously asking big questions will force you to think about the big ideas available in the culture. One of the best ways to solve a difficult problem is to apply that kind of idea to a question that genuinely matters to you.

Principle 5: *Do* Respect Your Unconscious

Have you ever faced a problem that defied all rational analysis? Scientists face this kind of problem more often than you would expect. As they have found, unconscious methods often succeed where conscious, rational analysis fails.

Tortoises and hares are both surprised when they learn the extent to which scientists rely on their unconscious. Hares often see themselves as artists and not scientists. They are therefore surprised to hear that scientists rely on their unconscious in much the same way that artists do. Unlike hares, tortoises often do see themselves as scientific. But they rarely put a lot of trust in mysterious entities such as the unconscious. It comes as a surprise to them that serious scientists put so much faith in anything so intangible. What you actually see in the laboratory puts in question their popular image of being cold, logical, and objective. On the contrary, the practice of science is what the eminent biologist Stephen Jay Gould called "a gutsy human enterprise."

What do successful scientists say when they publicly discuss their own thought processes? Over and over again, they talk about how much their unconscious has contributed. The American Nobel Prize–winning geneticist Barbara McClintock described her unconscious mind as a kind of computer. This "computer" processed and integrated data far more complex than anything you can consciously perceive. In describing her most productive period of research, she said that she was conscious of nothing except "looking at these fine strips of recessive tissue"; the "computer" did the rest.

The French mathematician Henri Poincaré saw the conscious and unconscious minds as partners. The job of the conscious mind first and foremost is to understand the problem. The unconscious does all the work of devising possible solutions. The conscious mind reenters the process later as a kind of quality-control inspector: it verifies whether a candidate solution actually works.

Respecting your unconscious means letting it make its contribution. Recognize that you still may stand a good chance of solving your problem through the work of your unconscious, even after conscious, rational methods have failed. Scientists sometimes talk about problems having an incubation period. You have to leave enough time to allow this kind of incubation to take place.

The time you leave for your problem does not all have to be work time. You might well do better to sleep on it instead of trying to solve the problem in one sitting. Robert Stickgold and his colleagues at Harvard Medical School have conducted extensive research into the effects of sleep on simple learning and memory. In a typical study, they show subjects two patterns that have rotated letters embedded in a field of horizontal lines. The subjects' job is to say whether or not the two are the same. The researchers train their subjects for a short period of time but ask them to come back several hours later for retesting. What do they find? Subjects do better on average when retested but only if they have had a chance to sleep on the problem. Getting six to eight hours of sleep helps. The same number of wakeful hours does no good.

Many people find, like Poincaré, that "sleeping on it" aids complex problem solving as well. Sleeping gives your brain time to digest and integrate. When you wake up, you sometimes immediately see the solution to a problem that seemed intractable the day before.

Principle 6: *Don't* Ignore Your Peers

Even the most brilliant problem solver sometimes makes mistakes. It is much better if your friends point out the mistakes that you yourself miss rather than have your mistakes come out in public. The latter can cost you part of your reputation or even your job.

The principle of peer review is one of the pillars of modern science. As a matter of course, scientists subject their ideas to critical examination by other scientists before the public ever has a chance to see them. The peer review process indeed is almost always the harshest and most thorough examination that ideas receive.

Why is peer review such an important part of scientific practice? It protects the good name of both the individual scientist and the scientific community as a whole if they do their own internal quality control. Concerns about reputation exist in all other walks of life as much as in science.

Why is it that peer review usually functions well within a scientific community? The main reason is that all members are to a large extent like-minded. They usually share similar goals and values, and they usually share the same basic image about the current state of knowledge. When this consensus begins to break down, peer review no longer functions nearly as effectively.

Scientists are not the only people who listen closely to the opinions of their peers. Doctors, lawyers, actors, journalists, writers, teachers, business executives, engineers, and members of almost every other occupation do the same thing. They all have associations to which most members of the profession belong. They almost all feel pride when their peers recognize their accomplishments and shame when their peers criticize their performance.

Both tortoises and hares usually benefit by paying more attention to their peers. Hares are often so individualistic that they refuse to listen to their peers. It does not matter how constructive the criticism or how useful the suggestions. Tortoises can also shut themselves off too easily from their peer group. The peer group often picks up new ideas before they get written into the book. For a tortoise, listening to peers is a good way to stay up to date.

The principle of peer review goes beyond even occupational groups. Most people see it as just common sense to consult with friends and family members in the process of making a big decision.

Principle 7: *Don't* Be Intimidated by Setbacks

According to Dante, the doorpost of hell reads, "Abandon all hope, ye who enter here." This observation applies squarely to problem solving. Working on a problem becomes hellish as soon as you lose hope of finding a solution. You never know for sure whether you will actually solve your problem until you have the solution in hand. For this reason, you need a deep reservoir of hope to sustain you during the time you spend working on your problem.

Once you have gotten into the problem, the most common obstacle you face is loss of morale. *Morale* is just another name for *hope*. Watch other people as they work on a problem. As long as they feel hopeful of a solution, they work constructively. See what happens if they begin to lose morale. If they are tortoises, they find it increasingly difficult to work step-by-step. If they are hares, their inspiration dries up. Their minds begin to stray; the quality of their ideas deteriorates; progress on the problem slows down and eventually stops.

What makes you lose hope? In the context of problem solving, seeing your plans go wrong saps your morale the most. The worst case occurs when some unforeseen factor ruins an otherwise well-constructed plan. A major setback can easily discourage you to the point that further work seems like an utter waste of time.

Significantly, scientists face long-term setbacks in their work quite often. Keep in mind that scientists often devote their lives to a particular problem, such as finding a way to treat a serious illness. Somehow they manage to keep working, even after years and decades full of frustration and setbacks. How do they retain their hope?

Their most successful method of sustaining morale, by far, is to be prepared in advance. Most scientists know beforehand that coping with setbacks is the real essence of their work. When an obstacle arises in the course of solving a problem, they are prepared to see it as an interesting challenge instead of a reason for despair.

Young scientists face harder and harder problems in the course of their training. As problems get harder, the setbacks along the way become more difficult to overcome. As a result of their training, good scientists become prepared for the serious obstacles that often block progress.

There are other practices that help you to cope after things start to go seriously wrong. Try these:

- **Take a break.** Either work on a totally different problem or take the afternoon off. This is a great time for a massage or a workout. Progress comes more easily when you are able to return to the problem with a fresh mind.
- **Talk to a friend.** Maintain a network of friends and peers who work on problems comparable to your own. That is one of the main reasons why scientists almost always belong to a community of peers. Count on these people for support and encouragement when things go wrong.
- **Use a fresh approach.** When you return to the problem, approach it as differently as possible from the way you did before. If you look at science, you see that good new theories typically seem diametrically opposed to the ones that came before. As an example, consider the study of animal behavior. In the mid-twentieth century, the dominant paradigm in the field was behaviorism, with its emphasis on environmental influence. What changed? The Nobel Prize–winning research of Nikolaas Tinbergen and Konrad Lorenz underscored the influence of innate genetically determined action patterns. Today

almost all experts in animal behavior have abandoned behaviorism in favor of ethological and sociobiological theories, both heirs to the tradition established by Tinbergen and Lorenz.

Finding the opposite of a failed theory is one of the best ways to discover a new theory that will work for you.

Principle 8: *Don't* Wait for a Eureka Experience

Most people associate the moment of sudden inspiration with the experience of solving a major scientific problem. It may surprise you to learn that the eureka experience, when it occurs, is a cumulative effect of slow, steady, hard work, not a sudden inspiration that can hit anyone at any time.

Hares in particular are likely to wait for a eureka experience. Tortoises usually know better. In this, the tortoises are on the right track. Waiting for a eureka experience is like waiting for Godot—you can wait forever.

The myth of the eureka experience was popularized by the story of the nineteenth-century German chemist Friedrich August Kekulé. Kekulé is famous for having discovered the structure of the benzene molecule. According to Kekulé, a dream helped him to make this historic discovery. In the dream Kekulé saw six snakes. He saw the first snake take hold of the tail of the second in its jaws. Then the second took hold of the tail of the third. The third held the tail of the fourth. The fourth held that of the fifth. And the fifth held the sixth. At this point the six snakes formed one long chain. Then the last snake came around and took hold of the tail of the first snake so that the chain of snakes became a ring. At this point in the dream, Kekulé suddenly woke up with the flash of insight that benzene has a ring structure.

Many people came to believe that Kekulé saw the answer to this intractable scientific problem in a dream. Thus they concluded that inspiration was the source of his solution and that the long years he spent in the laboratory were time wasted.

Nothing could be further from the truth. On the contrary, no other person, not even another chemist, would have thought of benzene's structure after a dream like that. What made Kekulé different? Kekulé gained his rich understanding of the benzene problem as a result of his many years of hard work. His detailed knowledge and intense interest made him see the solution in a dream about snakes.

Like Kekulé, you may see solutions to problems in your dreams. But do not confuse the climax of your discovery with the process of searching itself. An inspired answer will be a useful answer only if you have done enough legwork in advance. Waiting for inspiration almost always is a waste of time; working on finding a solution is usually time well spent.

Principle 9: *Don't* Be Surprised by Interactions and Side Effects

You've probably heard the phrase "A whole can be more than the sum of its parts." Sometimes a whole is much better than the sum of its parts. Other times it is worse. It is sometimes (but rarely) neutral. Finding a solution to one problem sometimes causes unintended side effects. Occasionally, the side effects are genuinely beneficial. But most of time they only make your work more difficult. Indeed, because of the side effects, the cure can easily become almost as bad as the disease. To keep your cool, you have to be prepared in advance for the fact that unintended negative interactions and side effects will sometimes occur. Then you can just breathe a sigh of relief when they do not happen. If, through some stroke of luck, the interactions are positive ones, you have every reason to jump for joy.

Interactions and side effects can be extremely harmful to both hares and tortoises. As more and more side effects appear, hares can start to give up on what was a legitimately good idea. In their case, the solution is greater persistence. For tortoises, side effects pose a different kind of problem. It often seems as if overcoming a side effect requires a kind of thinking that is awkward for a tortoise. You may believe, for example, that you have to work on the main problem and the side-effect problem at the same time in parallel. To tortoises, thinking in parallel often feels very unnatural.

The solution for tortoises is to find a method that circumvents the need for parallel thinking. Surprisingly, these methods do exist. One method is to keep a list of common kinds of side effects along with solutions to each one. To a hare, it might seem neurotic to maintain that kind of list. But to a tortoise, it often seems natural and helpful. If the method works, who has any right to criticize it?

Scientists and especially engineers have often had to worry about interactions and side effects. For example, when they first designed moving vehicles, such as cars and trains, the act of turning did terrible damage to the wheels. You see why if you compare the inside wheels with the outside wheels during a turn. The outside wheels have to go a lot farther during the same amount of time. But since carmakers attached both inside and outside wheels to the same axle, they both turned at the same speed. That made the outside wheel scrape along the ground, wearing it out, and resulting in a terrible grating sound. The solution turned out to be the addition of a special gear, the differential, which transferred energy between the two wheels. The differential made the outside wheel turn faster. Every car today has a differential. It has effectively prevented the side effects from recurring.

You have to deal with interactions and side effects in your personal life, too. This is an example of my own. My wife and I recently purchased loft space for a home in the middle of Manhattan. One of our main objectives was to make every square foot count. A dilemma we faced was where to place the coat closet. A second quandary was how to use corner space in our kitchen. In this case, we turned out to be lucky because my wife discovered a positive interaction.

She noticed that the foyer next to our front door shared a common wall with the kitchen. Her creative idea was to move the walls of the kitchen so that the corner space became part of the foyer instead of the kitchen. In this way she turned almost useless kitchen corner space into a coat closet, something we badly needed. Through noticing an interaction, she turned the whole into something much better than the sum of its parts.

Principle 10: *Don't* Be Afraid to Reinvent the Wheel

Reinventing the wheel is supposed to be such a waste of time that the expression itself has become shorthand for *redundancy*. What could be less useful than to reinvent something that was discovered thousands of years ago? The experience of science disproves this cultural cliché. Contrary to what most people believe, rediscovering an old idea can be just as revolutionary as developing an entirely new one.

In science some of the most important innovations are nothing more than rediscoveries of something very old. Consider the idea that the earth rotates around the sun instead of the other way around. That idea was so important that it set off perhaps the greatest scientific revolution of all time. Many people learn in school that the Polish astronomer Nicolaus Copernicus discovered this idea in the sixteenth century. In reality this idea is thousands of years old; astronomers knew it in ancient Greece. But it got lost during the Middle Ages. The cause of the Copernican revolution was an old idea rediscovered, not a new one.

Hares and tortoises as a rule are both far too reluctant to reinvent the wheel. Why is this? Hares are often so future-oriented that they regard the past as a collection of tired ideas. They never realize how many good ideas get discarded prematurely. Tortoises usually have more respect for the past than hares do. Their problem is that they have an idealized picture of what the past was like. The most familiar ideas from the past are usually the ones that have been overworked. You can often find fresh insight by looking for ideas that never caught on the first time.

What good does it do to reinvent the wheel? Recent discoveries can sometimes give an old idea a new lease on life, beyond what it ever had in the first place. Greek astronomers knew that the earth revolves around the sun but did nothing with that knowledge. On the other hand, Renaissance astronomers had new instruments, such as telescopes, and new mathematical tools. Because of this they could apply ideas familiar to the Greeks, to map the orbits of the planets and to discover the fundamental laws of motion.

Think of all the drafty old buildings with leaky plumbing that someone successfully restored with the help of modern materials. Ideas are no different. Recondition a fine old theory, and people will consider you a great inventor.

Four Questions to Ask When You Face a New Problem

If you work on difficult problems, it will probably help to have a set of boilerplate questions that you routinely ask from the start. These will serve you in two ways. First, they help you to overcome inertia. Getting to work on an unfamiliar problem can be hard regardless of whether you are a tortoise or a hare; a start-up routine gets you far enough into the problem that you are able to begin developing plans specific to the problem at hand. Second, good questions alert you to potential sources of difficulty. Thus you are able to guess at the very start where you will have to concentrate your attention.

Here is a sample start-up routine that involves four important questions to ask:

1. Am I sure I know what the real problem is?
2. Are standard methods enough or should I look for a creative solution?
3. Do I know how much time to budget?
4. Do I need a structured plan?

You should see these questions as offering a model that will prove most useful to an average problem solver. The specific questions you ask depend on your problem-solving style and on the kind of problems that you yourself usually face. Following are some suggestions about how to go about finding answers to each one of the four questions.

Am I Sure I Know What the Real Problem Is?

Perhaps the most common reason why people arrive at the wrong solution is that they were answering the wrong question. This happens to hares more than to anyone else. They can easily jump to an answer before they have really understood what the problem is. Take time to become as certain as possible that you know what you are supposed to find.

The Swiss psychologist Piaget devised many different problems in which children made mistakes because they were answering the wrong question. Here is an example. Piaget made a bouquet with six tulips and five daffodils. Then he asked the children if there were more tulips or more flowers. Especially around the age of six or seven, most children incorrectly answered that there were more tulips. You get a good idea of why they gave the wrong answer if you ask them to repeat back the original question. What do they say? They think you asked whether there were more tulips or more *daffodils*. They answered that question correctly—but it was not the question that Piaget had asked.

The same thing happens to adults. You give a routine answer to what seems to be a straightforward question. You discover later that there was a trick or complication that made the problem deceptively difficult. A little more care originally in understanding the problem would have let you discover the right answer.

How can you be sure that you understand the problem? If you are a hare, try borrowing some methods from the tortoise. You can ask yourself to say precisely (even out loud) what is required in the solution, what facts are given, and what conditions, if any, constrain any possible solution. Then compare what you said to yourself with the problem's actual wording. To avoid misunderstanding a problem, self-knowledge helps as well. Know the reasons why you may have misunderstood problems in the past. You will know to be especially careful if the problem at hand reminds you of others that you may have misunderstood before.

Are Standard Methods Enough or Should I Look for a Creative Solution?

Can you find the solution with standard methods? Tortoises usually push standard methods as far as possible to avoid betting their solution on something risky and unproven. Hares often have the opposite problem. They begin immediately devising creative solutions. Meanwhile, they have totally overlooked some simple standard method that would have worked perfectly.

If you have enough of something else, creative ideas may not be necessary. Think about all the problems you can solve with enough time, money, or hard work. Nevertheless, a small amount of creativity can often save a large amount of some other resource.

Psychologists sometimes see solving a problem as analogous to climbing a hill. Their idea is that each step up brings you a little closer to the top, until you finally reach it. Hill climbing is the method of the tortoise. It works quite well as long as the problem is as uniform and predictable as an even and gradual slope. Imagine, though, that the slope suddenly became incredibly steep. Wouldn't it be better to find an alternative path? In this case, creativity may not be necessary; nevertheless, it would make the solution much easier.

There are many other scenarios in which you absolutely require creativity. Imagine that while going up the hill you reach a sheer cliff that is perfectly vertical, too steep even to think of climbing. Most tortoises have no idea what to do at this point. Even many hares find themselves lost. Most people fail to realize that slogging away will never solve a "precipice" problem. You will find the solution only if you realize the futility of "brute force" and look for a more inventive idea.

A final shortcoming of hill climbing is that it can give you a false sense of security. Reaching the top of the first foothill might lead you to believe that you are nearing the end of your climb. You might feel that you have just about got the solution to your problem because your next step in any direction heads downward. But in reality, you have only just begun—there is so much more climbing to be done before you reach the mountain summit (the solution).

Like hill climbing, routine methods bring you to your objective only sometimes. Ask yourself at the beginning whether an alternative might not be more effective.

Do I Know How Much Time to Budget?

Can you make an educated guess of how much time your problem is likely to take to solve? It will help you to estimate in advance if it is likely to take a few minutes, a few hours, a few days, a few weeks, or a few years. Hares are notorious for having a hard time with time management. A hare can leave a few weeks for a problem that ends up taking months!

Here is an example of how inaccurate time estimates can be. Even as a young man, Piaget saw himself as primarily a philosopher. At the age of twenty-two, he had the idea that observing children might help him to answer philosophical questions. So he planned to devote five years to studying children. In the end, Piaget's research with children took him forty years instead of five. Thus he was well into his sixties before he returned to the questions that had motivated his research in the first place.

Why is it helpful to estimate time? If a tailor were going to alter an outfit for you or if a mechanic were going to repair your car, you would ask beforehand when the work would be ready. The same logic applies when you are solving a problem. You often need to know in advance when you will be able to deliver the solution to a boss or a colleague. Furthermore, you almost certainly need to know how much time to leave free.

Surprisingly, it helps just to ask yourself how long it will take, even if your estimate turns out to have been wrong. Here is a case in point. During the 1950s, at a time when they were building the first computers, a number of scientists became intrigued with the possibility that we might one day be able to build computers that are genuinely intelligent. One of these scientists was Herbert Simon, who later won the 1978 Nobel Prize in Economics. Simon rashly predicted that it would take about ten years to develop genuinely intelligent computers. He forecasted as well what these intelligent computers would be able to do. He thought, for example, that they would be able to converse in a language such as English and also that a computer would be chess champion of the world.

Although the time scale was wrong, Simon's intuition was still amazingly right. Fifty years later, computer programs are indeed good enough at chess to defeat world champions. But it would not have mattered, even if Simon's predictions had all proven wrong. His estimate served to galvanize researchers' energy and attract attention. It was surely responsible in part for the rapid progress in the fledgling science of artificial intelligence.

Do I Need a Structured Plan?

Tortoises typically draw up a plan before they begin solving their problem. On the other hand, hares usually just dive in. If your problem is complicated, think about whether a plan might help you. Even if you are a hare, some degree of structure can bring you closer to a solution. Something as simple as writing down a list of steps on a piece of paper is sometimes useful. Check off each step as you complete it. Plans help people to remember what they have finished as well as what steps they have left to do. And, very importantly, plans help keep you from leaving out any steps.

A related question is whether you might want to use a formal mathematical technique or a computer program. (You can see both of these as structured plans that an expert has prepared for you in advance.) Tortoises usually feel reasonably comfortable with formal methods. But they can be useful for hares, too. It goes without saying that scientific, technological, and business problems often require mathematical techniques. It may surprise you to learn that mathematical techniques can be useful as well for solving everyday nontechnical problems.

If you are a hare, when should you think of using a plan, a computer program, or a mathematical technique? It depends on how comfortable you feel with formal methods. But getting used to at least using simple math can significantly increase your options. The right computer program can also substantially reduce your workload.

Plans are useful when you have to keep track of a lot of parts and details in coming to your solution. You should think of using a mathematical technique or a computer program if you know that there is one specifically for the kind of problem you face. Most people think of using mathematics for calculating numbers and measuring. Apart from that, the most common time to use formal mathematics in everyday life is when estimating the probability of an event. Computer programs are widely available for various tasks that involve bookkeeping, organizing reports, and performing complex calculations. You can use computer programs to create business plans, to complete income tax returns, to generate graphs and charts from numerical data, and to perform various kinds of statistical analyses.

Rethinking What People Think About Scientists

How large a part of mind magic does problem-solving ability represent? How you answer this depends to some extent on your view of intelligence. Traditional thinking says that it is a very large part—indeed, the largest part. Some people even used to think that intelligence and problem-solving ability are the same thing. Today many people want to broaden our view of intelligence to include skills that are notably different from solving problems. Nevertheless, even those people grant that problem solving is quite important. They just view it as not being quite as large a part of intelligence as most people thought at one time.

But something has to change in how you look at problem-solving ability. In particular, you can no longer see it as being a gift that some people simply lack. On the contrary, it is a skill like any other skill. Learning problem solving is essentially no different from learning any other skill. People who do not know how to solve problems have simply never had the opportunity to learn this skill.

You can go one step further. In this chapter you have seen thinking techniques used by scientists. Suppose that you learn these methods thoroughly. Would this mean that you are able to think as well as a scientist? If so, it implies that scientific problem solving is not so far away from ordinary thinking. In the past most people accepted that scientific thinking is exceptionally difficult. They saw it as demanding unusual intelligence. And they saw mathematical thinking as even harder. If most people can learn to think like scientists, then scientific thinking may not be that exceptional after all.

Why do so many people find science so daunting? One reason is that it is unfamiliar. Learning science is like learning a foreign language. If you live in the West, you will quite likely have a hard time learning to speak Russian or Chinese. But that does not imply that people who speak those languages are more intelligent. They have the same difficulty learning English. Learning to speak foreign languages is difficult because they are unfamiliar. The same is true of science.

A second reason people find science to be such a challenge is the sheer quantity of scientific knowledge. To master such a large body of knowledge demands years of study. That amount of study in turn requires a great deal of persistence. Furthermore, it takes unusual dedication to seek to advance that knowledge in a way that will improve human life.

What makes scientists exceptional may not be their mind magic but rather other qualities. Among these traits are dedication, perseverance, and a commitment to progress. Scientific ways of thinking are skills we all can acquire. The human qualities of an outstanding scientist can also help any of us become successful in our own field.

CHAPTER 7

MAKING AN ASSET OF YOUR EMOTIONS

Are emotions an asset or a liability? The jury still appears to be out. No one seems to have a neutral opinion about emotions. But experts are far from agreeing about whether their influence is good or bad. On the one hand, brain scientists and evolutionary biologists generally have a positive view of emotions. They point out that our emotions have evolved over millions of years. During that time emotions have generally proven effective in regulating our behavior and ensuring our survival. The limbic system, regarded by brain scientists as the seat of our emotions, is essential to us. It contains brain centers associated with pain and pleasure, along with ones that regulate hunger and thirst, fighting, fleeing from predators, and reproduction. Without it, life would be impossible.

On the other hand, business professionals and psychotherapists typically see emotions in a more dubious light. According to many investment advisers, the behavior of losers is governed by emotions, such as greed and fear and the herd instinct. The "smart money" relies on logic, research, knowledge, and judgment. Psychotherapists also worry about the influence of emotions. Psychologists and psychiatrists often observe the effects of irrational fears, obsessions, and impulses. Being too emotional can get you into deep trouble.

Shakespeare had his melancholy protagonist Hamlet also praise reason over emotion. He wrote, "Give me that man / That is not passion's slave, and I will wear him / In my heart's core, ay, in my heart of heart." That man whom Hamlet considers not to be passion's slave is his friend Horatio.

How can we reconcile the two perspectives? Instead of saying that emotions necessarily are either bad or good, we will look for ways to maximize their benefits and minimize their risks. The people most worried about emotions often seem to suppose that you have only two options: either you keep your emotions under control or they will control you. In this chapter I will argue in favor of a third option: your emotions should act as a guide and a source of information rather than as a master. They should influence your actions but not to the point that they paralyze your mind. As in other chapters, the key concepts are mind consciousness and mind magic. See how to interpret and manage your emotions. Transform a potential liability into a blue-chip asset.

Emotional Awareness: The Mind Magic of Emotions

We have seen that mind consciousness can help you in numerous ways to make better use of your mind's intellectual power. Can we apply the principle of mind consciousness to emotions, too?

Even to ask this question seems superfluous. Helping people to become more conscious of their emotions is so well established that there hardly seems to be any need to defend it. All insight-oriented forms of psychotherapy have emotional awareness as their main goal. Much of literature, drama, music, and art seek to increase people's emotional awareness. There seems little question that self-knowledge can help people in dealing with fear, anger, stress, anxiety, disturbances in personal relationships, and various kinds of emotional conflicts.

Does emotional awareness also help with intellectual issues, such as problem solving, information management, creative thinking, learning, and adapting to change? That suggestion is more surprising. Aren't these processes purely intellectual? Do they really include an emotional component as well? Conventional wisdom says "no." In this chapter you will see that conventional wisdom is mistaken.

Psychotherapists and poets have addressed the question of emotional awareness, the affective counterpart of mind consciousness, in different contexts. Here we will ask how emotional awareness increases mind magic. As you will see, thinking and feeling in everyday life are so inter-twined that we experience them as a seamless web. Can mind consciousness help you to manage your emotions as well as your thinking? There is every reason to believe that it can.

How You Feel About Information Affects How Well You Manage It

Let us begin our examination of emotional awareness by considering a context in which almost everyone can find it useful. This context is the skill of information management.

Schools of education spend large blocks of time teaching future teachers to introduce new information in an interesting way. The time is well spent. You surely know what a difference it makes when you find information interesting. Mastering boring information is slow and painful. Mastering interesting information often seems more like fun than work.

What happens when you are interested and engaged in a body of information to make it come alive? New facts start to form networks and connections with each other and with the rest of what you know. When you are bored, new facts remain inert, unrelated to anything important to you. In the words of alienated students, they are irrelevant.

Bringing Information to Life

Trace the creation of networks of knowledge in the mind of a person who is engaged. The process involves feelings as well as thoughts.

MIT mathematician and learning theorist Seymour Papert offers a vivid example. He recalls as a child that he developed an intense involvement with automobiles. Before the age of two, he learned the names of many car parts. He was especially proud of knowing about the parts of the transmission system, the gearbox, and especially the differential. As he came to understand how gears work, he became fascinated with rotating one circular object against another in gearlike motion. He would turn wheels in his mind as a way of making chains of cause and effect. He was particularly intrigued by the differential because of its ability to distribute motion in many ways to the two wheels instead of following a simple linear chain. Later in school he came to understand equations in two variables by making a mental gear model of the relation between x and y. Figuring out how many teeth each gear needed made the equation as comfortable for him as a friend.

Papert believes that playing with differentials contributed more to his mathematical development than anything he did in elementary school. Why? The reason, according to Papert, is that it involved feeling as well as understanding. Without emotional involvement, his experiences with gears would have lacked power.

Papert's experience is an extreme case. It is rare that an attachment to a particular object so decisively shapes an individual's education and career choice. Nevertheless, attachments to people, places, and things affect what and how almost everybody gains knowledge, even if their influence may not be life changing.

Landmarks in Conceptual Space

Papert used the gear as a reference point for understanding new ideas. Seeing something new (such as an equation in two variables) in terms of gears helped him orient himself in a new conceptual world. It happened in much the same way as a major landmark, such as the Eiffel Tower in Paris or the Empire State Building in New York, serves as a reference point to people in those cities. Apart from its being a terrible human tragedy, one may speculate that people reacted to the destruction of the World Trade Center in part because of their emotional investment in a landmark that had dominated lower Manhattan.

In terms of mind magic, landmarks are important as anchors for large networks of information. They play this role regardless of whether they are features of a landscape, such as a prominent building or a mountain, or personal possessions, such as a differential gear. They can even be books or theories or characters and concepts that they contain. What matters is that you develop enough of an emotional investment that you return to them when you are trying to make sense of something new.

The concept of a landmark is directly related to the subjective experience of understanding an unfamiliar notion. Sophisticated learners usually want to feel that they understand new ideas. What do they mean? They can recognize the point when they achieve understanding; nevertheless, although they know in their bones what helps them to understand, they usually have great trouble explaining it to someone else. Let me suggest that people usually gain the feeling that they understand when they can relate the unfamiliar to one of their established landmarks. Seeing how the two fit together makes a new place or concept seem friendlier and more familiar.

From Landmark to Networks

The concept of a landmark fits the spatial language that we so often use in describing the way we come to understand new concepts. For example, when people think that they lack understanding, they often describe themselves as feeling lost. Being lost literally means not knowing the physical location of where you are. If you describe yourself as lost when reading a technical report or solving a math problem, you are appealing to a spatial metaphor. People do this, perhaps, because coming to understand ideas feels so much like finding your way around in physical space.

Identifying a major landmark is only the first step in getting to know a place. The next step is to come to understand the relationships among landmarks. Once a newcomer to New York City has gotten comfortable with the Empire State Building as a reference point, he or she can find its relationship to other landmarks, such as Times Square, Central Park, the Statue of Liberty, and the United Nations. By this point the Empire State Building has come to serve as an anchor for building a "cognitive map" that includes a network of locations and the relationships among them.

Knowledge of abstract domains grows in the same way as our understanding of physical space. I first saw this a number of years ago in a case study of how people come to understand narratives. My subject, a teenage boy named Jason, would come to our lab at Harvard, watch an episode of an unfamiliar television drama, and then participate in a clinical interview about his experience. Over a period of two months, it was apparent how his understanding of the series grew into a network of interrelated facts and themes. Early on he developed what he called an attachment to the protagonist, a visitor from outer space. He became especially interested in the question of whether or not the spaceman's behavior was realistic; in other words, would a visitor to Earth really act the way he did. With time this one character came to serve as a reference point for Jason in understanding the behavior of other characters, just as the Empire State Building might serve as a reference point for a visitor to New York. Jason used it at first to analyze other characters in the series. Later he began to reflect on how realistic various incidents were. He then generalized the concept of realism to entire episodes. By the end of the study, he was using the protagonist as a reference point for thinking about characters in other television programs as well as in books and movies.

Regardless of whether you are learning about a particular place, a narrative, an academic subject, or any other kind of knowledge, networks of information are far more useful than isolated facts or concepts. No wonder people say that it helps them if they "see the big picture" and "understand" what they are learning. Having landmarks in your mental space matters because they serve as catalysts to make networks of information grow.

You Can't Make Yourself Form the Right Attachments But . . .

Emotions matter in the process of information management. For example, landmarks engage your emotions as well as your thoughts. People form bonds or attachments to them. They become familiar and secure, and people feel comfortable returning to them. Later on, people gain a subjective sense of understanding new structures, processes, and ideas by seeing their similarities, differences, and relationships with these favorite landmarks. Thus building an information network involves emotions as much as thinking.

Does this mean that you should actively try to form attachments to landmarks when you want to master a body of knowledge? That hardly seems realistic. Trying to form attachments to landmarks is like trying to fall in love. It is not the kind of experience you can make happen just by trying.

If trying is futile, how can mind magic and emotional awareness help you? First, they help you to avoid unproductive work. People often tackle a new subject by reading whatever they can get their hands on. Reading a random list of loosely related books or articles, however, is usually an inefficient strategy. A much better use of your time is to follow the landmarks that grab your attention. What got your attention is the first text that you read. Choose next to read something that deals with that topic, too. Using the attention-grabbing feature of the first text as a reference point, you will start to build a network of connected ideas instead of a random list.

Second, mind magic helps you to evaluate your own success in mastering a new subject. Many people judge their progress in mastering a new knowledge domain by how much they read or how much time they spend on the subject. Although time spent on average correlates with progress, the correlation is weak. A more valid measure of progress is how rich a network of connections you have been able to build. And your success in building this kind of network depends directly on forming attachments to landmarks.

Read Your Emotions, Don't Just Respond to Them

The process of forming attachments and building networks of knowledge exemplifies the third option mentioned earlier in this chapter. As it illustrates, everyday learning is not coldly unemotional, but neither do your emotions overwhelm you. Your feelings guide, but they do not control.

Many people let their emotions take control. They feel hungry and they eat. They feel happy and they smile. They feel angry and they yell. An alternative is to experience your feelings, note them, but not act on them immediately. Go away and think about how you want to react. Do not be impulsive.

Here is an example in which reflection worked better than instinct. Brad was applying for a new job and noticed on the application that he had to write an essay explaining why he wanted the job. His first reaction was anger. The question seemed insulting and demeaning. It seemed like something that would be asked of a child in elementary school, not an adult. Furthermore, Brad had always found essay writing difficult. His first reaction was to tear up the application and forget about applying for the job. Instead of acting on impulse, he put the application in a drawer for a week. When he took it out, he wrote the essay, slowly and unhappily but nevertheless completely, with assistance from his wife. He later received an interview.

Here is a more unsettling example. Sally is a diagnosed manic-depressive who had been taken by a friend to a psychiatric facility during a manic episode. At one point she found herself handcuffed, in transit to a locked ward in a psychiatric hospital. A slight woman of five feet four inches, weighing 120 pounds, she felt intimidated by the two large male police officers escorting her. Her fear increased when they separated her from her friend. After the incident, she wrote:

> *Because I had been a consultant for a rape prevention program, the possibility of sexual assault became my paramount concern. I remembered that men were less likely to attack a woman if they could identify with her, so I immediately began to make appropriate small talk.*

Regardless of whether her feelings about these men were justified, the fear was nevertheless real. Under the circumstances, it would have been easy for Sally to panic. The fact that she did not shows the strength of emotional awareness even during a psychotic breakdown.

Learned Helplessness

It is important for all of us that we can successfully integrate our knowledge and our feelings. Think of the intense emotions experienced by people in high-stress occupations, such as race car drivers, air traffic controllers, and high-stakes investors. Effective performance requires that they can use their knowledge to modulate the fear and the thrill evoked by their work. Does it also matter for other people? Some of the best evidence comes from work with people in quite ordinary occupations. Like most high-stakes investors, these people experience high levels of stress in their everyday lives. But unlike professional investors, they have not chosen this way of life.

During the late 1960s, the American psychologist Martin Seligman began systematically studying the psychological consequences of uncontrollable stress. As he observed, prolonged exposure has the effect of making people despondent and apathetic. He called this phenomenon *learned helplessness*. Seligman defined it as "the giving-up reaction, the quitting response that follows from the belief that whatever you do doesn't matter."

The experience of learned helplessness illustrates the kind of circumstance when following your emotions will lead to trouble. When your emotions tell you to give up, they have stopped serving your needs. What is the alternative?

The principle of mind consciousness tells us to understand and manage our thinking to make it work to our best advantage. The principle of emotional awareness tells us to do the same thing with our emotions: understand and manage them.

Learned helplessness is not the only experience in which raw emotion leads us in the wrong direction. Nevertheless, it is all too common and illustrates the point well. How can emotional awareness help people cope with a problem such as learned helplessness?

Are You an Optimist or a Pessimist?

Common advice tells us to be honest with ourselves and face our problems. Most of the time, this is good advice. But at times of high stress, a certain amount of self-deception, at least temporarily, may be a good idea. How do you know when this is the case? Emotional awareness can help.

Although most people underestimate their problems, there is a small but significant minority who see their problems for what they are or worse. These people systematically try to avoid self-deception. They pride themselves on being realists. Do you belong to that minority?

Realists are able to make a unique contribution to the world because they often see and begin trying to solve problems well before the rest of us catch up. But as a society, we often treat them roughly. We do not want to hear their sobering message until we have no choice. The effect on such a Cassandra can be terrible. For someone prone to see the world in tones of gray, the stress of rejection can result in a case of learned helplessness.

Research shows that realists are more susceptible to learned helplessness and depression than other people are. Are you surprised? For one thing, they often understand problems at a time when no one else is willing to do anything to help. When they cannot solve the problems on their own, it is understandable that they should feel discouraged.

For another thing, realists are not always as free of self-deception as they believe. On the contrary, they often deceive themselves by overestimating the seriousness and intractibility of a problem. Most people see the world as better than it really is. Realists err by often seeing an admittedly difficult situation as worse and harder to manage than it really is. When this happens, they are prone to feeling helpless.

Here is one useful principle of emotional awareness: know whether or not you belong to this pessimistic minority. If you do, recognize that you face a somewhat elevated risk of depression. If necessary, be prepared to take appropriate action. If you are like most realists, you feel, as Hamlet did, that we should not be "passion's slave." Can you put your philosophy into action? By all means listen to your instincts telling you to face your problems squarely. But also take into account the mind magic principle that tells you to make instincts your guide and not your master.

For more than half a century, there have been methods available to help people overcome the effects of harmful instincts, such as Albert Ellis's Rational-Emotive Behavior Therapy. Victims of one-sided pessimism may want to consider working with a professional therapist, especially if they suspect that they may be crossing the boundary that separates healthy realism from clinical depression. But before stresses reach that point, you can use emotional awareness to modulate the effects on your own.

As Ellis points out, adverse experiences typically lead us to formulate explanations for why things went wrong, and these explanations in turn affect our subsequent behavior. Confirmed pessimists usually come up with terribly depressing explanations. But are these the only plausible explanations one could propose? There are nearly always other possible alternatives just as consistent with the facts.

In his 1991 book *Learned Optimism*, Martin Seligman provides the following example. Katie has been dieting for two weeks. One night she goes out with some friends and eats some of the nachos and chicken wings that they ordered. When she gets home, she interprets her behavior as a sign of weakness. As she sees it, she had made a glutton of herself after two weeks of dieting. Feeling that her diet is now blown, she goes to the freezer and eats an entire chocolate fudge brownie cake.

The real problem was not Katie's behavior at the restaurant but rather the interpretation that she offered herself later at home. It would have been just as consistent with the facts if she had seen herself as incredibly strong for having kept to her diet for two weeks and only slipping a little on one night. And if she had believed this second explanation, she would never have eaten the cake.

As an effective antidote to a pessimistic explanatory style, Seligman has developed the technique of *disputation*. How does it work? Disputation is essentially ordinary arguing, but in this case, your argument is with yourself. First, identify a pessimistic explanation that you currently accept. Next, make up a less pessimistic alternative. Finally, as an exercise, create the most convincing case that you can in favor of the alternative.

To make things easier, Seligman proposes that you ask a friend to assume your normal viewpoint. Ask your friend to articulate your normal pessimistic explanation and to do so as clearly and cogently as possible. Your job then is to propose the alternative and defend it. The exercise forces you to see and understand a perspective that you would normally not consider.

How is this exercise beneficial? By offering you a degree of emotional awareness, it can help to head off a debilitating emotional reaction later on. As a realist, you should understand that facing problems squarely is futile if it undermines a person's ability to cope. You should be willing to temporarily grant yourself a small amount of what may seem to be optimistic self-deception. When the period of risk has passed, if you choose, by all means resume being your sadder but wiser self.

Intelligent as You Feel

Learned helplessness is the subjective sense that you lack control over the external world. It is the public face of feeling powerless. There is a private face as well. It occurs when people begin to feel that they cannot use their own minds in a directed purposeful way. They feel not helpless but instead incompetent. *Learned incompetence* can undermine your ability to work productively and to learn. Emotional awareness can offer support in coping with feelings of incompetence as well as helplessness.

A pilot study that I conducted in the early 1990s graphically brought this point home. The study compared two groups of university students. One group consisted of top students, all of whom were math majors. The other consisted of weaker students, all of whom had previously been diagnosed by an assessment team as having a mathematics learning disability.

The experimenter asked all of the students to solve a series of brain-teasers. The problems demanded logical reasoning, but they were quite different from the mathematics that the students had seen in the course work. The problems did not build, at least in any obvious way, on what students might have learned from math courses.

You will not be surprised to discover that the math majors were far more successful than the "math LD" students. You may be surprised, however, to know why.

Because the problems were difficult, both groups of students made a number of mistakes. The difference between the groups was how the students responded to their own errors. The math majors were able to take them in stride. The math LD students did not.

One of the math majors was a young woman named Thalia. When Thalia made her first mistake, she glanced up and said, "Look at that, a brilliant person like me making a mistake." Then she went back to work. She made mistake after mistake until she finally got the answer half an hour later. After each mistake, she shrugged and then continued working.

Anthony is a young man diagnosed as suffering from a learning disability in mathematics. His first mistake on one of the research problems was the same as Thalia's—but his reaction was just the opposite. Anthony looked up and said, "You see how bad I am at math. I'm always making mistakes." With some encouragement from the experimenter, he agreed to go back to work. Nevertheless, he made another mistake in a couple of minutes. This time he was so discouraged that he could no longer continue.

Was the only difference between the math majors and the LD students that they differed in their sense of personal competence? Clearly, it was not. The fact remains, however, that it was one important difference. It is hard to behave competently unless you feel competent. Success depends at least as much on this emotional aspect of intelligence as on any logical aspects of it.

Why Are Learning Disabilities Disabling?

Anthony's sense of incompetence seemed to me especially sad because I was never convinced that he really lacked the ability to do well in mathematics if only it were taught in a way that suited him.

Anthony is one of many millions of students diagnosed as learning disabled. How common is this diagnosis? Approximately one student in five at some time is considered to have a learning disability. How many of these students suffer from a real and permanent impairment in their ability to learn reading or mathematics or another academic subject, and how many of them could learn effectively with the right teaching methods? No one knows.

Most learning disability specialists believe that some kind of impairment in brain function causes a learning disability. How common is this kind of impairment? Does it affect the majority of students diagnosed as learning disabled or only very few, perhaps less than 1 percent? Anthony was surprised to learn that the estimate of less than 1 percent may be more accurate.

We do know that there are common differences in the brains of people diagnosed as learning disabled when compared with the general population. Many people tend to think that a brain difference associated with poor performance implies brain impairment. But this is not necessarily so. Sometimes brain differences have nothing to do with how well a person thinks and manages information.

Consider another example of brain difference, left-handedness. There are significant ways in which the brains of lefties are different from those of other people. Furthermore, in many societies lefties are less successful than their right-handed peers are because many cultures discriminate against left-handers. In our culture we retain the antilefty bias in our language. The words *sinister* and *gauche*, which have negative connotations, originally meant "left." When we call a compliment "left-handed," we mean that it is insincere.

Being left-handed, however, is not in itself a disability. It only becomes a disability when society makes it into one. So, might many learning disabilities really be similar to left-handedness? Yes, some people have brains that work a little differently. Nevertheless, we might think there was nothing wrong with them if our society treated them differently.

Considering the weakness of evidence in favor of the brain-science explanation of learning disabilities, it is disturbing that Anthony came to feel so negatively about his own abilities. Indeed, he may have developed a case of learned incompetence just because of prevailing bias. For Anthony, understanding this fact should provide a means for better managing his conception of himself as a learner. In his case, greater emotional awareness holds promise of reducing his personal sense of incompetence. In turn, a greater sense of competence may increase his success in mathematics.

Mind Consciousness and Emotional Awareness— Achieving Synergy

Another question is whether Anthony's problem is really intellectual and academic or emotional. The question is difficult to answer. On the one hand, there is clearly an emotional dimension. Anthony feels demoralized and discouraged, perhaps even depressed. His sense of himself as a learner, a significant part of his personal identity, is badly damaged. These are classic symptoms of an emotional problem.

On the other hand, solving the emotional problem will not in itself correct his learning problem. In addition to emotional awareness to overcome his affective problem, Anthony also needs mind conscious-ness to correct his learning problem. Neither one nor the other on its own is enough. He needs both of them.

In this respect, learning problems are not unique. Intellectual prob-lems and emotional consequences quite often go together. The synergy is greatest when you have been working on a problem for a long time with little sign of progress. The intellectual problem itself remains, but now poor morale, a negative sense of your abilities (learned incompe-tence), and even symptoms of real depression emerge as well.

You can describe this pattern as a *negative self-defeating spiral*. The more trouble you have with the practical or intellectual problem, the worse you feel about yourself. And the worse you feel about yourself, in turn, the greater your difficulty with the original problem. With time the negative spiral digs deeper and deeper.

When this happens the solution also has to involve synergies, but this time they have to be positive. A small bit of mind consciousness should help you make progress in solving the practical problem. This small bit of success, in turn, should make you feel a little bit better about your-self. So you become able to achieve a small amount of emotional aware-ness. Gradually, a positive spiral should replace the negative spiral. When this happens you are well on your way to overcoming both intel-lectual and emotional problems.

This is known as the *synergy principle*. According to this principle, to overcome a problem that includes intellectual and emotional com-ponents, you need both mind consciousness and emotional awareness working in synergy. To solve many serious problems, this principle is crucial.

Can You Overcome a Learning Disability?

The synergy principle has been found to be extremely useful in help-ing people with serious intellectual problems. Helping adults diagnosed as learning disabled may be the best example.

In the past most specialists have believed that you can manage a learning disability but not overcome it. Is this true? Perhaps not. For half a century, the Israeli psychologist Reuven Feuerstein has reported amazing results in treating learning disabilities. More recently, Canadian therapists Joshua Cohen and Barbara Arrowsmith have reported a comparable degree of success. My colleague Mary Louise Bat Hayim and I wanted to see if principles of mind magic might help people in overcoming a learning disability.

In working with students like Anthony, psychologists have observed how often emotional factors undermined people's ability to learn and solve problems effectively. Typically, students with a learning problem face years of failure in at least one academic subject. The effect is a tangible feeling of helplessness and despair when they must deal with this subject and a hopeless sense of their capacity as learners.

How do you cope with a learning problem? Bat Hayim and I felt strongly that learning problems are hard to overcome unless one addresses both the intellectual and emotional dimensions and helps students break out of a negative spiral. We developed Learning Therapy, a method of treatment that combined the two dimensions. On the one hand, our clients received counseling to help them understand the intellectual difficulties that made learning hard for them. On the other hand, they participated in a support group to help gain emotional awareness of how a negative image of their abilities and symptoms of learned incompetence made their learning problem more serious than it otherwise would have been.

The treatment of learning disabilities may represent a strategic point of reference for understanding how emotional awareness may be useful in dealing with other problems of learning, problem solving, creative thinking, and adaptation. It offers evidence that synergies between emotional awareness and mind consciousness can be substantially more powerful than mind consciousness on its own. Might we find synergies in other domains? There is every reason to expect the answer to be "yes."

Might Emotional Awareness Help You More than Mind Consciousness?

Apart from its role in forming synergies, what is the potential of emotional awareness as a component of mind magic? Is it useful to most people primarily in managing information and in reading emotions? In other respects, is it most helpful to people with special needs, such as students who have been diagnosed as learning disabled?

One possible answer comes from Piaget. He believed that the next major breakthrough in psychology would deal with the relationship between emotions and thinking. As has happened so often in the past, it is entirely possible that events will prove him right. Psychologists' investigation into how emotions affect adaptation may one day progress to the point that we actually understand emotions better than we understand thinking. If that happens, emotional awareness very well may help you to learn and adapt more than mind consciousness does.

In the meantime, emotional awareness is more likely to be especially useful to individuals with a particular personality type or outlook or to most people under special or unusual circumstances. It often seems as if emotions are more basic and primitive than other psychological resources. They are present and active during the first days and weeks of our lives. They also seem to have a longer evolutionary history. You can think of your emotions as your resources of last resort. When nothing else seems to work, it may be time to pay special attention to your emotions.

Five Rules for Making the Most of Your Emotions

Following is a set of principles of emotional awareness based on the preceding discussion. Each of these can help in solving intellectual problems.

1. **Follow Horatio's principle.** Do not ignore or repress your emotions, but do not automatically act on them either. Instead, read your emotions before responding. Remember Hamlet's friend Horatio, who was not "passion's slave." Hamlet respected him because Horatio knew to think first. (For his characters, Shakespeare sometimes chose names that emphasized their personal qualities. The name "Horatio" includes the Latin word *ratio*, which means "reason.")
2. **Look for something interesting in the information.** It is easier to learn material that you find interesting. If information bores

you, your mind will not engage with it and learning will be a challenge. When you have to acquire information that you initially find boring, try to find something interesting in it, even if that something is peripheral. One or two interesting points give you entry hooks to begin finding additional interesting features. The more you become engaged with the material, the easier you will find it to learn.

3. **Monitor your attachments to promising landmarks.** Once you become interested, you will automatically form what we have called *attachments* to selected features (or landmarks). As you notice this happening, you can become more confident that you are beginning to make progress. This happened with Allan Smith, the computer professional introduced back in Chapter 1, who, as a child, was diagnosed as having a mathematics learning disability. A turning point for Allan came when he began using his experience programming in BASIC as a reference point for solving algebra problems in school. Seeing the connection between the computer and algebra in itself was an important breakthrough. But even more important was Allan's awareness of this connection. By monitoring his own attachment, he began to develop confidence in his mathematical abilities.

4. **Look for synergies between knowledge and emotions, and respond to the ones you find.** This is a specialized principle that so far has proven most useful in addressing learning disabilities and other persistent problems. It can be beneficial as well to people who suffer from mental blocks. Consider the possibility that poor morale, emotional conflict, or your sense of who you are (personal identity) might be affecting your success in learning and problem solving.

5. **Consider challenging your bias toward either optimism or pessimism.** Most people have a bias toward optimism or pessimism. In the absence of definitive evidence, some of us are predisposed toward assuming the best and others toward assuming the worst. Most of the time, this kind of bias causes us no particular trouble— it is just the way we are. But under certain circumstances, it can undermine our ability to function. For example, people with a pessimistic bias run the risk of depression at times when optimists are better able to cope. When your normal bias seems to be harming you, consider challenging it, at least temporarily.

Intelligence in Emotions

During the 1990s, Peter Salovey and John Mayer (and later Daniel Goleman) argued that there is a distinct kind of intelligence called *emotional intelligence*. Are they correct? Or are emotions, thoughts, experiences, and perceptions all part of one single large array?

It has always seemed to me that intelligence is one great big complex system. It includes thinking, feeling, acting, responding, perceiving, remembering, reasoning, and many other kinds of processes. Is there any point in separating out emotion or logic or any component of the mind and calling it a different kind of intelligence? I think not.

What clearly is important is for psychologists who study intelligence to pay more attention to emotions. To ignore them creates a false and disembodied impression of how our minds work. A deeper understanding of how emotions contribute to thinking and learning will surely expand our knowledge as well as our capacity for mind magic.

THE INDEPENDENT MIND RECAST

As a society and as individuals, most of us cherish the notion that we and our neighbors all possess our own independent minds. At the very heart of our social and political system lies the thesis that private citizens can use their minds to decide matters of public concern. We shudder at images of mind control and brainwashing with the same fear that we reserve for the most draconian methods of political oppression. We see the cultivation of an independent mind to be one of the most important goals of public education. And we reserve special admiration for thinkers who seem to have resisted all preconceptions and embodied the ideal of the truly independent mind.

But how independent a mind does any of us have? Perhaps the very concept of independent thinking is just an old-fashioned fiction. More than a century of social and psychological theory and research puts this idea seriously in question. Consider such influential theorists such as B. F. Skinner and Sigmund Freud. They seemed to agree about almost nothing. Nevertheless, they agreed that the idea of an independent mind was nothing more than an illusion. The academic consensus today is that a socially constructed worldview controls the way all of us think; therefore, the belief that a person may have an independent mind is charming but quaint.

The appeal of Jean Piaget and others who influenced the concept of mind magic in part is that their work seems to revitalize the idea of psychological and intellectual independence. This does not mean that they necessarily force us to ignore the contributions of psychoanalysis or behaviorism (even though Piaget himself had deep disagreement with both of these movements). But rather they went beyond the major currents of twentieth-century social science, perhaps paradoxically to offer a new conception of intellectual independence consistent with the findings of behavioral research.

As you have seen in chapter after chapter, believing in mind magic does not mean denying that there are laws and principles that govern how our minds work. On the contrary, understanding these laws and principles is what makes mind magic work. Neither, however, does it tell you to go with the flow nor to accept passively that you should avoid controlling what your mind does. It tells you to learn how your mind works precisely so that you can use this powerful instrument more effectively and responsibly.

This combination of prescribing active control with acceptance of deterministic theory makes mind magic different from and arguably an advance over earlier ways of thinking about the mind. To some people, it may seem paradoxical. It is certainly faithful to both the letter and the spirit of Piaget's work. It holds promise as well of vindicating the concept of independence of mind in a highly psychological age.

Independent-Mindedness: Reality or Illusion?

To what extent is it ever possible to have an independent mind? The answer depends on what exactly you mean by the question.

In the eyes of some people, such as the French philosopher Jean-Paul Sartre, concepts such as personal freedom and independent-mindedness are incompatible with any notion of psychological causality. If this is what you mean by an independent mind, then no form of psychology will give you comfort. The divide is total.

But is there any need to see the two as incompatible? The work of Piaget and other psychologists suggests that there is not. They rediscovered a side of human nature that an earlier generation of psychologists had disregarded. Piaget, for example, was interested in topics such as moral judgment, consciousness and purposefulness, the process of discovery, and, most fundamentally, the activity of the individual in determining his or her learning and behavior. These are the very experiences that most people have in mind when they talk about independent thinking. Furthermore, Piaget pursued these interests without in any way rejecting a scientific conception of mind.

To accept the concept of independent-mindedness is not to deny that there may be constraints on what we think. It implies, nevertheless, that we can push these constraints back. Absolute independent-mindedness may be an ideal that we can strive to approach but never entirely achieve. Instead, to use one of Piaget's metaphors, independent-mindedness may be like an asymptote to which we can keep getting nearer and nearer but never quite reach.

Some of these constraints of interest to research psychologists really should not matter for practical purposes. For example, most psychologists believe that there are limits to how much information you can hold in your head, meaning your active memory, at one time. Should this matter to you? Probably not. And if it does, there are tricks that let you function as if you could hold more information at a time. (For example, you can organize information so that it places fewer demands on your memory.)

On the other hand, other kinds of constraints should matter more. These three are especially powerful:

1. Effects of life experience and education
2. Effects of social role
3. Motivational and psychodynamic effects

First, consider the effects of life experience and education, for example. We may want to be able to imagine what it is like to be fifty meters under the sea, but our thoughts can be no more than an act of imagination without experience in deep-sea diving. Similarly, we may want to understand theoretical physics or higher math, but without the necessary education, that is usually impossible beyond a superficial level.

Even the period of history and the place in the world where we live affect our thinking. Imagine how people in Shakespeare's England would have reacted to the idea of a legal system that guarantees freedom of religion. The notion that people of many different religions could coexist happily as members of the same society would have been unthinkable. But in modern England, this idea is so obvious that it never raises an eyebrow.

Aren't there similar ideas that we cannot imagine today? Surely, there are political and social practices unthinkable today that will seem commonplace to our great-grandchildren. We can try to stretch our minds to imagine what they may be. If we succeed in doing so, we are making our minds a little more independent of social and historical constraints.

A second kind of constraint that should matter is social role. Factors such as our sex, age, occupation, and ethnic group have a powerful influence on how we perceive the world. Imagine what would happen if children could really see family dynamics as they look to their parents or if parents really saw the same interactions as they seem to their children. Imagine if men and women for one day could exchange points of view. The American psychologist Robert Selman has demonstrated that people show progress with age in their ability to adopt the point of view of another person. In doing so, their minds become freer. Nevertheless, the ability to transcend social role is extremely difficult to the point that many of us forever seem trapped in one perspective.

A third kind of constraint is motivational or psychodynamic. Both material needs, such as our need to earn a living, and psychological needs, such as our need to think well of ourselves and to get along with the people around us, affect what and how we think. Most people are reluctant to change their thinking if change implies significantly less profitable professional or business practices. Similarly, it is hard to accept ideas that entail a less appealing image of our own actions or of family members, friends, and other people important to us. One long-standing justification for psychotherapy is its ability to help people partially free their minds by accepting normally unwelcome truth.

It is never possible to eliminate experiential, social, or motivational constraints entirely. But does this mean that independent-mindedness is an illusion? It does not.

Independent-Mindedness in Everyday Life

When we think of a person as being independent-minded, what do we usually mean? We of course may have in mind a professional iconoclast, such as Bertrand Russell or Noam Chomsky. But most of us know these people only from newspapers and books. Aren't there people in our everyday lives whom we legitimately may consider to have independent minds? As an example, consider Barry.

As a teenager, Barry earned a reputation as an independent thinker by being critical. It went without saying that he was critical of the government. He was also critical of teaching methods in his school. He was critical as well of many of his class members, whom he regarded as snobs. People called Barry "the leader of the opposition." They expected that he would grow up to become a social activist or perhaps a university professor who would develop original ideas of public policy. Instead, Barry went to law school. But he never gave up his commitment to social issues. And as a lawyer, he became successful as a specialist in public interest law.

Was Barry an independent thinker? According to any ordinary understanding of the term, he definitely was. This is not to deny that the larger social context shaped his thinking just as it influenced everyone else's. But nevertheless, he stood out. He adopted a viewpoint never even considered by his more conforming and conventional peers. Furthermore, his teenage defiance was not just a function of age. It reflected a seriousness that became even more apparent in his later choice of career and lifework.

When we speak of independence of mind, should we include someone like Barry? I think so. Certainly, most of us have in mind people like Barry when we talk about independent thinkers. If there are philosophers who disagree, I suggest that they are no longer using language in the same way as the rest of us.

Six Steps Toward Becoming More Independent-Minded

Thinking independently is like thinking creatively, in the sense of being a skill that you can develop with an understanding of mind magic. Do most people naturally think independently? Well, yes and no. As Piaget's work showed over and over again, we all build up our basic sense of the world through the activity of our own minds. But constraints such as the effects discussed earlier eventually begin to take their toll. It is easy to become trapped thinking more or less the same thing that everyone around you thinks.

Is it possible to break free? As has been noted, not even the boldest and most independent of minds ever totally escape the influence of culture and society. On the other hand, as people like Barry show, it is certainly possible to become less accepting of prevailing trends and ideas and to begin to develop your own ideas.

The following is a sequence of steps that you might try. The goal of this process is similar to that of other chapters in this book. To become more of an independent thinker, you need to weaken the constraints on your mind's natural ability to build up ideas and perspectives. Each step should help in approaching this goal.

Step 1: Articulate Your Assumptions

It may seem paradoxical how greatly a clear statement of a rule or dogma helps you to free yourself from its control. Why? It is hard to free yourself of assumptions unless you know that they exist. A significant step toward independent-mindedness is to become aware of what your underlying assumptions are.

As a psychologist, I am aware of how much my own field has benefited from this kind of clear statement. A good example is the rise and fall of the behaviorist movement.

From 1910 to 1970, the behaviorist movement dominated the study of psychology in American universities. Although many psychologists still accept specific principles developed by behaviorists, their broad theoretical viewpoint is now considered outdated.

A basic premise of behaviorists' work was a principle called *operationalism*, proposed by the physicist Percy Bridgman. In essence, operationalism equated meaning and measurement: it specified that the meaning of a scientific term is equivalent to the operations involved in measuring what it refers to. By implication, if there is no way to measure, the term lacks meaning (and therefore should not be used).

Bridgman's influence was in many ways positive. It led researchers to define their terms more rigorously, thereby sharpening their thinking. But taken to extremes, its influence could be harmful. On the basis of this principle, behaviorists such as B. F. Skinner argued that psychologists had no business talking about mental states and entities. With a stroke, they banned the study of emotions, thoughts, memory, motivation, or the unconscious unless a researcher was choosing to use these psychological terms as shorthand for some form of observable behavior. In effect this meant that psychologists couldn't study psychology (unless they changed the definition of the word *psychology* to mean something like "the study of observed behavior").

Significantly, Bridgman's work in articulating the principle of operationalism was a great help to a later generation of psychologists who challenged behaviorism. The principle was so well stated that it was clear and visible and therefore easy to attack.

Are the liberating effects of stating your assumptions limited to psychology? Not at all. It works in fields as diverse as physics and philosophy. According to the eminent physicist Richard Feynman (1965), scientists during the Middle Ages believed that planets stayed in orbit because angels beating their wings pushed them. Isaac Newton was able to develop his alternative explanation in part because medieval scientists had articulated their theory so clearly.

Step 2: Question Your Questions

Is it possible that you are asking the wrong questions? It may seem presumptuous for someone to tell you to ask different questions. You are asking the question that you want (or need) answered. That fact in itself makes it the right question, doesn't it?

Not necessarily. We do not always ask the questions that will get us the answers we need. You sometimes can liberate your thinking by recognizing the problems inherent in your question and then "unasking" it.

The classic case of unasking a question was the revolutionary work of the Austrian-born U.S. mathematician Kurt Gödel. In the early twentieth century, mathematicians were seeking to develop a set of axioms and rules inference that would be consistent with each other and at the same time powerful enough to generate all the theorems or true statements that constitute mathematics. This bold project attracted some of the finest minds of the period, including Bertrand Russell and his mentor, Alfred North Whitehead. Gödel's remarkable achievement was to demonstrate the impossibility of success. He proved that within a theory rich enough to be interesting to mathematicians, no set of axioms could be consistent with each other and at the same time generate every theorem within it.

Did Gödel's theorem leave mathematicians upset and disappointed? On the contrary, while closing off an existing problem, it opened new directions for future mathematical inquiry.

There are several reasons why a particular question might be the wrong one. Here are some examples:

1. **It may in principle be impossible to answer.** Gödel's achievement was to prove that his fellow mathematicians were asking a question that in principle was impossible to answer. Similarly, a question may in theory be possible to answer but not within a reasonable amount of time. For all practical purposes, it is a bad question.

2. **It may be ambiguous or vague.** An ambiguous question is one that can be interpreted in more than one way. A vague question has only one interpretation that also happens to be muddy. Neither ambiguous nor vague questions can have a clear answer.

3. **The question may be counterproductive.** Questions that are good in the sense that they solicit valuable information may also be bad in the more important sense that discussing them obstructs vital social goals. For example, in the heat of a conflict, people sometimes ask inflammatory questions that could be answered but only at the price of intensifying anger.

4. **The question may be formulated in a way that unnecessarily limits your options.** For example, a question might be formulated in a way that forces you to select between two unacceptable options. A genuinely good answer might be some combination or compromise between both options, or alternately it might assert that neither alternative is acceptable.

5. **The question may be superficial or irrelevant.** A superficial question is one that asks about surface features instead of cutting to

the essence of what you need to know. An irrelevant question is worse: it requests information that you really do not need.

6. **The question may be tricky or paradoxical.** Gamesters and logicians often take delight in riddles and other questions that defy any straightforward answer. Unless you are specifically interested in paradoxes, the best answer is usually to recognize that the question is tricky and then quickly move along to something more productive.

Step 3: Examine Your Priorities

Is independent-mindedness really that important? The price of thinking independently is that you sometimes find yourself out of step with people around you. Some people, such as Barry, accept and enjoy standing out. Do you? Maybe you would be happier to go with the flow. It depends on your priorities.

It is striking how people who have a reputation for independent-mindedness often care more deeply than most of the rest of us do about public issues and causes. This was clearly the case with famous iconoclasts, such as Russell and Sartre. Barry, the critically minded teenager, never had to serve time in jail for his beliefs, as Russell did. Nevertheless, Barry's social commitments clearly affect important decisions in his life, such as his career choice.

If you want an easy life, you might prefer to be less independent-minded. Although independent thinkers sometimes win big, most of the time they experience higher-than-average levels of friction and frustration. Accepted ideas and opinions are like products that have proven their staying power in the marketplace. They have been tried over and over again and found to work acceptably well. If you want to have your own ideas, things will usually be harder.

Step 4: Recognize Your Commitments

There is a joke about how many psychologists it takes to change a light-bulb. The answer is "One, but it has to want to change." I recently met one who didn't.

My job was to act as coach to Jeff, a professional learning specialist who works for a nationally known American business organization. Jeff was developing a new online course for M.B.A. students. In reviewing Jeff's preliminary documents, I noticed that his course was top-heavy in theory and light in practical hands-on information. It seemed better suited for future business professors (like Jeff himself) than for future managers. I suspected and later was able to confirm that Jeff's course was similar to one that he had taken twenty years earlier, when he was a student at a prestigious business school.

I hoped that Jeff, as an early user of a new medium (the Internet), would jump at the chance to try out new concepts in course design. I therefore strongly advised Jeff to redesign his course with an eye toward making it more relevant to real-world decision making. Jeff resisted, eventually paying the price by being denied institutional approval to offer his online course. It never happened. As a result, Jeff never successfully made the switch from face-to-face to online course delivery.

Just as we have commitments to people, we also acquire commitments to established ideas, principles, and professional practices. We get them from our education, from the people we know, and from the books we read. Our involvement may deepen if it serves as a basis of our professional reputation and if it is widely accepted by colleagues we respect. It is important in most occupations to remain faithful to effective practice and not to jump at every new fad or trend. But some people, like Jeff, can become set in their ways. They stick to what they learned in school even in the face of newer and better ideas.

Step 5: Don't Be Afraid to Think Big . . . or Small

George Polya, the pioneer in the study of problem solving, observed that more ambitious plans might have a better chance of success. The advice to think outside the box, based on the work of Edward de Bono, expresses a similar notion. Both Polya and de Bono recognized that you risk recycling the same old ideas if you think on the same scale of magnitude as everyone else. Thinking big may help free your mind of shaky premises that everyone else takes for granted.

Less well known is the fact that thinking small can be just as liberating. It worked for Sherlock Holmes, with his eye for details that everyone else overlooked, and it can work for you. Noticing fine points can open up a whole new way of thinking.

Science is full of examples in which thinking big or thinking small changed history. Charles Darwin caused a social revolution by thinking big, on a scale of millions of years, when most people were thinking on a much smaller scale. On the other hand, Johannes Kepler and Galileo caused another revolution by paying close attention to detail. Kepler's careful description of the motion of the planets proved that their orbits were ellipses instead of circles, contrary to what medieval astronomers had believed. Why should the difference between a circle and an ellipse matter so much? Objectively, there is perhaps no good reason. But subjectively, an ellipse felt less perfect to astronomers than a circle. This subjective difference was crucial in moving astronomy from a divine explanation of planetary motion to a mechanistic explanation.

Step 6: See Your Heroes in Context

It's great to have heroes. People known as independent thinkers have had heroes at least since Plato followed in the footsteps of Socrates. But don't let your heroes trap you. Having an important thinker as a hero is a mixed blessing. On the one hand, it gives you a great starting point. Powerful thinkers set high standards for themselves and ask significant questions. Having a hero helps you appreciate what makes a piece of work good and therefore lets you become more demanding of yourself. On the other hand, your hero can overwhelm you. It is easy to look at your own ideas and feel that they are pedestrian and mediocre compared to what your hero did. All too often, bright young people end up feeling that they should provide support for a hero or mentor instead of developing new ideas of their own.

One way to free yourself of a powerful thinker's overwhelming influence is to see your hero in his or her historical context. Independent thinkers are often ahead of their times in the sense that they imagine possibilities inconceivable to their contemporaries. But even the bold-est minds nevertheless are products of the times in which they lived. For example, it is hard to imagine a thinker more independent than Freud. But Freud wrote about people from his era. The patients he saw suffered from conflicts and problems very different from what psy-chotherapists usually see in the twenty-first century. Freud also took for granted a social structure that seems terribly remote from the world of today.

Although Piaget belonged to a later generation than Freud's, his writ-ings also in many ways seem to come from a distant era. The children interviewed by Piaget, for example, often seem less mature and sophis-ticated than children today. Also, some of Piaget's ideas today seem skewed by intellectual battles that were fought and won long ago.

Admiring people does not mean that you have to slavishly follow what they said. Seeing your heroes in context often makes it easier to depart from what they said without feeling in some way disloyal.

What Makes an Independent Thinker Different?

What are the benefits to you of being an independent thinker? Two stand out. The first is a greater ability to adapt to change. The experi-ence of trying to think things through on your own provides excellent training in how to manage when there is no one to tell you what to do. The second is greater creativity. Even when you do not appreciate the value of your ability to think independently, employers, mentors, and colleagues can recognize and appreciate it. When I think of people who have worked with me, the most valuable have always been the most independent-minded.

Morgan worked with me as a research manager. When she started the job, she had a firm grasp of research methodology but little expe-rience with the demands and expectations of clients. Her great strength, though, was her willingness and ability to figure things out on her own. There were a few gaffes, such as neglecting details that seemed unim-portant to her and social niceties that she did not at first appreciate. But these mistakes became increasingly rare after a couple of months as she came to understand client needs. What remained was Morgan's ability to make decisions on her own and to cope with emergencies. Her habit of independent judgment made her far more valuable than someone who simply follows instructions and works only to please the boss.

Do Not Take It for Granted

Public discourse in our society treats independent-mindedness with special respect because of the important role that independent decisions, often by ordinary citizens, are expected to play in our political, legal, academic, and economic systems. It is therefore easy for us to take a high regard for independent thinking for granted. We should not. Independent thinking is not highly valued by everybody. Indeed, many cultures forcefully discourage it.

Away from the spotlight of public scrutiny, independent thinkers are frequently unwelcome, unless they happen to be the boss. When veterans tell their brash young colleagues, "Don't get any ideas," they usually mean it literally.

Educators committed to the ideal of independent-mindedness often feel frustrated when their community does not share the value that they attach to independent thinking and learning. For example, consider Anne, a professor at a liberal arts college in rural Nebraska. Most of her students grew up on the farm. Many are Lutheran descendants of immigrants from Germany; these students work hard and look up to their professors. Anne nevertheless feels frustrated. She would like her students to develop their own ideas, but she has had little success in encouraging independent-mindedness. The students feel such deep respect for their professors' learning that putting forth ideas of their own seems presumptuous to them.

I see the same frustration among some of the education students I teach at New York University. People may expect New York kids to be independent thinkers, but quite frequently they are not. Many of my students are committed to encouraging independent-mindedness and also to helping underserved, disadvantaged communities. They find, though, that parents in the communities where they work often do not share their belief in independent thinking. On the contrary, the parents believe that their children need discipline and structure and have to learn to defer to authority. The parents therefore often reject the innovative teaching methods that NYU education students enthusiastically embrace.

How much independence of thought exists even among highly educated professionals and academics? As social scientists have long known, you can usually predict what people think with a high degree of accuracy by knowing basic demographics, such as their age, sex, occupation, ethnicity, and the place where they live. This applies to questions of fact as well as matters of opinion. For example, do people think it is possible for the government to effectively manage a publicly financed health care system? Compare what Americans and Canadians think. It is hard to imagine two groups more alike. Nevertheless, almost all Americans will answer "no" and almost all Canadians will say "yes." It surprises few people to hear that social scientists use group membership to make highly accurate predictions. But look at the implication. If your ideas are predictable on the basis of group membership, it is hard to argue that much independent learning or thinking is taking place.

In an influential work, the sociologists Peter Berger and Thomas Luckmann argue that all of us live within a socially constructed worldview. According to these authors, what we see as reality is not an objective world but rather the product of cultural assumptions. How do we acquire this sense of reality? It comes not through any explicit instruction but rather because the media we watch, the books we read, and the people we know all seem to take them for granted. In turn, we take them for granted. This is why rich people and poor people, city dwellers and country dwellers, Americans and Europeans, who are in many ways so similar, quite often see the world so differently. We are influenced the most not by what people tell us but by what people find so obvious that it can be left unstated.

Does everyone buy into the worldview of his or her culture and community? Without sharing our culture's perspective to a large extent, we would feel isolated and would find it difficult to function. It is no surprise that sane people virtually always accept it. At the same time, some people, such as Barry, succeed in negotiating a working compromise with their society that allows them a measure of autonomy in what they think. Taking steps, such as the ones described earlier in this chapter, can expand this autonomy a little further.

Looking at the Long Term

As noted earlier, developing an independent mind has real personal benefits beyond offering personal satisfaction. Foremost among these is the ability to improve long-term learning and adaptation.

In many respects, independent thinkers are no more capable than anyone else is. But they do excel in certain spheres of life, especially the ability to learn over the long term. Why does timescale make a difference? Over the short term, being an independent thinker may not be an advantage and can sometimes even be a hindrance. Independent thinkers usually have trouble accepting the ideas of other people without critically evaluating them. If learning involves evaluating what you hear, it is going to take a lot more time than if you easily accept other people's worked-out ideas.

On the other hand, over a period of years, independent thinkers enjoy a definite advantage. Because they like to think through and evaluate what they are learning, they end up with a better understanding of its strengths and weaknesses. They can therefore modify their preexisting knowledge more easily in the face of new information. Over the long run, making regular changes and corrections is relatively quick and easy. It takes more time and energy if you have to assimilate a whole new way of thinking.

To see why, think about Barry. As a teenager (and perhaps even earlier), he was developing a set of values and a point of view that continued to guide his actions as a professional twenty years later. His adolescent habit of criticism gave him a chance to test his ideas, even if it sometimes annoyed adults and some peers. Because he lived and thought with his emerging viewpoint for such a long time, it became the center of a rich network of formal knowledge and everyday experience. Furthermore, he owned this viewpoint and therefore had the freedom to adjust it in light of life experience and changing social conditions.

Having ownership gave him flexibility that you do not have if you adopt the views and ideas of the people around you.

Why do people sometimes underrate the independent thinker? We usually look at learning over the short term. Schools virtually never take more than a few months of work into account when they assign grades. Corporations use the same short timescale in making performance evaluations. The only measures that truly take the long term into account are those of real performance in the world and in the marketplace. But aren't those the measures that truly matter?

We may also underestimate what long-term learning can achieve. As a culture, we still remain under the influence of the nineteenth-century idea that ability is innate and fixed. Well-established cultural practices, such as IQ testing, serve only to reinforce this belief. Many people still believe that *what* you think is learned but that *how* you think is innate. By failing to realize that you can learn ways of thinking, they also fail to appreciate the real value of long-term learning.

You can think of the mind becoming more powerful as being like a body developing stronger and stronger defenses. Your body becomes better at fighting disease as it develops more antibodies. Antibodies in turn develop through contact with bacteria, viruses, and other pathogens. An overwhelming challenge to the body's defenses can overpower them. When that happens the result can be serious illness. On the other hand, a moderate challenge will stimulate the body's defenses to fight back. Each time the body successfully defends itself, it becomes better able to cope with challenges in the future.

The mind also becomes stronger through coping with challenges. That happened to Barry as a teenager; by debating determined opponents, he developed clearer thinking, and his justification for his own viewpoint became stronger. What kinds of challenges make a difference? Each problem that an independent mind faces represents a new challenge. Each time you respond successfully to a problem, your mind becomes stronger. Furthermore, as it becomes stronger, you become able to face and deal with more complicated problems.

In response to every demand that it successfully handles, a mind becomes more complex. That complexity in turn makes the mind stronger and more stable. You will have developed a basic sense of confidence in your own viewpoint. After that you will see a sharp increase in your ability to gain from experience.

It does not matter whether experience takes the form of a challenge or of support. In response to a challenge, your mind may be able to fight it off, in which case you have developed additional defenses to fight off future challenges. Alternately, if the challenge forces you to change your thinking, it can bring you to a broader, more stable, and more realistic perspective. A supporting experience gives you new facts, evidence, examples, or ideas that confirm that you had originally been correct. They sometimes help you to see your original ideas in a new light and therefore understand them more fully. Other times they offer arguments in your defense available in the face of future challenges. Finally, they may suggest interest applications of your idea potentially worth pursuing.

You do not gain mind magic only by reading a few books or by taking a few courses, regardless of how helpful they in themselves may be. Instead, mind magic represents a change in your approach to knowledge. You never begin a new project or encounter a new subject expecting in advance to know the right way to think about it. On the contrary, you always expect the way you think to continually improve. You realize that mastering new ways of thinking is a normal part of any difficult project.

The analogy between strengthening the mind and strengthening the body has one further implication. People who commit themselves to physical fitness find that exercise eventually becomes an integral part of their life. The same is true for people who commit themselves to mind magic. Long-term learning can become as much a part of your everyday life as a regular workout. A day or a week seems to be missing something unless you do exercise your mind.

By that time, you no longer have to worry about mind magic. It is there no matter what. Your mind is continually searching for challenging problems and new opportunities to learn. The challenges of a new era become a source of stimulation instead of being a cause of stress. Mind magic lets you face new learning with greater confidence and hope.

CHAPTER 9

ARE THERE LIMITS TO WHAT YOUR MIND CAN ACHIEVE?

We often like to believe that we live in a society where anyone can achieve his or her potential. The lesson of life experience is not so sweet. Most of us face real obstacles, many of which are difficult if not impossible to overcome. Is the sky really the limit? The short (and perhaps glib) answer to this question is "why not." No one knows the limits of your potential.

A more sober answer is less grandiose. Yes, there may genuinely be certain real obstacles that limit what you can achieve. Nevertheless, they are fewer than most people believe. Furthermore, the limitations that actually exist still leave room for far greater attainment than you probably realize. You do have the ability to achieve a great deal. But to do so, you must be prepared to learn how to use the assets you have.

Limits: Real or Imaginary?

It is important to be able to perceive the difference between real limits and artificial ones. What is a real limit? A good example is lack of educational opportunity. If you want to excel in a field that requires highly specialized training it will be hard to acquire the most up-to-date knowledge and gain access to the most rewarding job. What is an artificial limit? Paradoxically, the concept of potential may itself represent an artificial limit. The word *potential* suggests some high point beyond which you cannot expect to go. But there is no evidence that such a high point exists. Why shouldn't you aspire to go beyond all limits, including any conception of your potential?

Since the 1970s, the field of psychology has witnessed growing controversy about such concepts as ability, potential, and even intelligence. One source of skepticism has been growing doubts about the validity of IQ tests. A second is research, including that of Jean Piaget, which has put in question the notion that intelligence is innate and fixed. A growing number of psychologists are coming to embrace the idea that intelligence can change and perhaps increase as a result of life experience. This fundamental change in perspective has opened the door to theories of mind magic and mind consciousness with their goal of increasing people's mind power.

Nevertheless, you will not use mind magic effectively if you have an unrealistic conception of what limits you genuinely face. Mind magic shows you what your mind can do and by implication what you can hope to accomplish with it. You will undermine your own best efforts if you believe in fantasy limits that do not really exist, such as a fixed, unchangeable level of intelligence. On the other hand, you will set yourself up for frustration if you ignore true obstacles and limits that actually exist.

The IQ Myth

Perhaps the most common fantasy limit is the myth of low IQ. What is this myth? Many people believe that a low IQ test score implies a lack of innate intelligence and, therefore, a poor prognosis of future success. This myth has become deeply embedded in our culture and language. Indeed, everyday usage treats *IQ* as shorthand for potential. Is there any truth to this myth? In fact, IQ test scores have no predictive value of long-term life success. Nevertheless, for many decades the notion persisted that IQ tests measured some deep innate ability. They do not.

The late Stephen Jay Gould, a leading thinker of his generation, argued that IQ tests are essentially a device to maintain social hierarchy, not a measure of real talent. How do IQ tests serve to maintain the social structure? According to Gould, they do so by playing on two key assumptions widely accepted in our society. The first is that your level of achievement depends on your ability, which means mainly intelligence. The second is that IQ tests accurately tell you how intelligent you really are.

Suppose that you have an "average" score on an IQ test. If you fall for the IQ myth, you will accept an average level of achievement as your destiny. What happens to people whose IQ test score is "below average"? If they accept the IQ myth, then they may see a below average level of achievement as their fate.

The IQ myth even harms people with a high IQ. They risk feeling that their success depends on their test score rather than on what they produce and contribute. So they may devote their energy to puzzles and problems that maintain their test scores instead of to something productive.

IQ tests are useful instruments but only as long as we use them correctly. They can be helpful for identifying children and adults with special needs. They are valuable as well in helping to diagnose certain kinds of brain damage and a number of major clinical disorders. We abuse them, however, when we rank people according to their IQ. We misuse them further when we mistakenly treat IQ as a deep unchanging attribute.

Seven Limitations That Can Affect Anyone

If obstacles and limits are an unavoidable fact of life, is there anything you can do about them? Yes. First, know the difference between obstacles that can be removed and limits that you cannot expect to overcome. Second, confront and accept the consequences for what you can and cannot do. Third, do what you can do so that you come as close as possible to achieving what you ideally would want.

Many people get discouraged because they have a self-defeating conception of what a limitation is. They see it as a kind of imperfection, like a flaw in an otherwise perfect diamond. They think that they could achieve more if only they worked harder, were more disciplined, or had a more resolute character.

In reality, limitations are more like undeniable laws of nature. You may want to be a basketball player, but you may be too short for the game. Social and cultural factors limit your potential for intellectual and artistic achievement in the same way that physical factors limit your potential for athletic achievement. You may have the ability, the discipline, and the commitment to achieve what you want, but you may fail nonetheless. Why? The reason is the set of objective circumstances into which you were born. Perhaps your ideas do not align with what is currently in fashion, good as they may be. Maybe somebody else made your great discovery before you had the chance. Whatever the cause, you need to accept the consequences.

Following is a list of seven common limitations that many people face. Most of the seven probably limit you at least to some extent. Understand what limitations actually exist. Then look to see what remains. Unless some real barrier stands in your way, is there any reason not to pursue your goals?

1. Health and material means
2. Family and friends
3. Learning opportunities
4. Larger social context
5. Motivation
6. Self-concept
7. Intrinsic ability

Health and Material Means

Do you have the means to achieve what you want? If we have them, we usually take them for granted. Others are not as fortunate. Poverty, illness, or some other material obstacles can throw people's life plans far off course. You may have the talents to contribute an enormous amount. But first you have to meet your basic needs. Poverty and illness are far from being the only external obstacles that sometimes stand in people's way; nevertheless, they are certainly quite common. It is difficult for people to think about trying something new and creative as long as they remain victims of some terrible tragedy.

Do you want to advance in a company, an institution, or a community? The more you have to worry about meeting basic needs, the less you are likely to feel able to take the risks often necessary for advancement. You do not have to be rich to achieve a great deal. But your means usually have to be greater than subsistence. Otherwise, you could not be able to afford to make the necessary investment in time, energy, and thought. This luxury is rarer than you may think.

Family and Friends

You have no choice over your family, and you have little choice over your society, especially when you are young. You do have choice over your friends. Both family and friends can influence whether or not you achieve your goals.

Is your family an asset or a hindrance? Psychologists have studied the effects of families on student achievement. The results are surprising. Is the family consistently a source of encouragement and support? It is not. For example, students who have trouble in mathematics, especially girls, often hear from an early age that they are not mathematical. When they do poorly in math at school, family members simply shrug. But why do these students do poorly? Quite often they suffer from no lack of mathematical ability. Instead, they suffer from a lack of self-confidence. Why? From an early age, parents and siblings have been telling them that they have no head for numbers. Is it any surprise when these statements become a self-fulfilling prophecy?

A family who understands and supports your ambitions can be an invaluable resource. A family who does not support your ambitions can also be a great asset if those ambitions are not realistic. In some ways, your family may know you better than you know yourself. Or they may know something about the world that you do not. They may see that your goals are unrealistic when you do not. On the other hand, some families are liabilities. Maybe you are right and family members are wrong.

In any case, things will be much easier if your family does support you. Taking risks is hard enough at the best of times, and it becomes much harder over the opposition of your family. Without the support of either family or friends, the stress can be great.

More important perhaps even than emotional support are the knowledge, values, and experience that you can gain from your family. Do you come from a musical family? It will be much easier for you to succeed as a musician if you do. Do members of your family have business experience? If so, you have probably been learning about business ways of thinking for years even if you did not realize it. Do you come from a family of university-educated people? You have probably been influenced by academic values that will make it much easier for you to succeed in an academic setting.

Learning Opportunities

It is a truism within our society that education is the gateway to success. But like many truisms, there are good reasons to wonder at times if it may be false. Many parents are willing to spend tens and hundreds of thousands of dollars to send their children to a prestigious university. Yet little of what you study in college has much practical use. It certainly has much less practical utility than what is taught at a technical college. Is attending a university right for you?

The standard argument in favor of a liberal arts education is that it teaches you better ways of thinking and broadens your experience. But there are other ways to gain breadth of experience. (Travel is a great way.) Does a university education teach you better ways of thinking? For most people, I think it does. Nevertheless, there are certainly many extremely successful people who never finished their formal education. For example, no matter how different they are in other ways, Bill Gates and Margaret Atwood are both Harvard dropouts.

What matters more than course work is having learning opportunities. An institution such as a school or university offers many people the setting they need to devote a few years primarily to learning. Nevertheless, some people are able to learn what they need outside of any institution. How do they do it? They may have enough personal enthusiasm and good judgment to find the right books and experiences. Think of the biologist Stephen Jay Gould, long before he was admitted to college, spending his weekends as a teenager at the Museum of Natural History. Maybe these people belong to a network of friends who learn together. Maybe they grew up in a family that provided learning experiences richer than what any school could offer. Maybe they learned through the practical experience of making or starting something.

Are you the kind of person who learns best in an institution or on your own? It may depend on what kind of career you hope to pursue. In some fields, such as the professions or experimental science, a university may be the only realistic alternative.

What is the real limit? It is the lack of adequate learning opportunities. Whether or not they involve formal education is less important.

Larger Social Context

Is society ready for you? You may be talented and educated and have something wonderful to contribute. But you will not succeed without a good fit between what you have to offer and what society is prepared to receive.

What larger social factors can limit your success? The politics of race, sex, and ethnicity are part of everyday discourse. But subtler forms of discrimination are less well known. Consider the subtle barriers that confront female scientists. Evelyn Fox Keller, a historian of science, has argued that scientists engage in a subtle, unconscious form of sex discrimination, in spite of consciously and sincerely trying to ensure equal opportunity. According to Keller, the standards used to evaluate scientific research favor a thinking style that is typically male. Scientists attach lesser value to work that reflects a thinking style more typical of women. She argues, furthermore, that there is no good scientific reason for this discrepancy.

These subtle forms of discrimination are quite common. As a society, we have deeply ingrained stereotypes of the typical practitioner in most occupations. Think of the cynical, tough-minded business executive; the narrow, detail-oriented accountant; the flaky, bohemian painter; or the socially awkward computer programmer. Such stereotypes are so much a part of our thinking that we usually do not realize that we have them.

For people whose personality fits the stereotype, finding a career can provide a comfortable niche. What happens if you are interested in a particular career but you do not fit the stereotype? Imagine that you enjoy painting but you also prefer a bungalow in suburban Omaha instead of a loft in Greenwich Village. In the eyes of many people, you will not *seem* like an artist. Will that affect your career success? It will certainly make things harder.

Motivation

People often fail because they misjudge their own motivation. They may think that they want to do something ambitious or creative, but they change their minds when they discover the real costs involved. Among the most liberating forms of self-knowledge is to know what you really want, as opposed to what you thought you wanted.

You can face substantial costs in trying to pursue a grand ambition. Ask yourself, "Is achieving my goals really worth the costs involved?" Some of these costs are tangible: years of study, cost of training, and the purchase of equipment and space. There are also psychological costs: self-doubt, risk of shame or failure, the need to face your weaknesses as well as your strengths, and the costs of success.

Ask yourself honestly if achieving your goal truly matters enough to you to justify the sacrifices it would require. Achievement usually involves years of preparation and an exceptional amount of work. Furthermore, the rewards themselves are often modest. You may not be able to justify this large an investment of time and energy in terms of the expected payoff.

Self-Concept

Can your opinion of yourself limit your success? Shakespeare's observation that "all the world is a stage" is frustratingly correct. We assign ourselves roles and then dutifully play them. It is extremely hard to step out of character and achieve a level of success that conflicts with our sense of who we are. The constraints of self-concept can be as strong as iron shackles.

Here is a surprising example of the effect of self-concept. When offering training workshops for coaches, the tennis expert Timothy Gallwey sometimes asks a novice player to demonstrate how he or she generally serves. As you would expect, the serve is usually weak and unimpressive—after all, the player is a novice. Gallwey then asks to see the player's best serve. This time it may be a little better, but the difference is negligible. Gallwey will then name a professional tennis player and ask the novice to demonstrate how the pro would serve. What does Gallwey find? Of course, the serve is not nearly as strong as that of a real pro, but it is much stronger than the student's own "best serve." The audience of coaches is visibly impressed. Then finally, Gallwey once again asks the student to demonstrate his or her best serve. Once again, the serve is weak—in no way comparable to when the student was playing the role of a tennis champion.

Why was the serve so much improved during the role-playing exercise? The answer is that when the student was not playing the role of the tennis pro, he was playing the role of himself. Because he thought of himself as a poor tennis player, his self-concept constrained the quality of his performance. Does this happen only on the tennis court? No. You can see it in everyday activities.

A case in point is the difficulty faced by many girls in learning mathematics. Although academic problems and learning disabilities are in general more common among boys than among girls, many girls seem to have a problem specifically with mathematics. Why is that? One reason is that we often teach mathematics in a "girl-unfriendly" way. For example, examples and word problems frequently come from activities (such as mechanics) that do not interest many girls. But even after we change our methods of instruction, many girls still seem to have more trouble with mathematics than with other subjects.

It is possible, of course, that girls for some biological reason are less talented at mathematics. But Jacquelynne Eccles and her colleagues at the University of Michigan (1986) offer an alternative explanation. They find that girls with mathematics problems are from an early age quite often told (at home) that they are not good at math. This message becomes a self-fulfilling prophecy. These girls have become so convinced that they are weak math students that they play the role of weak math student every day at school.

Intrinsic Ability

Last and probably least among the seven common limitations under discussion here is intrinsic ability. How important really is it? Many people believe that a lack of innate ability is the ultimate barrier to success. Are they right? Significantly, psychologists are generally far more skeptical about the concept of ability than are most other people.

Consider first hard evidence. Yes, there is evidence for the existence of some special abilities that set certain people apart. Nevertheless, these abilities are few in number and are rather specialized. What is an example? One intrinsic ability is perfect pitch. Most people have a sense of only relative pitch. If they hear two notes, such as a B-flat and an F-sharp, they can tell only which one of the two is higher. People with perfect pitch can also tell you the exact pitch of any note they hear. If they hear a B-flat, they know immediately that it is a B-flat. Even with training, most people are unable to recognize a note's exact pitch. Perfect pitch is definitely an asset for a musician. Furthermore, people with perfect pitch are more likely to pursue careers in music than are other people. But there is no evidence that they are more likely to be successful. Many people without perfect pitch become distinguished composers and performers.

Aren't there many other more familiar kinds of abilities? Don't we know people with an innate talent for mathematics, drawing, sports, or chess? There are certainly people who excel in these and many other pursuits. But there is no reason to suppose that their talent is innate. Typically, these people devote a vast amount of time to their talent. Couldn't their high level of skill be the result of practice? They also frequently receive superior instruction. Their educational advantage surely must contribute to their level of performance. Quite often these people come from families in which other members have shown similar talents. Isn't it possible that they might have learned from observing the people around them? Finally, these are people who normally think of themselves as being quite talented. It is hard to doubt that their high self-esteem plays an important role in their success.

Conversely, does a lack of innate ability represent a significant barrier to success? There are certainly activities in which specific innate attributes can make a decisive contribution. Successful football linemen are usually big and strong. Successful jockeys are usually small and wiry. If you have the physical attributes of a football player, it would be hard to succeed as a jockey and vice versa. For the majority of activities, how important is a distinctive innate ability? According to all evidence, its influence is small.

Face Limits but Overcome Obstacles

Confirmed optimists may tell you that anything is possible and the sky is the limit. Are they right? A quick look around shows you a more somber picture. You do indeed face real limits and obstacles. Mind magic can help you to confront limits and to overcome obstacles. But not even mind magic can suddenly make real limits disappear.

How do you deal with limits? First, recognize the difference between limits and obstacles. A *limit* is a barrier that you cannot remove. If you face real limits, you have no choice except to change your expectations. If you are tall and muscular, you are not going to become a professional jockey. On the other hand, an *obstacle* is a barrier that you can remove. How do you remove an obstacle? This becomes an exercise in problem solving. Mind magic can indeed make a difference with obstacles.

Imagine, for example, that you are having trouble understanding and evaluating a book or an article in a field that you are generally quite knowledgeable about. You can try a "brute force" solution, such as reading the demanding passages over and over again. Most of the time, that will give you a headache rather than an answer. You could ask someone to explain it to you. A clear explanation can make the idea more accessible, but it does not usually give you ownership of a complicated idea without more work on your part. So what should you do? As you know by now, the theory of mind magic usually tells you to solve intellectual problems by giving your unconscious a chance to work. Much of the time, doing nothing aside from waiting until the next day will make the difficult concept less intimidating.

Does mind magic help in other ways to overcome this obstacle? Try effective problem-solving techniques. For example, think around the concept by trying to relate it to a similar concept that you understand well. If it seems overly difficult, learn about its history, to understand who developed it, what problem it was first intended to solve, and what its antecedents were. Finally, mind magic can help by suggesting the amount of work time usually entailed in coming to understand a genuinely difficult concept.

Your second step in dealing with limits is to recognize the difference between material barriers and psychological ones. Imagine you need learning opportunities that you do not have. Is the barrier material or psychological? It could be either one. What do you need to do to obtain these learning opportunities? Do you need to find particular books, courses, or mentors? If so, the barrier is material and objective, and problem-solving methods are likely to be successful in finding a solution.

On the other hand, the barrier may be in your head. Is that the case? Is it possible that all the resources you need are ready at hand and you simply need to make the decision to try them out? Here is another possibility. Maybe you thought the obstacle was a lack of learning opportunities, but it was actually a lack of motivation. Is it possible that your real goals are different from what you thought they were? Overcoming an obstacle can require emotional awareness as well as mind consciousness.

Addressing a psychological barrier often requires adaptation instead of problem solving. Recall the example of the tennis player. Imagine that a limiting sense of your own abilities is your real obstacle. Many people are surprised to discover how hard it can be to see themselves as potentially more skilled and competent than they had imagined. As psychotherapists sometimes observe, people often experience a disturbing fear of success when they contemplate raising their expectations of themselves. Increasing your level of competence may require that you face and overcome these feelings. Surprisingly, adapting to increased ambitions can be just as difficult as adjusting to reduced expectations.

Know Your Own Mind

Facing and understanding the real limits that you face can be extremely liberating. How? Once you know the real limits, you can free yourself of the artificial ones. For most people, the artificial limits are at least as great as any real ones.

According to official ideology, our society is supposed to be ambitious, forward-looking, optimistic, and confident. But outwardly confident people all too often inwardly see themselves as incompetents or frauds. Surprisingly, even highly successful people may privately suffer from enormous self-doubt.

I had this point hammered home while working many years ago as a teacher of expository writing to Harvard freshmen. Given the intense competition for admission to Harvard, you would expect these students to see themselves as the crème de la crème. How confident did they really feel? Like most writing instructors, I gave my students a short writing assignment during the first class. Then I devoted my first private conference to finding out how each student evaluated his or her performance on the opening assignment. The experience proved to be an eye-opener.

To establish rapport, I started each conference by asking students about their interests and background. Then we would look at their writing. I always began with the same request—that they tell me what was good about the piece they had written. Student after student had the same reaction. Each one began by criticizing his or her work. I kept telling them that I wanted to hear praise, not criticism. But that made them more uncomfortable. Self-criticism came easily; self-praise did not.

I have seen the same reaction in industry when I have interviewed employees at the time of a performance review. Most people find it effortless to criticize themselves, but people almost never find it easy to praise themselves. Some of the time, no doubt, people avoid praising themselves because they do not want to look like braggarts. Even so, maintaining a modest demeanor draws attention to your shortcomings, not your strengths. If you are continually talking and thinking about your failings, they come to dominate how you perceive yourself. No wonder that so many people suffer from low self-esteem. To think poorly of yourself is as American as apple pie.

Is this poor opinion justified? In fact, most of the students in my Harvard class were quite competent essay writers. Otherwise, they probably would not have gotten into Harvard! But they did not see themselves that way. They found it terribly difficult to think or say something positive about themselves. The same could be said of so many other people.

Since antiquity most people have taken the ancient Greek injunction to know thyself as a warning. If you did not know yourself, the ancient Greeks would expect you to pay dearly. What were you supposed to know about yourself? It was almost never the good things. Usually, self-knowledge meant knowledge of your flaws, failings, weaknesses, and shortcomings. A sad fact is that people in our culture have become deeply conditioned into accepting this negative conception of self-knowledge. For most of us, it has become second nature.

The inscription on the cover of this book could also read "know thyself." The intent, however, would be almost the opposite of the traditional one. You have seen time and time again that self-knowledge is a source of encouragement, not caution. Self-knowledge tells you that you have the ability to accomplish far more than seemed possible, not less.

What good is self-knowledge? It means power, mind power. If you understand yourself well enough, you can use your mind for your own purposes. If you want, you may even be able to change it so that it serves you better. Self-knowledge is what allows you to act on the basis of conscious purpose. It adds meaning to your own life while enabling you at the same time to contribute meaning to the lives of other people.

CHAPTER 10

BECOMING A
MIND MAGICIAN

A re you using mind magic already? Chapters 2 through 8 covered
how ideas grow in your mind before you become consciously
aware of them. You may not realize how much you are using the ideas
in mind magic until one day some surprising idea bubbles up. You wonder where that came from. Whether you realized it or not, you were
putting mind magic to work.

First Jean Piaget and later a generation of psychologists discovered
power in the human mind that no one before had suspected. The better you understand the power of the mind, the more you can consciously
and deliberately put that power to use. Is it an exaggeration to say that
you can do anything with your mind? You can definitely accomplish a
great deal—far more than most people believe.

Earlier chapters covered the concepts of mind magic and mind consciousness as well as principles of mind magic in action. Now we will
step back and look at the process of changing from a reader of mind
magic to a practitioner who uses it whenever helpful.

Many people find it interesting to read about mind magic but come
away feeling unsure how to begin putting it to use. Others will have a
specific problem or project in mind before they read *Mind Magic* and
know right away how to put to use what the book says. A third kind of
reader may not have had a specific project in mind; nevertheless, certain ideas capture that reader's imagination, and he or she wants to try
them out. How did you react?

If you know how you want to use mind magic, then by all means get
started. But what should you do if you have no clear idea what to do

with it? There are ways to get started and to keep up the momentum once you have tried it out.

How Do You Apply Mind Magic to Solving Real-World Problems?

One way is to look at an example. In practice, how do people use mind magic to solve problems more successfully?

The following example, reported in Donald Schön's book *Educating the Reflective Practitioner* (1987), illustrates how a master architect and a student, working together, developed a successful design for an elementary school. It is very much a real-world problem. Unlike textbook problems, there is neither a single correct solution nor a single correct method of finding a solution. On the contrary, the problem is messy, complicated. You need to use subjective judgment as well as technical knowledge even to determine when the problem is solved.

Finding a successful solution involved the kind of qualitative change in perspective reminiscent of Piaget's work. At the beginning, Quist, the master architect, and his student Petra saw the essential problem as creating a design to fit a space. In this case, the space was an irregular hillside. After failure and frustration, they gave up this goal altogether and created an entirely different plan based on one relatively minor feature of their initial design, the L-shaped classroom. The successful solution came from "softening" the second design to make it more responsive to features of the landscape without giving up its internal coherence.

A Solution That Worked in the Real World

Quist and Petra went through the following five steps to arrive at a solution that they and other architects could find acceptable:

1. Diving in
2. Defining the basic problem (first attempt)
3. Making the first correction

4. Making the second (successful) correction
5. Putting concept into practice

Each step in the process made use of mind magic. Note that their result was the concept for a solution, not a fully developed blueprint. As Quist said, their solution "worked slightly but was good enough." What did he mean? It would be necessary to work out many details before their solution would be complete. But he could see by this point how they would successfully finish the design. The hard part, creating a viable and appealing basic concept, was done.

Diving In

The first step was essentially brainstorming. Because their medium is architecture design, Quist and Petra's brainstorming involved both verbal description and sketches. Their dialogue presumed a two- or three-story school building with rectangular classrooms.

Commentary

Many of the principles of problem solving, discussed in Chapter 6, underscore the value of leaping into the void. For example, you should be willing to make a lot of guesses. And you should not be afraid to bite off more than you can chew. At this first stage, Quist and Petra offer a set of ideas, all of which will eventually prove to have been inadequate. Does that mean they should have been more careful? On the contrary, they never would have achieved a successful design later on had they not been able to work from these early guesses.

Defining the Basic Problem (First Attempt)

Quist and Petra quickly recognize that the irregular hilly landscape raises special problems. Petra suggests that their basic problem is to create a design for a building that fits this particular space. She suggests that they have to butt the shape of the building into the contour of the land. She finds it impossible, however, to implement this design successfully. At this point, she says that she feels stuck.

Commentary

In Chapter 2 we considered the yin and yang of learning, the yin being the expansive phase and the yang being the corrective phase. The experience of becoming stuck tells you that you need to switch gears and critically examine your existing ideas. Note, furthermore, that Petra reads her emotional response, as discussed in Chapter 7, and therefore does not become overwhelmed by it. Less-skilled problem solvers would see weaknesses in the initial design as signs of failure at the task or even as personal incompetence. Mind magicians know that becoming stuck is a normal part of problem solving. The best response is usually to sleep on the problem. It is often surprising to see the ideas that a new day will bring.

Making the First Correction

Quist and Petra begin to try to correct their initial design by questioning its elements. Petra observes that the rectangular classrooms in the first design lacked significance, meaning that the regular shape was uninteresting. As an alternative, she suggests L-shaped classrooms.

Commentary

Looking for features to change and assumptions to question is typical of yang thinking. The idea of the L-shaped classroom will eventually prove to be the key to the solution. But at the point when they first discuss the idea, they do not yet realize its ultimate importance.

Making the Second (Successful) Correction

Quist, the master architect, suggests that they should not think in terms of fitting the building to the contour of the land. In his words, the hilly land is too "screwy." Instead, he says that they should "impose a discipline." This means that they should create a design independent of the landscape and then find a way of imposing the design on the site. Based on this redefinition of the problem, Quist and Petra create a series of sketches that use the idea of the L-shaped classroom. The most successful have a large open space that they call a gallery, with an L-shaped classroom leading off it.

Commentary

Chapter 6 discussed the notion of questioning a problem's "psychology." In this case, the psychological bug was the initial definition of the problem, in terms of fitting the building to the contours of the land. Quist understood that the real problem was finding a coherent design and that fitting the contours of the land was just one means to achieving that end. They made progress by "unasking" one question and replacing it with another that is more fundamental.

In fact, they will return to the issue of fitting the contour of the land later on. Nevertheless, they were able to find an appealing solution only because they ceased to define it as the essence of their problem.

Putting Concept into Practice

Working from the concept of an L-shaped classroom, Quist and Petra began to see how to include other crucial elements of the building, such as a cafeteria and a gym. They had the idea of making the gallery into a broad staircase with L-shaped classrooms at different levels. Quist suggested that the ceiling should be on levels. Thus the distance between floor and ceiling would be uneven and include kid-sized nooks five feet high, a perfect feature to include in an elementary school.

During this phase Quist describes their work as "softening the concept." By this he means that they are backing off from the discipline that they had imposed earlier. The coherence of the building still comes from the geometry of the L-shaped classrooms. Nevertheless, the staircase gallery makes a clear concession to the contours of the land.

Commentary

After redefining the problem, Quist and Petra switch back to yin thinking. It is characteristic of yin thinking that one idea—in this case, the concept of an L-shaped classroom—provides a focus to which problem solvers attach a set of related notions. The successful solution therefore takes the form of a network of mutually supporting and interrelated concepts. Note how at each step the idea of the L-shaped classroom becomes increasingly important without any fanfare. As noted in Chapter 6, the crucial steps in solving a problem often happen quietly, without any eureka experience. That clearly is the case here.

How to Start Using Mind Magic—
A Six-Stage Process

How do you reach the stage where you can solve difficult problems as successfully as the master architect Quist and his student Petra? Just as thinking is a highly personal process, so is applying mind magic. Some people like to immerse themselves fully and try out mind magic in every aspect of their lives. Other people prefer to let the ideas sink in slowly and then emerge after they have started to feel familiar. No one way is right for everyone.

The six-stage process that follows suggests one possible direction. See it as a model or prototype of how people advance their skill in using mind magic. It may or may not fit your experience. Try it if you think it could work, or adapt it to suit your needs.

You can look at this process as a kind of fitness program for strengthening your mind. Does this mean that your brain will start hurting in the same way that many fitness programs make your muscles ache, especially at the beginning? For most people, mind magic is fun, not agony. But for a few, the beginning takes some work. As in a fitness program, with time you can expect the aches to go away and your endurance to increase. The more you work at it, the more skillful you will become and the more you can expect to find it exhilarating, not painful or uncomfortable.

Here are the stages:

1. The initial reaction
2. The incubation period
3. Trying it out
4. Creative engagement
5. Follow-up
6. Taking ownership

The Initial Reaction

How did you react at the very beginning when you first heard about mind magic? Did you want to learn more? Did you find it empowering?

Did certain concepts seem useful or promising? Did some of it seem impossible or unbelievable? Did some of it seem old hat? Did some of it seem boring or confusing? Did it seem brilliant? Was it love at first sight?

The concepts discussed in earlier chapters dealing with information management and knowledge acquisition apply fully to the subject of mind magic itself. Some people will love it and others will dislike it. Those who react positively from the beginning are not the only ones who will go on to use it successfully. People who are skeptical at the beginning can become the greatest enthusiasts once they truly understand mind magic.

In Chapter 7 we looked at the role of emotions in learning and how reacting emotionally helps in learning a new set of ideas, especially at the beginning. How does it help? When you react emotionally to a feature, it becomes more memorable. A good way to enter into a new body of knowledge is to use these features as hooks. You begin to understand the topic as you notice connections between these points of interest and familiar concepts. You begin to understand it more deeply when you start to find connections among these new points of interest themselves.

Sometimes, of course, people do form a quick attachment to a concept, such as mind consciousness, and it then becomes a dominant theme in their thinking. But it can work the other way as well. Some initial skepticism may pave the way for substantial success later on in the use of mind magic principles. Especially for people unfamiliar with the work of Piaget and other developmental theorists, the concept of mind magic may initially seem surprising and perhaps even counterintuitive. You may be able to appreciate mind magic only after working through the reasons for your initial skepticism.

Others may welcome the promise of increased mind power and the generally optimistic tone but at the same time worry that the concept of mind magic might be too good to be true. The need to think through your initial doubts is a sign of a healthy critical intellect at work. Very often it signals a deeper and more serious interest in the future.

A more typical first reaction, however, is milder and more moderate. Most people at first feel interested and intrigued. They may be working on a problem at the moment and think that one or another fact or principle from the book could be helpful. Similarly, specific concepts or methods may appear relevant to solving some anticipated problem or to working on some project planned for the future. Alternatively, some people may find certain ideas so intriguing that they will look for a problem or a project where they can try putting them to work. Or else they may just enjoy thinking about the idea and look forward to doing further reading on the subject.

There is no such thing as a correct initial response. How well and how often you eventually use mind magic depend far more on what comes later.

The Incubation Period

After your initial reaction sets in, should you expect to start putting mind magic to work immediately? Probably not. If you have a specific project or an important problem before you, you may find yourself using a great deal of mind magic. Otherwise, it will probably command relatively little of your attention, at least for a while. Does this mean that you are going to forget about mind consciousness and mind magic? No, it does not. What it means is that you need time to digest and organize a new family of ideas. Expect to come back to mind magic when you are ready.

Chapter 3, on adapting to change in your personal life and in the world around you, discussed the concept of a period of adjustment. Assimilating a new way of thinking, such as mind magic, also takes time. It is hard to adopt a new way of thinking all of a sudden. You need some time to understand the consequences.

What kind of changes do you need to make? Much of the process can happen unconsciously. Your mind looks for connections with other ideas you are familiar with. Does it seem similar to ideas that you know and like? If so, which ones? Does it have uses or implications that go beyond the old familiar ones? Are there any conflicts or contradictions between mind magic and what you have heard or read in the past? If so, how can you resolve those conflicts?

For most people, new ways of thinking, such as mind magic, start becoming part of your conscious thought processes at unplanned moments. You may be thinking about a problem when some concept, method, or principle associated with mind magic might suddenly occur to you. You may be reading an article or having a conversation when you come across an idea that makes you think of mind magic. You may be focused on a problem and find that nothing seems to work and suddenly wonder whether mind consciousness might offer a path toward success. You may find yourself in an argument and suddenly feel certain that the other person would see your point of view if only he or she knew something about mind magic or that perhaps mind magic could help you see the other person's point of view.

How long should you expect the incubation period to last? It could be hours or days or weeks or longer. You know that the incubation period has ended when you find yourself wanting to consciously and deliberately try out mind magic.

Trying It Out

Trying it out is a small but nevertheless crucial step toward a serious interest in mind magic. It represents the point when you move from the role of interested observer to potentially active participant.

You can compare knowing a theory, such as mind magic, to knowing a person or place. The initial reaction is like a casual introduction at a party or exchanging business cards at a conference. You may make a mental note whether you are interested in this person, but you probably do not do anything more at least for the moment. Trying out the theory is taking the next step. You are seeking to find out whether it might possibly play a meaningful role in your thinking.

A relationship with a person typically begins in earnest with some deliberate effort to get to know him or her. In a personal relationship, this may take the form of a get-together over coffee or a first date. In a professional relationship, it may take the form of an interview or a working lunch. The act of scheduling this kind of event in itself expresses a degree of serious interest. Of course, you do not know at first how well things are going to work out. You will use the event to gauge the other person. If things go well, you plan to follow up later.

Getting to know a theory or system of ideas, such as mind magic, works much the same way. When the point comes that you begin to feel interested, there is little cost in giving it a try. Exactly how you give it a try depends on what problems and projects are foremost in your mind. If you are trying to produce a creative work, you may want to try the methods outlined in Chapter 4 (on creativity). If you have a job in which you need to manage large quantities of information, you may want to refer to Chapter 5 (on information management). If you are facing a career change or a major adjustment in your personal life, Chapter 3 (on adaptation) may prove to be the most useful. If you are a student, you may want to discuss some aspect of mind magic as part of a term paper.

Just as a good date involves doing something that both people enjoy, a good try-out project does something that is genuinely important to you. Also, aren't the best first dates often the ones that defy the rules and let you be yourself? Similarly, the best try-out projects are often the ones where you do whatever you want with the mind magic, even if (or perhaps especially if) you think of something that seems to break the rules.

Sometimes a friend or an instructor may suggest a specific application to you. An introduction from an informed associate can lead you to a valuable intellectual project. Most of the time, however, people find problems and projects on their own. If the chemistry is there, the project works.

Does the try-out project have to be a success? If you feel some awkwardness, should you take that as a warning of future difficulties? You expect to become more comfortable and competent as you gain more experience. Some awkwardness at the beginning is normal. The crucial question is whether you like it enough to keep going. If so, investing the time to try it out a few more times is worth it.

Creative Engagement

A good try-out project leads to a second project in the same way that a good first date leads to a second date. Then a second can lead to a third and a third to a fourth and so on.

As you devote more time to mind magic, you will find that it begins to integrate itself more fully with the rest of your thinking. For one thing, you start becoming interested in different sides and implications of mind magic. If you initially became interested in using mind magic as a knowledge-acquisition tool, you may next become interested in trying out what it says about problem solving. If you first tried out mind magic to help you manage information, you may want to consider its implications for adapting to change. If the idea of mind consciousness attracted you at the start, you may later want to think seriously about emotional awareness.

You may also begin thinking about mind magic in a variety of contexts. If you first saw mind magic as a study aid, you may next think of applying it to your personal life. If you tried it out originally on a hard-to-define psychological issue, you may next think of putting it to work to help solve a concrete technical problem. If your initial try-out project involved a recreational hobby, you may next wonder whether it can be useful as well in solving professional and business problems.

The more you work with mind magic, the more of a feeling you get for how it can be used. How long should you expect to wait? An educated guess is that you will probably need to tackle three or four try-out projects. By that point at least one or two concepts or principles of mind magic will probably have begun to enter into your everyday thinking. You'll likely be making at least some connections between these new ideas and familiar experiences and concepts. You may have also started to make connections among the various mind magic concepts and begun to see how they all fit together. If so, you may already have formed the skeleton of a "cognitive map" of mind magic.

As you become creatively engaged with mind magic, what changes are you able to observe in your thinking? Your answer depends on what you originally found interesting about mind magic. Did you have a specific project that you wanted to pursue or a body of facts that you were attempting to master? Did you want to try out particular methods or principles? Were you trying to get at the essence of mind magic so that you could understand the system as an integrated whole? Were you interested in mind magic for some other reason? Whatever initially interested you about mind magic will affect the role that it subsequently comes to play in your thinking.

- **If you were originally interested in a specific problem, project, or set of facts:** Starting with a specific problem, project, or set of facts opens up multiple directions in which your thinking about mind magic can develop. First, your initial project or problem can act as a reference point for the future. When you start to work on other applications, you can see the potential relevance of mind magic more quickly by comparing them with the one you tried first. Second, you can go from the specific to the general: from a few examples, you may develop your own broad rules of thumb for when and how mind magic could help you. Third, you can look more closely at the details.

- **If you were originally interested in mastering concepts, principles, or methods:** As opposed to starting with a problem or concern of his or her own, some people start by focusing on the intent of the author. When they begin they are often careful to stick to the book. Is that how you began? As you gain experience, you will feel more and more that you understand the concepts, principles, and methods that you are using. Furthermore, as you feel more confident in your understanding of mind magic, you will also feel more comfortable adapting it to your needs. Your command of mind magic will become more flexible and more personal.

- **If you were originally interested in understanding mind magic as an idea or a system:** Some people are initially interested in ideas for their own sake, not in applications. Is that you? Mind magic can serve as an effective introduction to the body of cognitive theory and research represented by Piaget, Vygotsky, and other developmental theorists. There is one warning, however. Many of the ideas will seem counterintuitive or even confusing at first unless you already have some familiarity with related work. Indeed, understanding Piaget's theories involves the kind of qualitative changes in thinking that Piaget wrote about. If you choose this route, you should be prepared to invest time and energy. Be aware that you might experience the kinds of misunderstandings and conflicts at the beginning that Piaget considered a necessary part of intellectual development. With experience, however, you should expect to develop a clearer and more accurate sense of its real essence.

Relatively few readers start out interested in ideas and conceptual schemes for their own sake. Most are interested in practical applications and benefits. But as they try out mind magic more and more, their interests begin to broaden. Some think to themselves, "It works, but I do not really understand why. It seems weird. How do you explain it?" Others think that it seems neat and want to know more about the ideas associated with it. The sense that you are ready to go from practice to theory signals the beginning of the follow-up stage.

Follow-Up

According to MIT mathematician and learning theorist Seymour Papert, people learn by doing and by thinking about what they do. After trying out mind magic for a while, do you begin to feel that you want to understand the ideas that lie behind it? You may be ready for help not just in practicing mind magic but also in thinking about it. This may be a good time for further reading or to take a mind magic workshop.

Some people do best by reading a lot or taking courses and workshops before they even begin to try using mind magic techniques. If you are that kind of person, you belong to a minority. Most people succeed best by starting out immersing themselves in the practice of mind magic and only later (if at all) concentrating on theory. There is nothing wrong with either direction.

How do you begin to follow up if you are so inclined? The two main options are to either do further reading or take a workshop. Books are more readily available, but a seminar or workshop might address your concerns more directly. When is a seminar or workshop more helpful than a book? If you have questions that need answers and ideas that need discussion, you may prefer the kind of forum that a seminar or workshop offers. You may also welcome the opportunity to meet people with similar interests. If no seminar or workshop is available, or if you have no questions or issues to discuss, the better option may be further reading. I have included a list of recommended books for further reading. For relevant articles and more up-to-date reading selections, check out the mind magic website at power-your-mind.com. The mind magic website also contains listings of seminars and workshops.

Have you found that mind magic sparked or deepened a serious interest in the subjects of learning, intelligence, and/or cognitive development? If so, you may think of taking university-level courses on any of a number of subjects related to this book.

Consider first a course on Piaget. Most major universities offer courses that deal primarily or exclusively with Piaget's work. Piaget was the quintessential interdisciplinary thinker, and for this reason, various university departments offer excellent Piaget courses. You will find good Piaget courses taught by developmental psychologists, philosophers specializing in epistemology, and educators. There are also outstanding Piaget courses given by computer scientists, physicists, mathematicians, and evolutionary biologists. Keep in mind one warning, however. An instructor who teaches a course on Piaget should know Piaget's psychological research and also his philosophical theories about the nature of knowledge. An instructor whose background is exclusively psychology or philosophy may not be able to do justice to Piaget's work. You should therefore verify that a course you are considering will cover Piaget's contributions to both psychology and epistemology.

If you want to go beyond a Piaget course at your local university, think about attending a conference or an international workshop. Do you want to meet the professionals who use Piaget's work every day and know it the best? Attending a meeting is the way to do that. The experts will love to have you attend. For conferences and workshops in North America, contact the Jean Piaget Society through its website, piaget.org. Another possibility is to take a course or attend a workshop in Geneva, Switzerland, where Piaget himself worked. The Jean Piaget Archives at the University of Geneva offers summer workshops, as well as courses and seminars at other times of the year. You can find information at the foundation's website, unige.ch/piaget/Presentations/presentg.html.

There are also other academic subjects that can serve as follow-ups to mind magic. One is artificial intelligence. Its mission is to enable computers to do things that would be considered intelligent if done by a human being. What does artificial intelligence have to do with mind magic? According to a formal definition, artificial intelligence is a branch of computer science. On the other hand, from the viewpoint of mind magic, artificial intelligence is a source of many of the most interesting ideas around about human thinking and human intelligence. The insights of artificial intelligence researchers can substantially increase your mind consciousness and in turn your ability to use your mind effectively. If you are mainly interested in psychological issues, choose a course that emphasizes broad concepts of how intelligence works and that devotes less attention to technical programming issues.

Finally, you might want to consider a course in cognitive science. Cognitive science is a hybrid discipline that was created at a time when psychologists and artificial intelligence researchers were first discovering each other. Look for a course that devotes most attention to learning, problem solving, and the development of intelligence.

Taking Ownership

This is the point when you feel that you have got it. At the beginning, the idea of mind magic may have seemed interesting and even exciting but foreign nevertheless. The more experience you have, what previously seemed foreign or even somewhat confusing comes to seem familiar and perhaps even obvious. If the stage of trying out mind magic is like a first date, the stage of taking ownership is like a stable relationship.

It may even seem strange to you when mind magic does not seem obvious to other people. At the same time, the system as a whole seems more and more to fit together. When you first read about mind magic, different applications may have appeared to be unrelated to one another. Now you start to see that they are expressions of the same underlying principles.

Chapter 5 (on information management) talked about differences between borrowing an idea and owning it. If you own an idea, you feel at ease with it and have a sense of mastery. You feel competent to offer your own interpretation of what it means and to adapt its meaning to fit new circumstances. On the other hand, you never feel entirely comfortable with an idea that you have simply borrowed. You are always worrying that you might have gotten it wrong.

More and more, do you experience a subjective sense of unity and familiarity with mind magic? These are signs that you are beginning to take ownership.

What are other signs that you have taken ownership of mind magic? Consider the following questions:

- Do you feel able to explain specific mind magic topics (such as information management, problem solving, or creative thinking) or the concept of mind consciousness to friends and colleagues?
- If asked, would you feel able to present a short lesson or seminar on some aspect of mind magic?
- Have you developed personal opinions about mind magic? (Such opinions might address what is most significant about mind magic, what are its implications, what are related ideas that deserve attention.)
- Do you feel able to use the concepts of mind magic or mind consciousness creatively, by making your own observations about how your mind works or by finding original applications?

Answering "yes" to any of these questions is a sign that you are starting to assume control over the subject.

By this point, you will be using this book in a different way. You will probably have formed an initial reaction by having reading so much of the book. By the time you assume ownership, you might consult it as needed. Stanford mathematician George Polya developed the concept of a heuristic or rule of thumb with a proven track record. You may want to treat *Mind Magic* as a collection of heuristics to consult when you have to deal with a new kind of problem or project.

Working as a Mind Magician

Where do you go from here, once you have taken ownership of mind magic and feel firmly in control? By now mind consciousness has become part of your everyday thinking. Do you want to keep up to date and read new books and articles on mind magic as they appear? You may. Other than that, will the ideas in this book fade into the background, having become integrated with all the other basic knowledge that you take for granted but nevertheless use unconsciously every day? Or do you want to make something with mind magic of your own?

What you choose to do with mind magic depends on your circumstances as well as your goals and interests. If you are a student, your options are different from those of a senior business executive. If you have to work every day, your alternatives are different from what confronts the holder of a generous fellowship. Three ways that readers can work at mind magic are (1) pursuing formal study, (2) creating new educational programs and/or business concepts, and (3) conducting original research. Is one or another of these alternatives available and interesting to you?

Pursuing Formal Study

Mind Magic grew out of a number of well-established bodies of scientific and scholarly research. If you are pursuing or expect soon to pursue studies at an undergraduate or postgraduate level, you may want to consider one or another of the academic disciplines influenced by Piaget and his followers.

Of all major academic fields, developmental psychology usually offers students the greatest opportunity to study Piaget's work in depth. Piaget's theory and research provide much of the foundation for the field and therefore must be included in any comprehensive course. You should expect a quarter to half of a developmental psychology course, even at an introductory level, to deal with Piaget.

A second alternative is to study the philosophical questions that motivated Piaget himself. Piaget called himself a genetic epistemologist, not a psychologist. (Epistemology is the branch of philosophy concerned with the nature of knowledge.) If you are interested in Piaget's philosophical work, you should look for epistemology courses that include a broadly interdisciplinary focus.

A third option is to select an academic discipline related to mind magic that does not focus specifically on Piaget. What are your choices? Readers interested in such topics as problem solving and information management may want to consider courses in cognitive science. If you are interested in practical applications, you may want to consider education courses. Other courses to consider include adult learning, mathematics and science education, and early childhood education.

Creating New Educational Programs and/or Business Concepts

Do you have an educational or a business background? If so, you may want to consider developing new programs and services that help people understand and use the potential of mind magic.

If you teach at a public or private school or work in the administration of a school system, there may be opportunities for new course development. The education world is coming more and more to recognize the importance of teaching students to use their minds more effectively. Look at the proliferation of courses in thinking skills and learning skills. Would your students benefit from a course in mind magic? If so, you may consider creating one.

How can you apply mind magic in business? Principles of mind magic ought to help people in most positions to do their jobs more successfully. Beyond that, whatever specific opportunities exist depend on the industry and the company in which you work. Companies in most sectors of the economy recognize the value of educated, thoughtful, and motivated employees. Many of these companies would appreciate workshops and courses on a subject such as mind magic that help their employees to use their minds more effectively. You may want to approach the training department of your company and offer to provide workshops on mind magic. If you are highly entrepreneurial, you may want to consider starting your own seminar company.

Does your company develop educational products (such as teaching aids, educational software, textbooks, and educational television programs) or deliver educational services (such as tutoring, course and curriculum development, teaching training, after-school program management, school management, educational conference planning, and distance education)? If so, mind magic could provide the stimulus for a new product or service. The education business is a growth industry of the twenty-first century. There are clearly opportunities for new programs and better ideas.

Conducting Original Research

A third and potentially profoundly exciting opportunity is to conduct original research. This could allow you to contribute to the actual development of mind magic.

It should be clear that mind magic is a work in progress. We are only at the beginning of understanding how our minds think, learn, and adapt, let alone how to put this knowledge to practical use. Where are the research opportunities? Mind magic deals with fundamental theoretical questions with wide-ranging applications. Consider five academic fields where mind magic has a direct contribution to make: (1) cognitive development, (2) cognitive science, (3) organizational psychology, (4) education, and (5) clinical psychology and mental health. Work based on mind magic should have applications in all of these fields.

Cognitive Development
Cognitive development is the branch of psychology concerned with how knowledge and intelligence grow and develop throughout the life span. Specialists know a great deal about the stages through which children and adults pass during the course of development. But what causes movement from one stage to the next? This remains a major outstanding research question where mind magic concepts could make a contribution.

Cognitive Science
Cognitive science is a growing field at the intersection of cognitive psychology, artificial intelligence, linguistics, and brain science. It addresses all questions related to knowledge, thinking, information processing, perception, and memory. Cognitive science has significantly influenced the ideas in this book.

Of particular interest to readers of this book is the branch of cognitive science known as the learning sciences. As the name suggests, it is concerned specifically with questions of learning, as well as other changes in thinking and knowledge. Ideas in *Mind Magic* could potentially advance basic theory in the learning sciences. There are research opportunities as well in applying the learning sciences to practical problems in the areas of general education and special education.

Organizational Psychology

Organizational psychology is the subdiscipline most directly concerned with applying psychological knowledge to problems of businesses and not-for-profit agencies. Its main concerns include adult learning and change management. Mind magic can potentially assist organizational psychologists to train workers to manage information and solve problems more creatively and effectively, thereby increasing their value to their employer. Furthermore, knowledge about the process of adaptation has direct relevance to the management of organizational change.

Education

Education and mind magic are a natural fit. The business of students is to learn and exercise their minds. A program designed to help them use their minds more effectively could help a great many students.

In the world of education, there are active programs of research with precisely this goal. A leader in this field, Harvard researcher David Perkins, characterizes their goal as being to "outsmart IQ." He means that an effective program should not only help students become more effective thinkers but also improve their scores on IQ tests.

Clinical Psychology and Mental Health

Clinical psychologists and other mental health professionals have become increasingly interested in such cognitive problems as learning difficulties, as well as affective and personality issues. The mind magic program of research should have direct relevance.

How Getting to Know Mind Magic Is Different

The six-stage process of getting to know mind magic presented here is notably different from the way in which you usually expect to learn a new skill or way of thinking. First, the process of getting to know mind magic is more naturalistic. It relies on an understanding of how people typically get to know a new set of ideas and methods rather than on traditional conceptions of course and curriculum design. It denies that you can expect to gain ownership of mind magic by taking a five-day or fifty-day course in thinking. Instead of being taught mind magic, you get to know it by using it and thinking about it.

Second, the process of getting to know mind magic is personal. It deliberately makes room for you to craft your understanding in a way that most effectively addresses your needs and learning style. Third, the process is holistic. It leads toward a broad enough conception of mind magic that you have a sense of ownership. The specific details that you master depend on your own interests and priorities.

Fourth, the six-stage process is self-referentially validating. In other words, it is consistent with the ideas and methods about how to use your mind effectively that make up the theory of mind magic. It is clearly a case of practicing what you preach.

Indeed, it is quite similar to what we have seen from other chapters to be the way people usually acquire knowledge. When discussing the role of emotions in learning (Chapter 7), we examined the role of points of interest and building connections between new ideas and familiar ones. In analyzing information management (Chapter 5), we probed the difference between borrowing an idea and owning it. While looking at adaptation (Chapter 3), we explored the emergence of new structures and perspectives that serve to guide a person's thinking. All of these processes potentially play a role in coming to know and understand mind magic.

In a number of other places, we considered Piaget's discovery that success typically comes before understanding. In the case of mind magic, this means that you cannot expect to thoroughly understand the theory until you have had quite a bit of practice trying it out.

Professional academics often ask if a model such as the six-stage process described here is prescriptive or merely descriptive. What do they mean? If it is prescriptive, then it tells you how you ought to learn. On the other hand, if it is descriptive, it tells you how people in practice do get to know mind magic regardless of whether it is the right way or not.

But ask yourself one question: is this distinction important? The six-stage model presents a process through which a typical reader might get to know mind magic. It is a description of what works. Beyond that, what else matters?

The Next Level: Mind Magic and the Challenge of the Future

The purpose of this book has been to introduce the concepts of mind magic and mind consciousness and to help you, the reader, enter into the world of methods and ideas that they represent. Once you feel that you understand mind magic and are comfortable using it, the question often arises of what comes next.

The answer in turn depends on two related questions. First, does it matter how effectively you use your mind? And second, if so, why? It surely matters to you how skillfully and effectively you use your mind. It may also matter to people who work with you directly, such as your teachers, students, customers, and employers. But should it matter to the rest of us? Why should everybody else care?

Throughout this book, we have seen examples of people who do not use their minds effectively and the consequences they have suffered. Some have been serious. Remember the people who suffer from learned incompetence, the inability to perform essential skills as a result of damaging experiences. Recall the increasing incidence of depression and other syndromes that reflect a lack of hope. Also reconsider the large numbers of students diagnosed as learning disabled. Think about future shock.

Other consequences of people not using their minds effectively are less dramatic but nevertheless frustrating and harmful to the victims. They include people overwhelmed by information overload, people unable to find solutions to potentially solvable problems, people unable to gain mastery over a new domain of knowledge, and people who feel that they lack the creativity and imagination to pursue an original idea or create an original work.

All of these people have a contribution to the world that they have not been able to make. Are you one of these people? The consequences are not just personal. If you fail to make some genuine contribution, not only do you suffer but other people who might potentially benefit from it also suffer.

Remember the numbers of people who believe that their future and that of their children will be more bleak and less rewarding than in the past. Perhaps you are one of these people, too. Why do people feel this way? Declining real wages, high unemployment, and evidence of increasing global dangers can certainly undermine people's confidence in the future. But these reasons are not the whole story. There is also the side that mind magic represents.

Using our minds in the old ways may have been good enough in the past. But as the challenges we face become more and more difficult, the old ways become less and less effective. Tougher problems require that we use our minds in better ways.

More and more people suffer from a private sense of powerlessness, the feeling that they can do nothing that will make a difference. On the other hand, the magic of mind magic is that it shows you how you can do more than you ever realized you could.

Mind magic is potentially a source of power and hope. But it will not fulfill this potential until people find constructive ways to use it. When you act positively, you are acting privately but positively in the direction of making things better rather than giving in to depression and despair.

A culture of hope can replace the culture of hopelessness only when more people once again begin to assume responsibility for building a better future. Do you have the psychological and material resources to do this? You do have that power if only you recognize that it is there and start putting it to use. That power is the magic of your mind. Understand it and use it well.

Piaget's greatest contribution to knowledge perhaps was the recognition of the power of normal everyday intelligence. It is a great gift. Do not squander it.

PART III

MIND MAGIC
AND CHILDREN

CHAPTER 11

GROWING MINDS: PUTTING MIND MAGIC TO WORK FOR THE FUTURE

Parents often wonder what they can do to help their children prepare for the future. How will today's children cope with life in the future when change exceeds its already seemingly breakneck pace?

While today's children will face a world that is quite different, the fact remains that children almost always adapt to change more easily and more quickly than anyone else does. Whereas we adults may struggle with information technology, most kids take to the computer easily and naturally. They have never known a world without computers, so having computers everywhere seems perfectly normal.

The situation of parents in the world of information technology is in many ways like that of earlier generations who came as immigrants to a new land. The language and customs of the new world are foreign. But look at their kids. They are speaking the language fluently and have no trouble adapting to new customs. Immigrants to America burdened by a thick accent had children who spoke English as easily as any native speaker. The new citizens of cyberspace are having a similar kind of experience today. Adults may need the computer equivalent of classes in English as a Second Language, but most kids do not. They pick up computer culture just by living in the middle of it.

Can Parents Foster Mind Magic?

Parents are continually seeking ways they can help their children increase their intelligence. The Swiss psychologist Jean Piaget, generally regarded as the twentieth century's leading authority on children's thinking, heard this kind of question so often, especially in the United States, that he called it "the American question." The basic answer to most parents is that they should just keep doing what they have done all along. Most of the time, their own instincts provide a more effective guide than listening to the experts.

The essential fact is that most parents usually know what their children need. Although there are many theories of how parents know this, no definitive answers exist. But look at children who grow up in a well-functioning family. You will find that caring, aware parents usually nurture the psychological growth of their children's minds as successfully as they nourish their physical growth.

Note that we are talking about ordinary healthy families, not perfect ones. What does this mean? A healthy family is one in which parents fulfill the responsibility of caring for children and children are given responsibilities consistent with their level of maturity. Parents are neither neglectful nor overly controlling. Rules are applied with reasonable consistency. Children do not have to fear psychological, physical, or sexual abuse. No family member suffers from a psychiatric or behavioral disorder serious enough to interfere with fulfilling his or her responsibilities in the family.

One could surely imagine a richer family environment more proactive in supporting the development of children's talents. Such a family might frequently purchase (or borrow from the library) children's books, make regular visits to museums and other educational community resources, make available a wide selection of software and Internet websites, and take their children on trips to interesting places. But intelligence develops normally without any special enrichment as long as the family remains functional. When does intelligence fail to develop properly? The usual reason is almost always either a congenital anomaly that interferes with the development of intelligence (such as Down syndrome) or some serious environmental stress (such as an abusive or neglectful parent). Lack of special enrichment is almost never an issue.

Does this mean that parents have absolutely no reason to worry that their children's intelligence might fail to develop normally? Not exactly.

Psychiatrists point out, for example, that neglect of the emotional relationship with a child, especially at an early age, can harm the development
of intelligence later on. Now as always, parents need to pay attention to
the basics. They need to meet their children's fundamental needs, both
emotional and physical. The important thing, though, is to make sure
that nothing is going wrong. Parents can provide a little help beyond that;
but in any case, they have already taken care of what matters the most.

It is more important to make sure that nothing goes wrong than to
actively intervene to make sure that things go right. In almost all
respects, children's intelligence will usually develop as fully as is possible, as long as nothing gets in the way of its normal development.

The principle of following your own instincts applies to most questions related to the care of children. Will children grow up to be more
intelligent if their parents are actively interventionist or more laissez-
faire? Any simple answer almost certainly is wrong. It depends on the
child and it depends on the circumstances. Sometimes parents need to
intervene more and sometimes they need to back off. As long as children have interests that they are actively pursuing, it is usually better to
provide helpful material, such as library cards, museum visits, and Internet access, and then give assistance only when requested. (Even when a
child asks for help, it is often a good idea to give only the minimum
amount of help that the child really needs.) More active intervention is
usually necessary with children who seem frustrated or bored. In general there is no better answer than to follow common sense.

There are many things you can do to prepare your child for the
future, but these things also depend on your child's interests and may
vary over time. Buying educational software may help a child who shows
a special interest in technology, but it might not help a child who shows
little interest in the subject. The same principle holds for other parental
practices, such as sending your child to a special kind of school or being
more permissive (or more strict). How you should behave depends on
what your individual child needs at that moment. A child who seems
bored much of the time probably needs greater stimulation; on the
other hand, a hyperactive child probably needs an environment that is
more orderly and predictable. You should not eliminate any of these

options out of hand, but neither should you believe that any of them can guarantee future success. Your own good judgment usually provides the surest guide to what your children need the most.

This is not to say that there is absolutely nothing special that parents can do to help their children in being able to succeed. There are some things. You will see a few of them later in this chapter. But the amount of additional good that they will do is small compared to the enormous good that comes from what parents ordinarily do every day.

What can you do if you feel that your family is not functioning well? The psychologist David Elkind has written a series of helpful books that address the problems of children who grow up in families under stress. Many parents would find his book *The Hurried Child* especially useful. Most serious problems may require the assistance of a family therapist. Your family doctor should be able to get you a referral. You can also find an experienced family therapist by contacting the American Association for Marriage and Family Therapy at aamft.org.

Natural Intelligence: The Magic of Children's Minds in a Well-Functioning Family

The term *natural intelligence* refers to the collections of skills and abilities that children naturally develop without any special enrichment or encouragement apart from normal love and attention. It provides the foundation upon which subsequent learning rests. This includes the development of mind magic through methods such as the ones described in earlier chapters of this book.

Psychologists who specialize in child development are continually dazzled by the complexity of abilities that children develop growing up in a well-functioning family. You see this in all societies, among rich and poor as well as female and male, in all ethnic groups and in all social classes, with parents who are educated or uneducated. There usually is almost nothing a child psychologist can say to parents that will be more helpful than advising them to follow their own natural instincts.

Is this surprising consistency and uniformity the result of biological maturation or some complex interaction between biology and experience? Intellectuals discuss this issue mainly for theoretical rather than practical reasons. We know for certain only that the intelligence develops inevitably and spontaneously as long as children receive enough physical and emotional nurturance. This is as fundamental as the fact that all healthy children will learn to walk or learn to understand language. Somehow parents just seem to know how to do the right thing.

Take an example of the way in which ordinary family circumstances allow intelligence to develop naturally—the fact that most children pass through the same recognizable stages. These stages of development are always the same and always happen in the same order. Babies in our society have to wrestle with the same problems of perceiving the world accurately and being able to handle objects as do babies in every other society. Slightly older children who are learning to speak and to play with their imagination as well are in the same situation as are children in other parts of the world. Children here who are old enough to begin school are similar in most respects to children in other societies when they begin mastering elements of their culture's established fund of knowledge.

You see certain processes in the development of intelligence only at particular ages or during particular periods. A good example is the development of imagination. The ability to imagine something other than the here and now is necessary even for an act as basic as using a word to stand for a thing. As you would expect, imagination begins to develop even before children first start using language. On the other hand, it requires intellectual sophistication and emotional maturity to appreciate that other people often see things quite differently from the way you do. You should therefore not be surprised to learn that this ability usually develops slowly until adolescence and even adulthood.

Other developmental processes happen over and over again but on different levels. As an example, think about how children gain a sense of control over their environment. If you watch the way babies try out all kinds of ways of grasping and holding objects, you can see them become increasingly flexible in how they handle things and are more and more able to use them in a purposeful way. They are gaining a greater sense of control. Now think about the way children around the age of seven or eight become interested in some element of the physical world: the planets, dinosaurs, insects, computers, or some other aspect of nature. They, too, are gaining an increased sense of control over the world. But in their case, the sense of control comes from scientific knowledge rather than from physical dexterity.

As another example, look at how children create a personal sense of what the world around them is like. You see this happening on different levels at different stages of life. Children are relatively young when they establish a reasonably firm image of what the physical world is like. But they first gain a clear image of the social world in middle childhood. And you usually have to wait until adolescence for them to look beyond the intimate scale of their immediate experience to the large scale of society as a whole.

Before embarking on any deliberate program to teach mind magic, parents need to appreciate just how successful they already are in nurturing the development of intelligence. By trying to fix what is not broken, they can easily run the risk of doing more harm than good.

When parents do go wrong, most errors involve features of their children's world that are significantly different from what the parents themselves had to face growing up. For example, immigrant parents sometimes fail to read to their children because books and reading were not essential for success in the old country. The same may be true of nonimmigrant parents who grew up in a geographically or culturally isolated community. Parents who grew up without computers often fail to make adequate technology available to their children even though computer literacy has become a basic academic requirement. Parents may also go wrong because of their own fears and inexperience. Parents who disliked a subject, such as mathematics, when they were young often pass this fear along to their own children. Paradoxically, teaching methods for many subjects have changed fundamentally over the last generation. Mathematics is a prime example. So these same parents might have enjoyed mathematics if they were going to school today.

Even parents who make certain mistakes are nevertheless in other respects doing exactly the right thing. It may be true that natural intelligence does not encompass all aspects of mind magic. But it does cover a great deal. Parents need to recognize how much they normally do right before they even think of doing things differently. That means knowing at least something about the many aspects of intelligence that usually develop without any special intervention.

Five Components of Natural Intelligence

Here are five components of children's intelligence, as it normally develops, that parents should understand.

Component 1: The Ability to Learn

Why is it that parents are such effective teachers even when they are not deliberately trying to teach and often so much less so when they are consciously trying to help their child? Watch even babies in the process of learning something new and you will see why. Children learn by following an agenda of their own, one that only sometimes matches their parents' agenda for them. Furthermore, the younger the child, the less he or she will respond to another person's educational agenda.

Some people mistakenly think that children's learning is trial and error. As Piaget first discovered, the truth is quite the opposite. Watch babies playing. You see that they are continually introducing more and more variations into familiar action patterns, to make them fit new circumstances, and bring them together, to build more complex patterns of behavior. This pattern of variation and integration is teaching the child new ways of acting on the world. During the first weeks and months of life, this kind of "playing" is the way in which babies learn.

Something that you see at almost every age, from the first days and weeks of life, is that children are continually reorganizing their action patterns and thought patterns in a way that makes their behavior more purposeful. At first babies will do things such as wave their arms or open and close their fingers, even when there is nothing for their arms to reach or their hands to hold. In the same way, small children will babble aloud, even when there is nobody to hear what they are saying.

But what starts out being random becomes more purposeful with time. For example, babies quickly learn to move their hands toward objects that they wish to hold rather than just for the purpose of exercise. Similarly, two-year-olds learn to make the sounds and then adopt the grammar that has meaning to people who speak what will become their native language, in place of random babble.

Babies' behavior also becomes more flexible as well as more purposeful. Consider again how they learn to grasp and hold objects. Babies start out with just one grip; they hold every object in the same way. They try to hold a balloon as big as their head in the same way as they grasp the handle of a rattle that fits comfortably into their fist. But watch how quickly they learn to vary the way they hold objects. Within a few weeks, they have acquired enormous flexibility in how they pick up objects. They grasp and hold objects in many different ways, depending on the object's weight, size, and shape.

Piaget often compared educating a child's mind to nourishing the body. As with the body, you need to provide the child's mind with a rich diet of healthy nutrients. But after that, most children can acquire almost everything that they need to know on their own. You do not need to micromanage the learning process.

Component 2: Imagination

Why do most parents fail to appreciate how much they are naturally doing right in how they handle their children? One of the main reasons is that they take for granted many of their children's most remarkable achievements. As a result, they do not see just how much they themselves are contributing to what are genuinely amazing accomplishments.

Consider the development of imagination as a case in point. Almost everyone realizes that children are naturally imaginative; as most adults know, one of the most effective ways to relate to children is to appeal to their imagination through pictures and stories. Nobody ever teaches children deliberately to have an imagination, but somehow they learn to be imaginative anyway. Is there something very right that parents do perhaps unconsciously that helps young children to acquire an imagination?

No other creature on earth is endowed with the power of imagination that human beings possess. Once a child's imagination has taken hold, it opens up a universe of ideas. Imagination is what lets children see a doll as a representation of a person rather than as just an assemblage of plastic and brightly colored materials. It is also what lets them see a toy truck as a child-size version of the trucks on the street and not just a piece of metal on wheels. Imagination is what gives you the ability to think abstractly and to talk about what you know. On a grander scale, it is what allows you to produce works of art and to make scientific discoveries. People need imagination even to be able to dream!

But imagination develops slowly. Do infants have imagination? It is hard to say. Babies as young as six to eight months usually show at least some memory of people. For example, babies notice and often become acutely disturbed when their mother has disappeared. In the same way, they notice it when you take away a toy. Piaget argued that babies younger than six months do not react to the absence of a familiar person (such as their mother) or the loss of a familiar toy because they do not remember or imagine a person or an object when she (or it) is no longer present. Around six to eight months, babies no longer remain passive when somebody important or some favorite object goes away. Six-month-olds do not have the rich imagination of a kindergartner. But, their reaction to absence hints at the beginning of what will develop later on.

A significant milestone occurs at the point when babies first acquire the ability to have something in mind that may be different from what they can actually see or hear. Soon after this, the growth of imagination takes off. Parents may start to notice that their children do not just respond to what is happening around them but might also begin talking about people and events of their own invention. Within a few years, evidence of children's powerful imagination is visible in their drawings, in their use of toys, in role-playing with other children, and in stories and fantasies that they make up.

Component 3: The Ability to Find Order in Experience

Imagination frees the mind from the here and now. At the same time that imagination is developing, children are also acquiring the ability to immerse themselves more fully in their immediate experience. Children are like scientists in the sense that they are skillful at perceiving order and organization in the world that they encounter. Does their understanding of the world come from the culture around them? Without minimizing the influence of language, media, and the immediate family, it is clear that children gain their sense of reality to a large extent through their own activity.

According to the nineteenth-century American psychologist William James, infants experience the world as a "blooming, buzzing confusion." Today we know better. From the first weeks of life, babies are discovering order in their experience. According to Piaget, babies are born not knowing even about the solidity and permanence of things and people. Nevertheless, they quickly become engaged in finding these and other features of the world around them. It takes until almost eighteen months of age before they know for sure that the world is made of many stable permanent objects, things that continue to exist even when they cannot be seen. Slightly older children become aware of aspects of reality that go beyond the here and now, for example, foreign countries, distant stars, or events that happened long ago such as during the time of Julius Caesar or the ice age. They may become interested in fantasy creatures, in aliens, or in religious figures. They may want to know more about the bottom of the ocean or places above the clouds.

Questions about the nature of reality, especially society, become most pressing during adolescence. How do things really work? Who has real power in society? Which people can you trust and who is untrustworthy? Even if these questions may seem abstract and distant to most older people, many teenagers experience them as personal and urgent.

Your sense of reality includes as well an idea of where things are going. This question may never seem more important than as an adolescent. The future for a fifteen-year-old extends much further than for a fifty-year-old because fifteen-year-olds can expect to live for many more years. It follows that their idea of where things are going must also be very different.

Parents, especially of teenagers, are often troubled when their children see the world in a way markedly different from their own. They sometimes wonder if their kids are really facing reality. Although some adolescents do not really face reality, many others perceive it at least as accurately as their parents do. Creating your own worldview as a teenager can serve as a precursor to becoming a more adaptable, independent, and creative thinker as an adult.

Component 4: Abstract Thinking

The case in favor of ordinary parental practices becomes even stronger if you look at how children develop the capacity to think abstractly.

How is abstract thinking different from imagination? Imagination, in essence, is the ability to think about the specific rather than the general. It deals with particular people, things, and events rather than about abstract ideas and universal truths. On the other hand, formal, or abstract, thinking is the ability to think in terms of the general rather than the specific. It is the capacity to think not just about particular people, events, and things but also about concepts, statements, propositions, theories, classes, and relations.

Some people argue that the development of imagination is caused entirely by biological factors; and it is true that genetic inheritance may have something to do with it. On the other hand, in the case of how abstract thinking develops, it is beyond question that parents can have a profound influence. Children can indeed learn to think abstractly from their parents, even if their parents are not consciously trying to teach them.

How can we be so certain of this? Compare children who grow up in a middle-class family with children from a society as different as possible from our own. You may choose a hunter-gatherer society or some other society in which there is little formal science. Unless they suffer from some kind of developmental disability, children from middle-class families by the age of eleven or twelve invariably show signs of being able to think abstractly. But children who lack the cultural background that we take for granted cannot do this, even as adults. Although probably every child you know will quickly learn to think abstractly, it is clear that this ability is not just the result of biological maturation. Abstract thinking is something children must learn.

The ability to think abstractly is an ability akin to speaking your own native language. Parents do not intentionally teach their children to speak, but children learn it anyway. (Language-conscious parents sometimes correct certain specific grammatical errors such as failure to use irregular plurals and past-tense forms. Children expand their vocabularies in part by hearing the words that their parents use. And parents often correct their children for impolite language. This teaching, however, represents only a small part of what children know about their native language, and it only happens after children have already mastered virtually all the basics on their own.) The same is true in the case of abstract thinking. Parents help their children by serving as models of adult thinkers, such as when they allow their children to see them in adult conversation. Parents also help their children by speaking to them as adults and by responding in an adult way to what they say.

Abstract thinking is part and parcel of the ability to learn from books, to program computers, and to do science and mathematics. It is the kind of thinking that most people in our society usually consider to be most characteristically "adult."

Component 5: Understanding Other People's Point of View

Parents' role as models for their children goes well beyond learning language and abstract thinking. Most significantly of all, they serve as models of how to deal with other people in a social context. So the unconscious teaching that parents impart to their children is especially important in the development of social intelligence.

One of the very real ways in which mind magic grows in children is in their expanding capacity to appreciate the existence of legitimate differences of opinion and perspective. As children get older, they come to appreciate that different people may perceive the same facts in entirely or subtly different ways and that doesn't necessarily mean they are wrong.

Listen to four- and five-year-olds who appear to be talking to each other. They may know the correct social form about how to engage in conversation, such as how to take turns and to face the person who is speaking. But if you listen closely to what each child is saying, it seems as if each one is engaged in his or her own private monologue. Each child is only slightly aware of the content of what the other child is saying.

You should not see children's absorption in their own point of view as a problem that you need to correct. On the contrary, it is an essential stage in the development of social intelligence. Children need to develop a firm sense of how they see things before they can appreciate other people's viewpoints.

It is normal for little children to live in a private world of their own. They do not differentiate between the world as they themselves know it and the world as it is seen by others. Most four-year-olds think that other people share their own perceptions even to the extent of believing that other people can see what they are dreaming. It takes children a long time even to learn how things look different from different physical perspectives let alone different social perspectives.

Ask a few four-year-olds how a collection of toy blocks would look from the perspective of someone sitting on the other side of a table. If you think that they may have a problem finding the correct language to describe the other person's viewpoint, then let them choose from a set of picture cards. One of the picture cards should accurately show what the other person sees. When asked to choose the correct card, almost all children of that age will select instead the picture that best represents what they themselves see. They do not yet have the idea that another person, with a different perspective, will see things differently. By the age of nine or ten, children will no longer make this error.

Awareness of differing perspectives in people's perception of social reality develops even more slowly. And once someone has this concept, he or she may still not recognize that different perspectives can be useful and legitimate. Even when they are old enough to enter college, most students remain confident a majority of the time that their own point of view is the only correct one, at least on important issues. And they feel able to dismiss alternatives out of hand. Only much later do most people begin to see their own viewpoint as just one among a number of perspectives that an intelligent person may legitimately choose.

Is There Any Way to Help Kids Increase Their Mind Magic?

So, do the facts of natural development imply that anything you do would be a waste of time? As you see, just following their instincts, parents normally raise children who have most of the components of mind magic that they will need in order to adapt to adult life, even in the information age. They have the skill in handling abstract ideas necessary for dealing with high technology. They have also the ability to modify existing knowledge so that it will fit new circumstances. But their capacity goes well beyond being able to master technical domains. They additionally have the capacity to understand differences between their own viewpoint and that of other people, so essential for citizenship in the global village. Finally, they have a well-developed imagination and have gone a long way toward developing their own vision of what the world around them is like.

So what can you do to help, beyond providing your children with a nurturing and loving home?

Natural development provides children with the raw material for becoming intelligent, thinking adults, but it does not fashion this raw material into a finished work. They have to do this for themselves. Natural development gives them means but not ends. And here is where you as parents can help them. To manage their natural intelligence in a productive way, children need a strong sense of purpose, combined with a clear conception of who they are and the ability to adopt a critical stance, when necessary, toward the world around them.

If they had grown up in an earlier time, they would have had the same natural abilities; but the society around them, almost certainly, would have decided how to put these abilities to use. In the world of the future, children will have the opportunity, and the responsibility, to become their own person. They will be able to use their intelligence to do what they think is best rather than what somebody else tells them to do. But natural development on its own does not give them the ability to make intelligent choices for setting their own direction. They will have to gain this kind of mind magic for themselves.

Three Components of Mind Magic That Kids Learn

The family can be helpful at the point where nature leaves off. Natural development does not usually teach people how to be intelligently crit-

ical, how to maintain a distinctive identity, or how to subordinate creativity to conscious purpose. You can help your children by encouraging these attributes.

Component 1: Learning to Question Assumptions

Kids growing up today will have to get used to questioning the assumptions that lie behind people's actions. In the computer age, things are
continually happening that most people neither expected nor even considered possible. If parents want to help prepare their children for the
future, they will have to prepare them for countless surprises. Not only
are the details of life constantly changing, but so are the rules. To keep
up, today's kids will have to be able to question not only their parents'
and their teachers' but also their own assumptions. There is no other
way for them to recognize when the old rules have disappeared and
something new has replaced them.

Many members of their parents' generation learned this lesson the
hard way during the 1990s. As wave after wave of downsizing jolted corporate America, suddenly millions of people, many of them highly
skilled, were forced to question one of their most cherished assumptions: that their skills and experience would guarantee them a job for
life. Having your job threatened is traumatic enough. This time, however, compounding the fear of losing their jobs was the worry that their
hard-earned skills and experience seemed no longer to be of any value
in the rapidly declining and competitive workforce. For many people,
the experience of downsizing flatly contradicted a fact of life that they
felt everybody considered certain. They had grown up with the assumption that having a university degree and being well trained would guarantee a job for life. Suddenly, this assumption was put in question.

Today's children can expect to learn often that the world does not
work the way they assumed. Sometimes, like workers faced with downsizing, they may find that it is harsher than they expected. Other times,
they will find that it is a nicer place than they had dreamed. But all big
surprises, good ones as well as bad, force people to adjust their worldview. For this reason, they will enjoy a significant advantage if they learn
the habit of questioning assumptions while they are still young.

The information age presents people with an enormous number and variety of seemingly impossible things. Most people thirty years ago thought that robots could exist only in science fiction; today they are found on assembly lines everywhere. The idea of a global village once seemed like the idle speculation of a crazy academic; today it is a fact of life because of the Internet. Scholars used to write learned tomes about the impossibility of computers playing expert chess; today computers can beat even the chess champion of the world.

At one time a quality education would provide children with knowledge that they could keep for life. Today that is much less true. Students have to become able to adjust their thinking as circumstances change. When necessary they need to be able to go beyond what it says in the books. The essence of the intelligent student is the capacity to listen and learn from authors and instructors, when what they are saying is helpful, without losing his or her own distinctive outlook.

What can you do to help kids learn to question assumptions? Try the following:

- Be supportive, not punitive, when kids could learn from their own mistakes. Piaget often made the point that mistakes are a natural part of learning. Having the chance to think about their mistakes and to consider alternatives, without feeling guilty or stupid, may be the best training in questioning assumptions.
- Explicitly model self-correction in your own behavior. Let children sometimes see you think critically about yourself when you may have made a mistake.
- Be prepared to question assumptions in discussing public issues from the news and private issues that come up in the family (without making the experience overly didactic).

Component 2: Learning to Remain One's Own Person

Alongside their desire for their children to succeed in the larger society, most parents feel strongly about their children having a clear conception of right and wrong. Parents hope as well that their children will carry with them, through life, the values and traditions that they learn when they are young. There is no reason, in principle, why personal values and occupational success should not go together hand in hand, but parents cannot expect children to know innately how to keep the two in balance. A rapidly changing society is also a society governed by fad and fashion. Parents have to teach their children to be able to resist the latest trend, on occasion, when it comes in conflict with values that they hold dear.

Entering a new school is one experience of earlier life that can help prepare kids for social change in the adult world. How are the two similar? In both cases, children face the same challenge of trying to reestablish a niche for themselves among a new group of people. If the family moves to a new neighborhood, kids have to learn to get along with a different set of peers. Even when they live in the same home for many years, a transition such as going from elementary school to high school forces them to deal with a different social environment.

The experience usually goes well beyond merely inventing a new public mask, or persona. It can even change them as people. Getting along with a new group of peers forces children and teenagers to come to terms with how the group's social norms relate to standards of their own. This confrontation of values can be a positive and broadening experience, but it can also be negative, especially if group norms conflict with significant principles learned at home.

Going to a new school is not the only opportunity for parents to teach children how to negotiate social change. Another is summer vacation, a time when children often meet children different from the ones they know at school. After-school and weekend programs provide similar opportunities. What children encounter when they enter into a new social group can serve as a model of how to cope with societal change later in life. Here are some ways that parents can help:

- Be clear to your children about what you believe yourself. You cannot expect them to adhere to definite values unless they can see that you do the same thing yourself.
- Tell them something about group dynamics. Your children will interact more successfully with their peer group the more they understand about how social groups work.

- Only in extreme cases should you treat conflicts between peer group and family norms as irreconcilable opposites. Expect most of the time that children will seek to find a way to synthesize or harmonize the two.

In a traditional society, people could go through life having to get along only with the same small group of people all the time. The information age poses new social challenges, of learning to get along with new communities, as well as new intellectual challenges. Success will require that today's children learn to cope with both. Natural intelligence did a good job at a time when our society was relatively stable. But the rapidly changing society of the future will demand something more. Our children will have to learn a new set of both interpersonal and intellectual skills to supplement what ordinary experience already provides for them. And this new skill set will have to include an enhanced ability to respond to change. They will use these new skills to deal successfully with the many different kinds of people that life in this new world will introduce.

Component 3: Learning to Be Consciously Creative

The ability to question themselves will help free today's children from the assumptions of the past. Having a clear but flexible personal identity will protect them from being swept along by each new trend. But to contribute something new, they will also need the ability to subordinate their imagination to conscious purpose.

As computers take over more and more routine work, creativity will emerge as among the most valuable resources for success in the information society. You may find it liberating that people will have greater freedom to put creative ideas into practice. On the other hand, you may find this thought intimidating. Do you know children who do not seem to have been born creative? Are you worried about them? You do not have to be. Creativity is also an aspect of mind magic that kids learn. It is a skill that they can deliberately acquire.

Just as our society has promoted the myth of the inspired genius, it also has popularized the myth of the naturally creative child. Do not be taken in by this legend. Creativity is a learned skill; it comes naturally to almost no one. Even the most famous artists and scientists had to learn to produce creative work.

Virtually all children are naturally imaginative but not naturally creative. Their imaginativeness can impress adults and cause delight. As an adult, you may know well the kind of startling ideas that you sometimes hear from children. But to produce genuinely creative work, children need more than just imagination and talent. They also require a sense of quality, the ability to recognize what makes a piece of work outstanding, so that they can consciously pursue excellence. People almost never have this sense until they have carefully studied the best work from the past, learned from it, and then gone ahead to do something distinctive of their own.

Suppose that you know a child who has some talent in drawing and painting and wants to be an artist. This kind of talent cannot develop in a vacuum. The best advice is for that child to practice drawing and painting and also to become familiar with works that have a reputation for being the best. Aspiring artists need to be familiar with great works even if they end up despising them. Why? Perhaps a budding artist will agree that a particular work is outstanding, at least in some way, and choose therefore to emulate it in part. And if the artist sees nothing good in the work, it will have at least negative value. The artist will be able to define what she considers good by way of opposition to what she dislikes. Today's creators are generally among the best critics of yesterday's masters. If students want to become creative, they need to identify the weaknesses, perhaps even more than the strengths, of famous works.

What is true in the arts is just as true in other domains. Do you know teenagers who want to invent a better computer game? Almost certainly, they will have to know virtually everything about the ones already on the market. A body of norms and standards exists as much in the world of computer games as in the world of fine art. To become a successful inventor of computer games, you have to come to terms with the computer game establishment and then go beyond what established game developers could have invented themselves.

Does this mean you should be encouraging adolescents to be more critical and judgmental? If you want to help them to become creative, then the answer absolutely is "yes." Adults are wrong if they think that most teenagers complain too much already. Youths need to actively question the status quo. Seeing what is wrong with the world of today serves as a catalyst for an imaginative child. It is the only way to become a genuinely creative adult of tomorrow.

Constructive responses to an assertive adolescent include the following:

• Within the family, distinguish between firm rules that have to be accepted and flexible policies that can be criticized and discussed.
• When you cannot be certain, assume that criticism is serious and not just ventilating.
• Distinguish between constructive and destructive criticism. A sense of a better way of acting or thinking stands behind constructive criticism. Destructive criticism is just an outlet for rage.
• Make the criticism itself a subject of thought. Expect the critic to handle likely responses to his or her criticism. Raise the question perhaps of how the people being criticized see the action in question and how they would likely reply. Consider alternative courses of action and the pros and cons of each alternative.

Learning to Learn as a Way of Life

A generation ago, there was a sharp division of labor between childhood and adulthood. Learning was the business of children, and working was the business of adults. But in the information age, a strict separation between learning and working is no longer tenable. People can no longer learn everything as children that they need to know as adults because science, technology, and society are changing much too quickly. As knowledge grows, people's minds must grow as well.

Natural development gives kids the basics. By the time they reach adulthood, they will have acquired a rich collection of intellectual resources. But without further help, they can easily begin to stagnate. You cannot reduce learning mind magic to acquiring a narrow set of problem-solving skills. Learning mind magic means learning to take control over life as a whole. Among other things, increasing the magic of one's mind means learning to take control at the point where natural development leaves off.

Before the computer revolution, increasing the magic of one's mind may not have been a necessity. Children could go on to live a happy and successful life, relying on the wisdom that their elders had taught them in their youth. But those days are over. More than anything else, helping children to develop mind magic means helping them to learn this lesson: that learning has to become a way of life.

How can you help? Here are a few ways:

- Make learning a way of life in your family. Include activities such as reading, travel, using libraries and the Internet, and visits to museums, cultural events, and historic sites.
- Be open to change in the home. Try out new foods, new recipes, new gadgets, new styles, and new ideas.
- When they have to choose academic courses, recommend that they include a few, such as mathematics and philosophy, that can help them become more effective thinkers and problem solvers over the long run.
- Suggest mind magic. Lifelong learning is essentially what mind magic teaches. Introducing ideas in this book can help your children as well in learning to use their minds more effectively.

Learning is as essential for mental fitness as exercise is for physical fitness. Kids need to grow up with the recognition that they will always have to be learning. If they fully understand this fact, then the magic of their minds will never cease to grow.

CHAPTER 12

TEACHING MIND MAGIC IN SCHOOL

Thinkers, such as Peter Drucker and Alvin Toffler, have repeatedly made the point that the information age has changed the nature of power. At one time you were powerful only if you had either physical might or great wealth. Today the mind has become a third source of power. This power comes from knowledge, information, and, most important of all, intelligence.

This new source of power, mind power, raises new opportunities for us, as a society, while it also poses new challenges. The academic system is the main social institution entrusted with the care and development of the mind. How will the information revolution affect it? Schools have the power to exercise enormous influence over the development of a child's intelligence. Their influence can be for good or for ill. The best teachers, when working under the best conditions, can empower their students to acquire the habit of seeking out knowledge actively and independently. On the other hand, poor teaching can have exactly the opposite effect. It can leave students feeling utterly dependent on other people for information.

What sides of intelligence are schools best suited to teach? In a normal environment, most aspects of intelligence develop rapidly on their own throughout childhood and adolescence. Schools can play the important role of filling in gaps that often arise in the course of development. Take the example of creativity. Students may naturally have the ability to think creatively. Nevertheless, they rarely know how to manage this ability in a purposeful way. This is something that schools can teach them.

Another example is the habit of thinking critically. The instinct to examine assumptions critically plays a role in many different domains of intelligence. You use it to solve problems, to adapt to changing circumstance, and to think creatively, just to name a few. Nevertheless, critical thinking comes naturally only to a minority of students. It is therefore a kind of mind magic that schools can teach.

Should schools offer new kinds of courses or adopt new kinds of methods in response to the demands for increasing mind power? According to some psychologists, such as David Perkins of the Harvard Graduate School of Education, the time has come when we should be making intelligence itself a school subject. They have therefore developed special courses for teaching intelligence. Their response to the challenge of the information age is highly theoretical. Students do learn a number of problem-solving methods from these courses. Nevertheless, their knowledge remains abstract and difficult to integrate into everyday life.

A better solution, perhaps, is to try to teach every class in a way coherent with the acquisition of mind magic. Instead of offering a whole new class in intelligence, we might modify our teaching methods so that students' mind magic is increasing all the time. Thus it becomes second nature for them to actively and creatively approach new problems and new knowledge domains.

A New Entry into the World of Abstract Thought

What is the secret for making schools "mind magic–friendly"? As with most problems in education, there is no simple recipe. The solutions instead come one by one as educators and researchers try to develop better methods for each subject one at a time. By now, however, mind magic–friendly methods are numerous. It is today realistic to think of opening an academy for mind magic. Each course in such a school would contribute in some way to the development of intelligence.

How might the courses in a school for intelligence be different from those in another school? The Logo Project at MIT provides just a glimpse of what can be possible. Logo is the name of a computer-programming language; along with BASIC, by 1985 it became the programming language most widely used in education. Why was Logo created? Significantly, the Logo Project team was concerned primarily with the development of intelligence.

Team members were primarily mathematicians and mathematics educators. As a group, they were deeply troubled about the state of mathematics education. The main reason for mathematics in school, supposedly, is to teach formal abstract thinking. Learning math should help to develop the mind. Nevertheless, as Logo team members saw it, most mathematics instruction did not do this. On the contrary, it served to deaden students' minds. It forced them to memorize arithmetic tables and to perform trivial calculations. At the same time, it gave students no exposure at all to the truly stimulating parts of mathematics.

Why was mathematics instruction not achieving its purpose? The problem, in their opinion, was arithmetic. Arithmetic was the only math that most students saw. This was particularly true in elementary school. As professionals, they knew that arithmetic is probably the most boring branch of mathematics. To use it to teach math is to anesthetize the mind in the name of stimulating it.

According to MIT Professor Seymour Papert, director of the Logo Project, Logo was the very opposite of arithmetic. Teachers used Logo to introduce math even to children as young as five or six. Furthermore, Papert and his colleagues tried to make Logo stimulating. They chose content with the goal of interesting students. And they were able to make the mathematics concrete and accessible by embodying it in the form of computer programs that move and act.

Does this mean that every school should start teaching Logo instead of arithmetic? Definitely not. It is important to see Logo as a pilot project that offers an entry into the future. It freed us from the trap of seeing arithmetic as the only way to teach elementary school math. Logo works wonderfully for some children, acceptably for others, and poorly for a few. It demonstrated one way to teach mathematics and at the same time to encourage active minds.

Synergy of Knowledge and Intelligence

The example of Logo shows how acquiring knowledge and developing mind magic can naturally go together. Indeed, one may argue, the best way to learn a subject is a way that simultaneously serves to expand your mind.

To understand why, consider the example of learning a foreign language, such as French. Most schools teaching French a generation ago followed a set curriculum. That still happens in quite a number of schools. This method has never served the goal of developing mind magic—but interestingly, neither has it been particularly effective in teaching French. Even students who did well in that kind of program year after year may have ended up knowing a lot of French vocabulary and many rules of French grammar. But could they speak French when they got off the airplane in Paris? No.

This happens similarly in mathematics. The old methods may have taught many mathematical methods and rules; nevertheless, they did not teach students how to use mathematical thinking except in the classroom and the examination room. In fact, the same thing happened in every school subject. Schools may have prepared students for the examinations but not for life.

What kind of education really does prepare students for the real world? Significantly, it is the kind that also serves the goal of developing mind magic.

Keep in mind the kind of challenges that the child will face as an adult. All aspects of mind magic—problem solving, creativity, information management, independent thinking, and adaptation to change—require you to have an active mind. Usually today, and even more often in the future, computers, not people, will perform the routine tasks. Education for the future means teaching in ways that continually make active thinking the top priority.

Learners equipped with an active mind do not depend on the teacher for knowledge. Instead, they figure out most of it on their own. How does the teacher help them? First, the teacher may direct their attention to new ideas congruent with their interests. Second, the teacher may help them with questions or problems that are clearly too difficult for them to answer on their own. Third, the teacher may occasionally point out serious or recurring errors. Fourth, the teacher can help them set goals.

In the old days, most people thought of teaching in terms of transmitting knowledge and information—that is, you explain it clearly and the student is supposed to absorb it. After you have studied the subject for a long time, you know it. If you study it for a really long time, you know it so totally and thoroughly that you become an expert.

In fact, that view of learning reflects at best a small part of the process. People do most of their learning not through knowledge transmission but instead through coping with reality. Furthermore, as you continue learning, the more you become aware of all the things that you do not know.

Teaching thus has more to do with advertising knowledge than with transmitting it. The teacher makes students aware that the knowledge is there and gives them reasons to go and get it. On a day-to-day basis, teachers need to force kids to keep thinking and showing persistence, even in the midst of confusion. Partial understanding is a fact of life for adults as well as students. Over the long run, the habit of active inquiry will serve them better than almost anything else that schools might teach.

Process Before Product

There is a basic difference between school and the work world. In an adult job, your priorities almost always are in the present. On the other hand, school priorities almost always are in the future. Often that future is distant. The difference between future orientation and present orientation changes the way you evaluate performance. It matters little how accurately or correctly students perform on a particular test or assignment in the here and now. Of importance is how much they have progressed over time. What matters is learning, ahead of performance.

Furthermore, putting long-term learning ahead of short-term performance forces teachers to be far more tolerant of mistakes than an employer would normally be. When you care primarily about performance, the work may have to be letter-perfect. But when you care primarily about learning, you need to accept errors as part of the process. Finally, if you care primarily about the development of mind magic, you will welcome errors as a positive sign. They serve as evidence that the students are trying to surpass themselves.

The leading expert on the development of intelligence, Jean Piaget, made this point more lucidly than anyone else has. For more than fifty years, he studied cognitive development across many different domains. They included language, play and fantasy, representation of space and time, and abstract mathematical and scientific reasoning. In every one of these areas, he found that errors were part and parcel of learning. Without errors, mind magic does not develop.

There are good reasons why making and then overcoming errors should be so important. For one thing, you can learn a great deal about learning and problem solving through the experience of correcting your own mistakes. There is a question, however, that may be even more important to answer. How will students learn to recognize their own mistakes by themselves? In adult life, you have to be able to recognize them on your own. After all, you no longer have teachers around to point them out.

A quality education should help students learn to be self-critical without being self-punitive. They learn this ability in part through the spirit in which teachers offer criticisms of student work. They learn it as well through seeing teachers in the act of criticizing their own work and improving it in light of criticism. Thus, an acceptance of mistakes as both normal and manageable is essential if students are to develop the habit of self-criticism.

How to Make Teaching "Mind Magic–Friendly"

As Papert pointed out, you can lead children to Euclid but you cannot make them think. Teachers can never make a child's mind become magical. Nevertheless, teachers can support and encourage intelligent habits that children develop naturally.

Keep this basic fact in mind: the art of teaching is to keep students' minds active. To a large extent, teaching involves maintaining students' interest. There are, of course, some students who are really not interested in learning; to help them is a much greater challenge. For the rest, good teachers concentrate primarily on giving their students a reason to care about what they have to learn. They will keep new material coming at a rate where students continue to learn and make progress but never so fast that they feel overwhelmed.

Here is a fact that will surprise a lot of people. Learning never has to be hard. Virtually any knowledge can be accessible as long as the teacher meets four conditions. First, make sure that the students have the necessary background. Second, divide what is to be learned into manageable pieces. Third, keep students from feeling threatened or intimidated. Fourth, give them a reason for being interested. The fourth condition is by far the most important.

Certain kinds of subject matter have a mystique of being intrinsically very difficult. Many students feel that calculus or Shakespeare or physics is just too complicated. Our culture makes them feel that way—but our culture is wrong. Usually, a subject seems difficult because it is alien to most people's normal ways of thinking. It is no more complicated than familiar ideas, however. It is just different. The real problem for the student—and the real challenge to the teacher—is to overcome that difference.

Think about the language in Shakespeare. To most of us, it is hard to understand. On the other hand, it seemed completely clear to the people who saw Shakespeare's plays during the late-sixteenth century, when they first appeared. If people of Shakespeare's day heard us talking, our language would seem at least as confusing to them as Shakespeare's language seems to us. Instead of being intrinsically difficult, Shakespeare's language in reality is merely unfamiliar. Therefore, the art of teaching Shakespeare, to a large extent, is, first, to point out the difference of language that separates our two cultures and, second, to give students a reason to care about crossing that chasm.

A sign of being educated is that you have experience in and skill at becoming interested in a broad range of knowledge domains.

A master teacher can be seen as an expert tour guide in the land of knowledge. In the role of a guide, the teacher typically begins by drawing students' attention to the existence of something worth visiting, even exploring. After that the teacher gradually weans the students away. When students have seen the most famous and obvious sights or start to become bored, the teacher may point out places off the beaten path. The teacher may also warn students of laws and customs, inherent in an unfamiliar knowledge domain, that must be respected. Over the long run, the teacher's goal is to make his or her own contribution superfluous.

Seven Ways to Teach Mind Magic in the Classroom

If you are like most people, you probably have no personal experience of a synergy between education and intelligence. You may therefore feel that the idea sounds wonderful in theory but at the same time feel skeptical that it could ever work in practice. It may seem plausible to teach art or history or literature in a way that encourages active inquiry and independence of mind. But can you teach the basics, such as reading and writing, mathematics, or science, that way?

Recall how most of us as children were taught in these subjects. Most methods of the time served to constrain mind magic instead of stimulate it. We therefore have nothing in our personal experience to show us a different way. Fortunately, there are visionaries who can show us something better. A new generation of innovators has developed new methods for teaching the most basic subjects. This new work emerged in the aftermath of Piaget's pioneering research. It shows that a different way is indeed possible.

Learning Mind Magic Through Learning Phonics

Surprisingly, one of the most interesting experiments in teaching mind magic involves a quite unlikely subject, phonics. It is common to see phonics instructions as the prototype of drill and practice. Is it possible to teach phonics in a way that encourages active inquiry? According to Mike Wood, the founder of LeapFrog Enterprises, Inc., the answer is "yes."

Mike Wood and his colleagues invented a new kind of interactive book that they call a LeapPad. How does it work? Children can make the book read to them either by pressing a button to read an entire page or by moving a sensor in the shape of a pen over a word or letter. What does this have to do with phonics? The product also includes a button that toggles the system between two modes. In one mode, it reads whole words when the child touches them with the sensor. In the second mode, it reads individual phonemes corresponding to letters and letter combinations.

The beauty of the product is that it can allow very early readers to read independently. Children do most of the reading on their own. That is a major advance over other reading instruction tools. Children can also choose to hear individual phonemes and words when they need them. What does this mean to a child? Suppose that a little girl can figure out every sound in a word except one. She can use the pen to tell her the one missing sound that will allow her to sound out the entire word.

What limitations does the product have? Right now it is far more popular as an educational toy for the home than as a teaching aid for the classroom. Experience suggests that it would have greater educational value the other way around. The problem is that few children spontaneously use it to help sound out words. Instead, they let the product read entire pages or else they use it to identify whole words. But in the classroom, the teacher could direct its use to what would genuinely be most educational. When used effectively, it could significantly increase the ease and speed with which children learn to read.

Learning Mind Magic Through Learning to Write

In the stern "hickory stick" school of the nineteenth century, reading and writing were the centerpiece of classroom activity. Today it is possible to teach their favored subjects in a way no teachers of that period ever dreamed. The best new methods are effective while at the same time encouraging creativity and independent-mindedness.

The village of Atkinson, New Hampshire, is a one-hour drive north of Boston. In the late 1970s, it became the site of one of the most innovative experiments in the world of education. Professor Donald Graves of the University of New Hampshire was the program director. His guiding slogan was "let them write." From the beginning of the first grade, the teachers required every child in the local school to spend half an hour per day writing. At the end of the period, they had to spend a short time in conference with the teacher explaining what they had written.

The students in the Atkinson experiment enjoyed a great deal of freedom; nevertheless, this freedom was far from absolute. For example, it was a firm requirement that each child spend thirty minutes writing. That was not negotiable. Students were able to remain in the program only if they showed the maturity to work within this kind of limit. This type of strict requirement is characteristic of mind magic–friendly school programs. It sharply distinguishes them from the old laissez-faire free school philosophy of the 1960s.

Skeptics wondered how children as young as five or six could write anything. They had not yet learned to read. They could not spell. They knew nothing about grammar or style. They did not know that you write (in English) from left to right and from top to bottom. Many children did not even know that you have to use letters and words when you write. Furthermore, no one had ever taught them this information.

At the beginning, their writing was even more chaotic and haphazard than the most convinced skeptic might fear. They used drawings as well as letters and words. They wrote in every possible direction: bottom to top, right to left, round and round in circles, as well as the conventional ways. They used spellings that had the most tenuous connections with the standard forms. Nevertheless, their writing slowly changed. Pictures began to disappear and only letters remained. Gradually, the children began to organize the page from left to right and top to bottom. Spellings became more conventional. Sentences, punctuation, and paragraphs appeared. Within several months, the children were writing real stories with a recognizable narrative structure.

Writing is an excellent subject for seeing the synergy between mind magic and knowledge. Why? On the one hand, writing is a basic academic subject; almost everyone agrees that it is an important skill to learn. On the other hand, learning to write brings into play all three learnable components of mind magic.

First, writing teaches conscious creativity. In writing even the simplest story, children have to use their imagination in the service of a purposeful goal. In this case, the goal is to construct an understandable text. Second, writing teaches students to be critical. As they write more and more, young writers improve by evaluating the various ways of conveying their meaning. They need to become critical of technique in published writers as well as in their own work. Third, writing strengthens their sense of who they are and what they represent. In the domain of writing, their sense of identity finds expression in their emergent writer's voice.

In talking to children who have participated in this program, you see how much maturity they have gained. During a visit to the Atkinson Academy, one boy in third grade took me to the school library. He showed me two books. He had read the first one, written by a commercially published author. And he had *written* the second. As the boy explained, the parents helped to bind the students' completed stories into booklets. The booklets were available to everyone who visited the library.

The boy went on to compare his own writing with that of the published author. He told me why he liked the published book. Then he told me in what ways he thought his own story was better!

Students at the Atkinson Academy progressed far more quickly than most other students in learning what we normally consider the basics. Even more important, however, is the effect of the experience on them as people. Through struggling with their own compositions, they were acquiring the ability to learn from their mistakes while gaining self-confidence. The experience was giving them the personal resources to cope effectively in the world they will know as adults.

Learning Mind Magic Through Learning a
Foreign Language

Writing is primarily a creative skill. You need to look into yourself to find the elements of your composition. In contrast, learning a foreign language is outward looking. You need to adjust your own habits of thought to fit the patterns of the language you are learning.

Is it possible to teach a foreign language in a way that keeps students' minds active? For foreign languages, the answer is the same as for writing. If you doubt it, look at how quickly and thoroughly immigrant children in America master English. Think about children from a country such as Holland. Most Dutch children, as a matter of course, learn to speak one foreign language fluently, namely English. A large minority also become fluent in French and German. There are places in the world, such as certain parts of India, where middle-class children routinely learn five or six languages as part of growing up.

North American children have good reasons to want to learn languages. There are millions of Canadians whose first language is French and tens of millions of Americans whose native language is Spanish. If you look beyond our national borders, the global village is a community of many languages. Nevertheless, most U.S. and Canadian children never learn to speak any foreign language. Even children who receive honors grades at school in Spanish or French rarely achieve *spoken* competence. Is there some biological reason why foreign languages are so hard for them? Or do our teaching methods cause the problem?

The answer is that we need teaching methods that engage their intelligence. Children do not acquire a language through learning vocabulary and grammar rules. Nor as a rule do they learn one by reading fine literature. To learn a language, speaking it needs to become part of their lives.

You may wonder how to make Spanish or French a part of your child's life if you live in English-speaking Denver or Toronto. The best way to do this is through an immersion program in school.

Why immersion? It makes sense that American children could learn Spanish or French in the same way that immigrant children learn English. Immigrants learn English by living in the language. Surely, American children could learn Spanish by actually living in Spanish.

In Graves's method of process writing, the one rule is that children are required to spend thirty minutes every day writing. In immersion, the rule, especially during the early grades, is that children can use only the immersion language. French immersion teachers will answer students only if the students address them in French.

From the start of first grade, children in French immersion take all their classes in French, including mathematics and reading. Beginning usually in second or third grade, they will devote some part of the day to reading and writing English. Unlike other subjects, their teacher conducts that class in English. Gradually, English takes up more of their day. By seventh grade, their program is usually half and half, English and French.

Research into immersion programs shows that they are a great success. They are successful in teaching the foreign language (without measurable deficits in other subjects). Furthermore, they are successful in supporting the development of mind magic.

How does learning a foreign language affect intelligence? Abundant research makes clear that it teaches students to become more flexible in their thinking. This is because learning a new language forces you to put something in question that you have always taken for granted, the right way to speak and communicate. You suddenly have to realize that you can express the same meaning, or similar meanings, in totally different ways. Let us say you study Spanish. Then you will discover that what English-speaking people call "cat" can have a totally different name in Spanish: *el gato*.

When you learn a new language, you become sensitive to subtle facts about how we express meaning, such as the effect of word order. (In English, word order is important. In other languages, such as Russian, word order matters little. Russians add suffixes to the end of words that do most of the work accomplished by word order in English. In languages such as Japanese, word order matters—but the correct order is quite different from English word order.)

Thus, learning a new language is one of the best ways to open students' minds to the possibility that what might be familiar is not always the only possibility. Increasing students' ability to adapt by becoming more flexible will surely be a great asset in the world of the future.

Learning Mind Magic Through Learning Math

Ask yourself how you learned to read fluently. You may recall a period every day that you spent as a child in a reading class. But reading classes merely got you started. People become fluent readers only because reading enters into so many different sectors of their lives. It is hardly an exaggeration to say that you live in Reading-Land. Every time you open a magazine or a newspaper or read the label on a package, you are practicing and improving your skill.

Most adults in our society are much better at reading than at math. Is that any surprise? Since they were six or seven years old, they have spent more and more time living in Reading-Land but very little time in Math-Land. Suppose that we wanted to educate a generation of children to be fluent in math in the way that their parents are fluent in reading. Would it be possible for them to grow up living in Math-Land?

If you know any four- or five-year-olds, you know that they, like most little children, are fascinated by the mathematics in the world around them. For example, most children enjoy playing with numbers. Piaget, more than anyone else, has shown that children naturally are interested in mathematical ideas. He and other psychologists have found precursors of many of these ideas in the thinking of little children. These include major branches of mathematics, such as geometry and logic.

Can you create a route that will link the mathematics of the five-year-old with the mathematics of the university? What used to be impossible has now become a reality. According to Papert, director of the Logo Project at MIT, the computer revolution has changed everything.

The Logo Project started from an insight that was critical in enabling it to design and implement Math-Lands. This insight was to recognize that computers are simultaneously concrete and abstract. On the one hand, they are concrete objects, like other children's toys. On the other hand, they are mathematical: computer commands are essentially no different from mathematical statements, and computers respond to them with mathematical precision.

Why is this fact so crucially important? It means that you can create a Math-Land with computers. Acting concretely with a computer contains the seeds of thinking abstractly. A child can play with a computer toy, a totally concrete act, and, at the same time, do the equivalent of proving a mathematical theorem, perhaps the most abstract thinking of all.

During the 1970s, Papert and his colleagues invented a cybernetic toy called a "turtle," which responded to Logo commands. By writing computer programs, children could determine the way the turtle moved around a room. People described the Logo language itself as having "no floor and no ceiling." It is so simple that four- and five-year-olds can use it—but it is so powerful that an MIT professor once earned his tenure by inventing and analyzing Logo programs!

Many people worry that children will lose their spontaneity, their underlying creative expression, when they acquire the structure and discipline inherent in logical, mathematical reasoning. From the beginning, the Logo group was successful in sidestepping this apparent conflict. Programming in Logo by its very nature was logical and mathematical. Still, it nurtured creative expression instead of suppressing it. How did it encourage creativity? As long ago as 1974, children were using Logo primarily for making pictures. They still do that today. But they also use it for making puppets, musical instruments, moving animals, and lots of other toys. The chance to program does not prevent children from making any of these things. On the contrary, it just makes the drawings and the toys more fun.

Does Logo help students to question assumptions as well? Surprisingly, the answer is "yes." An anecdote from one of the first experiments with Logo shows how this happens.

It took place at the Lamplighter School in Dallas, Texas. For a year, a class of fifth grade students was learning Logo during the period usually reserved for mathematics. The children enjoyed Logo much more than arithmetic. Papert tells the following anecdote about a conversation between two of them. One day they started talking about why they were doing Logo instead of the other mathematics. Then they went on to wonder what Logo had to do with math at all. One child said that Logo really was math, but not all the children could see this. Finally, one boy asked in frustration, "What is mathematics anyway?"

The children started out feeling sure they knew what math was. But the experience of Logo led them to put their certainty in question.

Regardless of their ultimate answer, just asking the question in the first place was a significant sign in itself.

Learning Mind Magic Online

The Internet places a virtual world of information at the fingertips of kids as well as adults. In parallel with the explosion of websites for adults has occurred a similar growth in sites for kids.

Kids' websites, like adult websites, come in numerous styles. Some are purely entertainment sites. Others are educational. Some promote a particular viewpoint or concern, such as traffic safety or healthy eating. Others present information on a broad topic, such as space exploration or twentieth-century painting. A few are portals designed to provide entry points to a range of kid-friendly resources on the Internet.

The Internet is particularly successful in supporting independent learning because it makes research so easy. Before the Internet there were three options available for a child who wanted to investigate a particular subject or find the answer to a question. Option one was to look it up in a print encyclopedia; option two was to ask a nearby adult (or perhaps another child); option three was to go to the library. The Internet has advantages over all three. It is larger and more up to date than a print encyclopedia—in fact, many encyclopedias can now be found online that update their content as often as any other website. It includes specialized knowledge that nearby adults may not have. And an Internet search usually takes much less time than a trip to the library and is available at all hours.

A good example of what the Internet offers is the website Ask Jeeves for Kids (ajkids.com). Ask Jeeves for Kids is a prototype of a search engine for children. It allows kids to ask any question they want in ordinary English (no special symbols or computer codes required). Within a few seconds, it will give either an answer or a list of kid-friendly websites where they can look for answers themselves.

An example of a more comprehensive kids' portal is MaMaMedia (mamamedia.com). MaMaMedia was developed for children between the ages of eight and thirteen. It offers a gateway to almost everything they might want on the Internet. Users have a choice between staying on the site or treating it as an entry point to surf the rest of the Web. The site itself features a variety of activities: drawing and construction projects, interactive virtual toys, online stories, and public forums where kids can share ideas. It also tells kids about other sites that they can visit. Some of these sites were chosen by the website developers. Others were recommended by kids who use MaMaMedia.

The educational value of the Internet goes beyond the fact that it contains such a wealth of information. Website owners have the capability of updating their site's content whenever they want, as often as they want, so information on the Internet is often more timely than that found in books. Furthermore, the low cost of operating a website makes available a much broader variety of ideas and points of view (thereby making it more important than ever to evaluate the source of the information). The Internet also allows kids from distant locations to communicate with each other as a group. Even the telephone does not usually allow that.

Learning Mind Magic Through Cognitive Science

Elementary school–age children for the most part learn by doing. Therefore, you want to fill their school day with a lot of activity. At that age, mind magic develops most successfully if it can be integrated into other academic subjects and activities outside of school.

High school–age students are far more self-conscious. They also have reached an age when they are able to analyze and think abstractly. That makes them particularly well suited to study the subject of intelligence, including mind magic, as a topic in its own right. The advantage of studying mind magic directly is the same as the benefit from reading a book such as this one. Students can strengthen their minds by making use of mind magic as part of everyday activities. But by studying mind magic explicitly, they can learn how to use the power of their minds consciously and purposefully.

Adolescence is probably the best time of life to learn about how the mind naturally works. It is also probably the best time to learn about mind management.

Cognitive science can help high school students to become more articulate about their own thinking. It can thereby empower them to have greater control over their own minds. It allows them to manage their minds more purposely and effectively by helping them understand their minds more fully.

One idea that high school students might learn as part of a cognitive science course is a distinction put forward by MIT Professor Sherry Turkle between two learning styles: top-down and bottom-up learning. She illustrates this distinction by describing how two students with contrasting learning styles use computers. Jeff, the prototypical top-down learner, has a reputation as one of the school's computer experts. He approaches the computer with determination and the need to be in control. When she meets him, Jeff is working on a space shuttle program. He begins by making a plan: the program will include a rocket, boosters, a trip through the stars, and a landing. Then he breaks the program up into manageable pieces.

On the other hand, Kevin is the prototypical bottom-up learner. Whereas Jeff is precise in his actions, Kevin is dreamy and impressionistic. Like Jeff, Kevin is working on a space program, but his programming style is markedly different from Jeff's. At the beginning, Kevin is mainly concerned about the aesthetics of designing a rocket with a red fireball at the bottom of it. He lets his plans change as he gets new ideas about how to produce interesting visual effects. When Jeff makes a mistake, he gets annoyed and rushes to correct it. On the other hand, Kevin is inclined to see mistakes as features and not necessarily as bugs. Mistakes often prompt him to explore the properties of the system and sometimes lead to interesting new ideas.

Top-down learners as a rule prefer to start with the most general principles and later fill in the details. Bottom-up learners usually feel more comfortable if they can start with the particular. Later on they can proceed to the more general.

It is useful just to know whether you yourself are mainly a top-down or bottom-up learner. For one thing, it can help you to choose the right class or program for yourself. You would choose one that suits your particular learning style.

A cognitive science class, however, can take you much further than that. Imagine that you have determined that you are a bottom-up learner. You might then find it especially useful to know that bottom-up learning typically happens through a process of emergence. This process is one in which independent parts of your mind gradually come together to form some kind of larger, more complex entity.

How would understanding the process of emergence help you? Top-down learners, like Jeff, are often convinced that their way is the right way. They therefore feel free to criticize bottom-up learners, who often feel bullied into giving up their natural learning style. Understanding their learning style can help bottom-up learners to defend themselves from unhelpful criticism. But knowing about bottom-up learning also entails a risk. Jeff may be wrong in criticizing Kevin for not having a plan; nevertheless, there are times when bottom-up learners really have stopped making progress. Because criticism from other people may often be misplaced, they need to be especially good at criticizing themselves so that they can keep from continuing too far down a blind alley.

You can gain even greater control over your thinking and learning the better you understand a process such as emergence. If you know how emergence works, you can sometimes catalyze the process so that you learn more quickly. You could even figure out how to cause emergence to happen at times when it normally would not. In effect, that means improving your ability to learn and increasing the power of your mind.

How? Many people discover that the technique of free association helps them generate ideas. They write down a word or short description at the top of a piece of paper and then below it write every idea that comes into their minds. People usually find that the top of their list includes mostly duds. But a few of the early ideas hold a grain of promise of something better, even if they may not be true solutions. As people continue to free-associate, their ideas become better and better. Free association can lead to solutions to relatively easy problems over the course of fifteen minutes to half an hour. For more difficult problems, it may be necessary to hold a series of sessions of free association spread out over a few days. People usually become more skillful at free association the more they use it.

Less well known is the practice of forcing a synergy between two ideas. The essence of the method is to free-associate simultaneously to both ideas. Ideally, you write both ideas, side by side, on the top of the paper and then list below every thought that comes to mind. Some people find that they can easily generate associations that are simultaneously related to both stimulus ideas.

What do you do if your associations are connected to only one idea or the other but not to both? You can improve your chances of success by forcing your attention back to whatever idea you may be neglecting. If your last association was connected to idea two, pick up your piece of paper and read your description of idea one. Do that after every association. People often find that their associations begin to connect both ideas to each other after a short time.

What if you still are unable to bring the two stimulus ideas together? At this point you may want to switch to a more structured process of problem solving. Look at your list of associations to one of the two stimulus ideas, perhaps idea one. Choose the best association from the list. Ask yourself what connections, if any, you can find between this idea and idea two. You might want to draw a circle around the association and a set of lines leading off your circle. You can write down descriptions of the possible connections on these lines. Do the same thing with other associations in your list. See if any of the connections that you propose seem to bring you closer to a solution.

Think back to Kevin, the bottom-up learner who was trying to create a space scene. Recall that Kevin created a design with a rocket and a red fireball below it. Kevin faced a problem when he tried to animate his space scene: as his rocket moved, the fireball got lost behind. He could not get the two images to move in sync. How could Kevin solve this problem? To try to force a synergy, he should write two stimulus ideas at the top of a piece of paper. Idea one is maintaining contact between the two images. Idea two is animating the rocket. By free-associating to both concepts, he can generate possible solutions that could make his animation work.

A high school class in cognitive science or mind management would cover many of the same topics as found in this book on mind magic for adult readers. They include problem solving, information management, creativity, and other related topics. But a course could cover a broader scope and be more thorough and rigorous. Here are five ideas that could be central themes of the course:

1. **Heuristics.** These are the useful rules of thumb that help you find the solution to problems. They help you to keep working on a problem, even after other people have given up. Free association and forcing synergies are both heuristics. So are other rules of thumb, such as the concepts of breaking a large problem into parts, finding a related problem, using examples to try out abstract ideas, and clarifying what is required for a solution.

2. **Debugging.** In computer programming, most of the work involves getting the errors (or bugs) out of programs. Getting rid of the bugs is part of everyday learning, too. Cognitive scientists sometimes say that bugs are friends, because you only learn by first having them and then dealing with them.

3. **Representation.** Finding the right representation can be the clue that solves a problem. Should you use a picture, a symbol, or a word? If you are technically minded, you may prefer a graph, an equation, a frame system, or a neural network. A sophisticated learner should know about many kinds of representations and be able to choose the best one for the problem at hand.

4. **Emergence.** Knowledge comes not just from top-down planning and deduction. Sometimes it comes from the unconscious interactions among ideas in your mind through a bottom-up process of emergence.

5. **Epistemology.** The term *epistemology* refers to the understanding of knowledge itself. You have control over knowledge only if you understand how it develops, how reliable or authoritative it is, and how much freedom you yourself have to change it. Knowing about knowledge itself may be the very best way to gain genuine control over your own learning.

Learning Mind Magic Through Studying Literature

Perhaps the most surprising fact about teaching mind magic in high school is that literature classes may be more helpful for doing so than any other traditional high school subject. It depends, of course, on how the subject is taught. At one time teachers assumed that there was one correct interpretation of a serious book. They expected their students to absorb it. That kind of teaching suffered from numerous shortcomings. First, it presented a false picture of what literature really is like. At the same time, it also served to constrain, instead of encourage, the growth of real intelligence. Most literature teachers today recognize that serious works support multiple interpretations and therefore ask their students to formulate an independent viewpoint. They also expect the students to support that viewpoint with sound argument.

During a time when social change happened slowly, there may have been no link between teaching literature and learning mind magic. In the information age, all that has changed. More than ever before, independent judgment lies at the very heart of what constitutes real intelligence. Furthermore, you need a clearer sense of what you yourself represent to preserve your identity in the face of constant change. Literature is better than any other high school subject for teaching this kind of emotional intelligence.

The Brazilian educator Paulo Freire and other specialists in the development of the mind have offered two contrasting images of the teacher, the difference between which can help clarify why literature is often better than math or science at teaching mind magic. The first is the image of the teacher as banker. The second is that of the teacher as midwife. The banker-teacher deposits knowledge in the learner's head. This knowledge is supposed to wait there until it comes out at test time. On the other hand, the midwife-teacher assists students in giving birth to their own ideas, in making their own ideas explicit and elaborating on them.

The present reality is that many high school literature teachers come close to the model of the midwife-teacher. On the other hand, math teachers even today remain close to the model of the banker-teacher. It is therefore hardly surprising to see which subject is better at teaching mind magic.

How to Be Critical and Constructive

You see the same forces at work over and over again. As long as students' minds remain active, their intelligence will develop. If their minds become stagnant, the process will stop.

What teaching methods are the best ones for teaching mind magic? Some of the best methods are the most concrete. They teach a practical skill, such as writing, reading, speaking a foreign language, and computer programming. They force students continually to invent procedures and to interpret experiences. Students constantly have to improve their understanding of events happening around them. To remain involved, their minds have to stay active. Other times students strengthen their minds by becoming more critical and self-conscious. The grasp of consciousness becomes the vehicle for learning mind magic.

Freire has argued that we need to look closely at the object of knowing. He writes in his 1970 book *Pedagogy of the Oppressed*, knowledge is "a medium evoking the critical reflection of both teacher and student." Even in adolescence, students' minds can begin to ossify. According to Freire, critical reflection is the best way to keep their minds alert and active.

Is Freire right? Without denying the value of critical thinking, it seems, nevertheless, that he is telling just a part of the story. Critical thinking may help you to see the problem, but it does not help you to find a solution. For that you need to have learned constructive skills. You need a degree of self-consciousness as well. For one thing, it will help you to manage your psychological resources more successfully. It will also help you to develop and maintain a stable sense of who you are and what you stand for.

A large part of mind magic is becoming critical enough to see the problems. But recognizing the problems has only limited value unless you can also create solutions. Finally, it is difficult to bring together critical and creative intelligence unless you have enough self-awareness to be able to manage your mind effectively.

The question is not whether school can help to teach these three important components of adult intelligence. Rather, the question is when it will take up the challenge.

RECOMMENDED READING

Here is a list of books that I recommend to readers who liked *Mind Magic*. These books are all quite different from one another. Each one addresses a unique topic or viewpoint related to mind magic. They are all written in a style that should be accessible to a nonprofessional. The list includes classic texts as well as recent books, major works as well as titles that have not yet received the recognition that they deserve. I have listed them in alphabetical order by author.

Bartlett, Frederic C. 1932. *Remembering: A Study in Experimental and Social Psychology*. Cambridge, England: Cambridge University Press.
Sir Frederic Bartlett's classic work on human memory belongs on any list of great books in psychology. It is full of brilliant insights and observations and remains as useful and original as when it was first written. It is the best book on memory ever written.

Boden, Margaret A. 1979. *Piaget*. London: Fontana Books.
This book is part of the Modern Masters series published by Fontana Books. Boden takes on the theoretical and philosophical questions that lie at the heart of Jean Piaget's work and makes them accessible to a broad readership. This is an outstanding introduction to Piaget for readers who want to understand what he was really trying to say.

Flavell, John H. 1963. *The Developmental Psychology of Jean Piaget.* Princeton, New Jersey: Van Nostrand Reinhold.

Flavell's book offers the first and most comprehensive overview of Piaget's body of research. It is valuable as an introduction to Piaget's work and as a reference, the main limitation being that it does not include research conducted after its publication date.

Gould, Stephen Jay. 1981. *The Mismeasure of Man.* New York: W. W. Norton.

Gould offers a stinging indictment of our accepted view of intelligence as the equivalent of what Plato called a "noble lie."

Hofstadter, Douglas R., and Daniel C. Dennett. 2001. *The Mind's I: Fantasies and Reflections on Self and Soul.* New York: Basic Books.

Hofstadter and Dennett address classic questions about the nature of self and mind in light of the new viewpoint that cognitive science has introduced. Readers interested in the philosophical questions underlying mind magic should read this intriguing volume.

Kuhn, Thomas S. 1962. *The Structure of Scientific Revolutions.* Chicago: University of Chicago Press.

This is the book that introduced the terms *paradigm* and *paradigm shift* into mainstream discourse. It may well be the most important academic work of the last fifty years. Not only does it describe how fundamental changes in thinking take place, but it also produces a fundamental change in the thinking of readers who understand it. Kuhn's ideas apply not just to scientists but to all of us.

Levine, Mel. 2002. *A Mind at a Time.* New York: Simon and Schuster.

Dr. Mel Levine is the leading authority on learning disabilities in America. His work combines the insight and analytic skill of a first-rate diagnostician with a realistic conception of the untapped ability of children diagnosed as learning disabled.

Minsky, Marvin Lee. 1986. *The Society of Mind*. New York: Simon and Schuster.

Minsky may well be the greatest living theorist of mind. In this book, he presents the most credible comprehensive theory that exists of how the human mind works. It consists of a collection of page-long essays. They are written simply enough to be understood by a general reader. Nevertheless, they also rely on a deep technical understanding of psychology and computation to make them required reading for a specialist.

Polya, George. 1945. *How to Solve It: A New Aspect of Mathematical Method*. Princeton, New Jersey: Princeton University Press.

How to Solve It is the bible of problem solving. Polya introduces his seminal concept of a heuristic, a rule of thumb that often helps in finding solutions, along with a dictionary of heuristics that have proven themselves. This is a standard reference for anyone with a serious interest in problem solving.

Schön, Donald A. 1987. *Educating the Reflective Practitioner*. San Francisco: Jossey-Bass.

Is judgment an attribute that you develop only after years of experience? According to Schön, it is not. The problem is that professional schools treat their subject as a technical skill. In fact, professional practice requires the ability to integrate numerous human, aesthetic, and technical considerations. His views of how to teach "professional artistry" have a clear resemblance to many ideas in mind magic. Here is a revolution in professional education waiting to happen.

Seligman, Martin E. P. 1991. *Learned Optimism*. New York: Knopf.

Seligman, a former president of the American Psychological Association, is a pioneer who helped bring cognitive psychology into clinical practice. This book introduces his theory of learned helplessness to nonprofessionals.

Simon, Herbert A. 1969. *The Sciences of the Artificial*. Cambridge, Massachusetts: MIT Press.

Simon was a scientist and scholar of remarkable breadth. He was a leading thinker in cognitive psychology and computer science as well as being the winner of the 1978 Nobel Prize in Economics. In this thought-provoking volume, he argues that psychology, economics, biology, and engineering are fundamentally different from classic sciences, such as physics, because they concern goal-oriented systems. This perspective allows him to offer surprising insights into the structure of a complex system, such as the human mind.

Tobias, Sheila. 1978. *Overcoming Math Anxiety*. New York: W. W. Norton.

Tobias is a pioneer in understanding the role of emotional awareness in academic learning. Her book was a major influence on the discussion of emotions in mind magic.

Turkle, Sherry. 1984. *The Second Self: Computers and the Human Spirit*. New York: Simon and Schuster.

Turkle is a sociologist, psychoanalyst, and winner of the MacArthur "genius" award. In *The Second Self*, she introduced and developed the interesting distinction between "top-down" and "bottom-up" learners.

REFERENCES

Barthes, Roland. 1957. *Mythologies*. Frogmore, St. Albans, England: Paladin, p. 68. Extract from *Mythologies* by Roland Barthes used by permission of the Estate of Roland Barthes, the translator, Jonathan Cape as publishers The Random House Group Limited. *Mythologies* was first published in French by Éditions du Seuil in 1957.

Berger, Peter L., and Luckmann, Thomas. 1966. *The Social Construction of Reality: A Treatise in the Sociology of Knowledge*. Garden City, New York: Doubleday.

"Data Smog: Newest Culprit in Brain Drain." *APA Monitor*, 29 (3), March 1998, pp. 1, 42.

Eccles, J. S., and Jacobs, J. E. 1986. Social forces shape math attitudes and performance. *Signs: Journal of Women in Culture and Society* II (21), pp. 367–89.

Elkind, David. 1981. *The Hurried Child: Growing Up Too Fast Too Soon*. Reading, Massachusetts: Addison-Wesley.

Feynman, Richard. 1965. *The Character of Physical Law*. Cambridge, Massachusetts: MIT Press.

Freire, Paulo. 1970. *Pedagogy of the Oppressed*. Translated by Myra Bergman Ramos. New York: The Continuum Press, p. 67.

Goleman, Daniel. 1994. *Emotional Intelligence: Why It Can Matter More Than IQ*. New York: Bantam Books.

Polya, George. 1945. *How to Solve It: A New Aspect of Mathematical Method*. Princeton, New Jersey: Princeton University Press.

Salovey, Peter, and Mayer, J. D. 1990. *Emotional Intelligence: Imagination, Cognition, and Personality.* New York: Harper.

Schön, Donald A. 1987. *Educating the Reflective Practitioner.* San Francisco: Jossey-Bass.

Seligman, Martin E. P. 1991. *Learned Optimism.* New York: Knopf, p. 210.

Shakespeare, William. *Hamlet* III, ii, 75.

Toffler, Alvin. 1971. *Future Shock.* New York: Bantam Books.

INDEX